WAR BY OTHER MEANS

In *War By Other Means* Carlyle Thayer has given a splendidly fair and detached verdict on the origins and policies of the National Front for the Liberation of South Vietnam. He refutes the dogmas of left and right propounded during the Vietnam war by showing both that the formation of the Front had significant local support in the South and that it came into being very much as a result of decisions taken in the North. Based on prodigious research, the book gives clear and convincing insights into the plight of the Communists in the South after the 1954 Geneva Conference, the strengths and weaknesses of Ho Chi Minh's government in the North, and the way in which wider Soviet concerns about improving relations with the West led them to do little for their friends in Hanoi.

Dr Thayer skilfully unfolds the series of events which led to the Chinese taking a line which the North Vietnamese were able to exploit in favour of a more militant policy against the government of Ngo Dinh Diem. The reader can easily understand the consequences: first a quiescent period in the South after Diem's crushing of the sects which led many observers to give him more credit than he deserved and the Americans to feel that they were supporting a stronger cause than was the case; and second the timely creation of a powerful organization deeply rooted in both the North and the South which was able to withstand the tests of a harsh war over the following fifteen years.

Thayer's treatment of these issues provides a fuller understanding than we have had to date of why the Vietnam war was fought with such tenacity and hideous cost over so many years. His book is to be recommended strongly for all who are teaching or studying the conflict in depth.

Robert O'Neill
Chichele Professor of the History of War
Oxford University

BOOKS OF RELATED INTEREST

Australia's War in Vietnam
Frank Frost

All The Way
Australia's Road to Vietnam
Gregory Pemberton

Nation in Arms
The Origins of the Peoples Army of Vietnam
Greg Lockhart

In Search of Southeast Asia
A Modern History
Edited by David Joel Steinberg

Southeast Asia
An Illustrated Introductory History
Milton Osborne

A History of Malaysia, Singapore & Brunei
C. Mary Turnbull

The Ties That Bind
Intelligence Cooperation between the UKUSA Countries
Desmond Ball & Jeffrey T. Richelson

War by other means

National Liberation and Revolution in Viet-Nam 1954–60

CARLYLE A. THAYER

ALLEN & UNWIN

Sydney Wellington London Boston

959.704
T 369w

To the memory of
Colonel Alan P. Thayer, USA

© Carlyle A. Thayer 1989
This book is copyright under the Berne Convention. No reproduction without permission. All rights reserved.

First published in 1989
Allen & Unwin Australia Pty Ltd
An Unwin Hyman company
8 Napier Street, North Sydney, NSW 2059 Australia

Allen & Unwin New Zealand Limited
75 Ghuznee Street, Wellington, New Zealand

Unwin Hyman Limited
15–17 Broadwick Street, London W1V IFP England

Unwin Hyman Inc.
8 Winchester Place, Winchester, Mass 01890 USA

National Library of Australia
Cataloguing-in-Publication entry:
Thayer, Carlyle A.
  War by other means : national liberation and revolution
  in Vietnam 1954–60.

  Bibliography.
  Includes index.
  ISBN 0 04 820045 X.
  ISBN 0 04 370187 6 (pbk.).

  1. Vietnam — History — 1945–1975. 2. Vietnam — Politics
  and government — 1945–1975. I. Title.

959.704'2

Library of Congress Catalog Card Number: 89–83595

Set in 10/11pt Times by Times Graphics, Singapore
Printed by Chong Moh Offset Printing, Singapore

Contents

Tables

Maps

Acknowledgements

The Viet-Nam War still lives with us, a decade and a half after the withdrawal of American and Australian troops. In recent years, a renewed interest in the history of the conflict has led to a veritable flood of books on the market. Few of these have focused on the Communist side, and, remarkably, no comprehensive account of the origins of the conflict has appeared. Those writers who have attempted to redress this neglect—Ralph Smith, George Kahin and Gabriel Kolko—have relied in part on unpublished research conducted by me over a decade ago.

The impetus for publishing this study arises from this renewed public interest and encouragement given by my colleagues and my publisher, John Iremonger. In writing this book, I have revised substantially my two volume PhD dissertation and incorporated documentation which has since become available. Most of the new material has been published in Hanoi and confirms previous research based on captured Communist documents and declassified intelligence reports. I have benefited from discussion with Party historians in Ho Chi Minh City arranged by the Viet-Nam Social Sciences Committee.

Research for this book was conducted in Viet-Nam, Australia, Republic of China (Taiwan), Thailand, France, England and the United States. I would like to thank Douglas Pike for granting access to his documentary collection, then housed in US government premises in Taiwan and now established as the Indochina Archive at the University of California at Berkeley. The late William Gausmann, then editor of *Viet Nam Documents and Research Notes*, was enormously helpful during my 1972 visit to Saigon. I would also like to thank the staffs of the National Library of Australia (and especially its Advanced Studies Reading Room); the Menzies Library, Institute of Advanced Studies, the Australian National University; National Library of the Republic of Viet-Nam; Ministry of Open Arms, Republic of Viet-Nam; Sterling Memorial Library, Yale University; Library of Congress; Widner Library, Harvard University; South-East Asia Treaty Organisation, Bangkok; and the Chatham House Library of the Royal Institute of International Affairs, London, for their professional services.

Over the past two decades I have accumulated numerous intellectual debts to friends and colleagues. In particular, I would like to thank the following for assistance in preparing this study: the late Harry Benda, John Girling, Huynh Sanh Thong, King C. Chen, Robert J. O'Neill, the late Karl Pelzer, Gary Porter, Jeffrey Race, William S. Turley, Geoffrey Warner, Christine P. White and Lee E. Williams. I also owe a special debt of gratitude to Alvaro Ascui, Shirley Ramsay and Jenny Crook for technical assistance in the preparation of the book manuscript. Special thanks go to the staff of the Defence Academy's Computer and Audio-Visual Centres. Last but not least, I must record my very special appreciation to my wife, Zubeida Bibi, for her patience, understanding and support during my trips overseas and long absences from home.

Abbreviations

ACDC	Anti-Communist Denunciation Campaign
AEZ	Agriculture Exploitation Zone
ARVN	Army of the Republic of Viet-Nam
CATO	Combat Arms Training Organisation
CCP	Chinese Communist Party
CIA	Central Intelligence Agency
CIP	Commercial Import Program
CPC	Communist Party of China
CPSU	Communist Party of the Soviet Union
DMZ	Demilitarised Zone
DPRK	Democratic People's Republic of Korea
DRVN	Democratic Republic of Viet-Nam
GVN	Government of Viet-Nam
ha.	hectare
ICC	International Control Commission
ICP	Indochinese Communist Party
MAAG	Military Assistance Advisory Group
MSU	Michigan State University
NATO	North Atlantic Treaty Organization
NFLSVN	National Front for the Liberation of South Viet-Nam
PKI	Communist Party of Indonesia
PAVN	People's Army of Viet-Nam
PRC	People's Republic of China
RLR	Royal Lao Government
RVN	Republic of Viet-Nam
SEATO	South-East Asia Treaty Organisation
TERM	Temporary Equipment Recovery Mission
TRIM	Training Relations and Instruction Mission
US	United States
USIS	United States Information Service
USOM	United States Operations Mission
USSR	Union of Soviet Socialist Republics
VCP	Viet-Nam Communist Party
VNA	Viet-Nam News Agency
VNQDD	Viet-Nam Nationalist Party
VWP	Viet-Nam Workers' Party

Preface

This book is concerned with the formulation and execution of Communist policy on the theme of national liberation in South Viet-Nam, from the period following the 1954 Geneva Conference, until the creation of the National Front for the Liberation of South Viet-Nam in December, 1960. An understanding of events during this period is vital for a full comprehension of decisions taken by the Communist Party to initiate a 'war of national liberation'. All too often, ignorance of this period has led writers to underestimate the importance of continuity in the revolutionary struggle in Viet-Nam.

This book traces the fortunes and changing objectives of the Communist movement in South Viet-Nam following the regroupment of military forces and the partitioning of Viet-Nam in 1954. The account is basically chronological and it is structured around the Communists' decision-making process, the regularly scheduled plenary sessions of the Party's Central Committee. Decision making is viewed as an interactive process in which three separate sets of factors were weighed and analysed in determining policy priorities: external, and northern and southern political and economic developments.

The division of Viet-Nam in 1954–55 posed unique problems for the Communist Party. It was compelled to devise and implement two completely different strategies: towards socialist construction in the north and towards national democratic revolution in the south. In the period under review, the paths of these twin goals rarely ran parallel. Priority was given to the consolidation of the north, and Party officials in the south repeatedly had to adjust their activities to take this into account.

This study challenges long-held views about the origins and nature of the Viet Cong. The struggle for 'national liberation' in Viet-Nam did not suddenly materialise as a result of decisions taken in Hanoi in 1959–60 'to conquer the south'. It was, in part, a product of a larger transformation and modernisation of Vietnamese society, set in train by the effects of colonial rule and the repeated attempts by Vietnamese political groups to expel the French and establish their own order. One consequence of this process was the emergence of a bewildering variety of political groups, each claiming legitimacy and each asserting its right to construct a new order. By 1954, if not earlier, it was clear that the Communist Party, with its associated military forces, front groups and village-based administration, was by far the largest and most popular of these groups.

The 1954 Geneva Agreements explicitly recognised the power and influence of the Communist movement by according it political control over Viet-Nam north of the 17th parallel. But the Geneva Agreements, although bringing about a ceasefire, did little to address the long-standing political conflict between the Communist movement and its opponents in the south.

One key issue facing the Party was how to pursue the national democratic revolution in the south. This study reviews the failure of purely political means, that is, political struggle under the terms of the Geneva Agreements, to achieve the aim of national reunification. The study then focuses on the life-and-death struggle between the Diem regime and the Communist movement, and the gradual evolution of Communist policy on the use of force: from reliance on armed sect units, armed self-defence, systematic political assassinations and combined political and armed struggle, to a period of simultaneous uprising and the development of regular forces.

The events of this period have been reconstructed from a wide variety of source material. This account relies mainly on contemporary Communist materials published in Vietnamese, such as the party's newpaper *Nhan Dan*, daily radio broadcasts by Voice of Viet-Nam/Radio Hanoi, internal party documents, and interviews with party officials and defectors. This has been supplemented by other sources such as contemporary media accounts, radio broadcasts, diplomatic dispatches, official documents and formerly classified intelligence reports prepared by US and Republic of Viet-Nam government agencies. A large number of individuals, including scholars, government analysts and journalists, were contacted and interviewed. In addition, exhaustive use has been made of the secondary literature, both popular and scholarly.

Author's note

The Vietnamese language was romanised by Catholic missionaries in the 17th century. Traditionally a hyphen was used to indicate when two words were being combined to express a broader or more complex idea. For example, the country of Viet-Nam is formed by combining the words 'viet' (the name of the people) and 'nam' (meaning 'south', that is, the Viet people to the south of China). In the 1950s and 1960s the use of the hyphen was quite common; this is less so today, especially when Vietnamese words are printed in English. There are, for example, three different ways of spelling Viet-Nam: with the hyphen, without the hyphen (Viet Nam), and as one word (Vietnam). I have adopted the hyphenated spelling throughout except when it is spelled otherwise in a direct quotation.

The Viet-Nam Communist Party was founded in February 1930. It has undergone several name changes since. In October 1930 it was renamed the Indochinese Communist Party. In November 1945, for tactical reasons, the ICP was officially dissolved and its members went underground. The party reappeared in March 1951 under a new name, the Viet-Nam Workers' Party (VWP), or Lao Dong Party. After reunification, the party reverted to its original title, the Viet-Nam Communist Party. Despite the changes in nomenclature, all these names refer to the same organisation. For stylistic reasons the Viet-Nam Workers' Party is referred to in the text in a variety of ways: the VWP, the Lao Dong Party, the Communist Party or simply the Party.

On September 2, 1945, Ho Chi Minh declared Viet-Nam's independence and established a government, which he called the Democratic Republic of Viet-Nam (DRVN), to rule over the entire country. The DRVN did not obtain state power until 1954, when it was given control of northern Viet-Nam above the 17th parallel. The Republic of Viet-Nam refers to the government created by Ngo Dinh Diem in October 1955 which replaced the State of Viet-Nam headed by ex-emperor Bao Dai. The RVN governed southern Viet-Nam below the 17th parallel from 1955–75.

In 1956 Le Duan, a key Communist official in southern Viet-Nam, wrote a major policy document entitled *Duong Loi Cach Mang Mien Nam*. This has been translated into English variously as *On the Revolution in South Viet Nam* or *The Path of Revolution in the South*. In the text, I have translated the document as *The Line of Revolution in the South*.

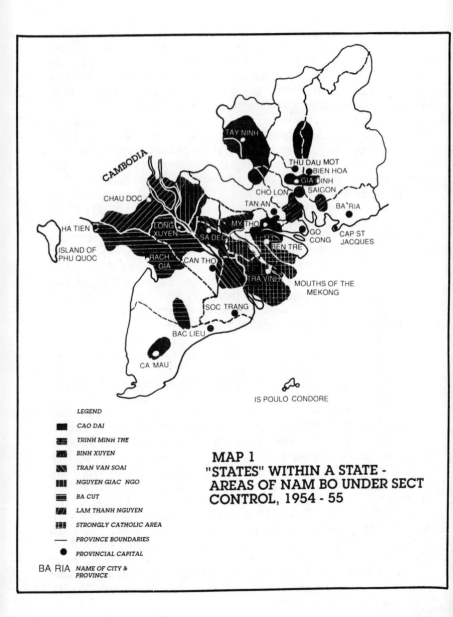

LEGEND

CAO DAI

TRINH MINH THE

BINH XUYEN

TRAN VAN SOAI

NGUYEN GIAC NGO

BA CUT

LAM THANH NGUYEN

STRONGLY CATHOLIC AREA

—— PROVINCE BOUNDARIES

● PROVINCIAL CAPITAL

BA RIA NAME OF CITY & PROVINCE

MAP 1
"STATES" WITHIN A STATE -
AREAS OF NAM BO UNDER SECT
CONTROL, 1954 - 55

Introduction

On December 20, 1960 an organising committee of Vietnamese revolutionaries met in Xom Giua hamlet, along the Vam Co river in Tay Ninh province near Vietnam's border with Cambodia. The committee proclaimed the formation of the National Front for the Liberation of South Viet-Nam (NFLSVN).[1] After nearly six years of trying to unify the country through political means, at times coupled with the use of armed violence, Viet-Nam's Communist leadership had concluded that a major reorientation of the revolutionary movement was necessary. The new objective was the overthrow of the Ngo Dinh Diem government of South Viet-Nam, and the liberation of South Viet-Nam from the grip of 'US imperialism'. To this end, a new Communist-led front was formed: the National Front for the Liberation of South Viet-Nam (NFLSVN: *Mat Tran Dan Toc Giai Phong Mien Nam Viet Nam*). The armed conflict that followed is now known as the Viet-Nam War.

The formation of the NFLSVN immediately attracted foreign attention. In January 1961, President John F. Kennedy read and was deeply troubled by a text of a speech in support of wars of national liberation delivered by the Soviet Premier Nikita Khrushchev. The new American President linked the growing Communist-led insurgency in Viet-Nam to this statement and concluded that 'wars of national liberation' were a new instrument of Soviet policy designed to upset the status quo and alter the global balance of power.[2]

During the Kennedy presidency, counter-insurgency planning became the order of the day as American crisis managers studied ways of coping with this new threat to international order and security. One of the first US responses was to increase military and economic aid to the Republic of Viet-Nam (RVN) in order to bolster the beleaguered government of Ngo Dinh Diem. Perhaps the best known symbol of America's commitment to South Viet-Nam at this time was the dispatch of the Green Berets, or Special Forces.

Needless to say, the decision by the Kennedy administration to intensify its military commitment to the RVN was controversial. As the facts became public, a debate erupted over the justifications advanced by the US government for its actions. Echoes of this debate resounded in Australia as the government of the day decided to follow the American lead and commit an Australian Army training team, veterans of the Malayan Emergency, to South Viet-Nam.

One of the most contentious issues of the war concerned the origins, causes and nature of the insurgency movement directed against the Diem government. The debate quickly became polarised as the protagonists simplified the facts of Vietnamese history and political development to fit their particular viewpoints. Supporters of Western intervention argued that the insurgency in South Viet-Nam was a war of aggression waged from without by Communist North Viet-nam. For example, in late 1961 the United States government issued a White Paper, *A Threat to Peace—North Viet-Nam's Effort to Conquer South Viet-Nam*, to justify its actions.[3] According to this document:

> The basic pattern of Viet Cong (Vietnamese Communist) activity is not new, of course. It operated, with minor variations, in China, and Mao Tse-tung's theories on the conduct of guerilla warfare are known to every Viet Cong agent and cadre. Most of the same methods were used in Malaya, in Greece, in the Philippines, in Cuba, and in Laos. If there is anything peculiar to the Viet-Nam situation, it is that the country is divided and one-half provides a safe sanctuary from which subversion in the other half is directed and supported with both personnel and materiel.
>
> What follows is a study of Viet Cong activities in South Viet-Nam and of the elaborate organization in the North that supports those activities. The Communists have taken the most elaborate efforts to conceal their role and to prevent any discoveries that would point an accusing finger at them for causing what is happening.

On the other hand, opponents of the war argued that the insurgency was essentially a civil war, a product of conditions within South Viet-Nam, with only minimal support and direction from Communist North Viet-Nam. George Kahin and John Lewis, in one of the most influential books[4] written during the war years, argued:

> In sum, the insurrection is Southern rooted; it arose at Southern initiative in response to Southern demands. The Liberation Front gave political articulation and leadership to the widespread reaction against the harshness and heavy handedness of Diem's government. It gained drive under the stimulus of Southern Vietminh veterans who felt betrayed by the Geneva Conference and abandoned by Hanoi . . . Hanoi, despite its reluctance, was then obliged to sanction the South-

erners' actions or risk forfeiting all chance of influence over the course of events in South Viet-Nam.

A close examination of the historical record, based on material that has since become available, reveals that neither of the above views is entirely accurate and that the interplay of events was far more complex than portrayed.

THE MODERNISATION OF VIET-NAM AND THE SEARCH FOR POLITICAL COMMUNITY

The view that the creation of the NFLSVN and the ensuing Second Indochina War was simply a continuation of a struggle between Communists and anti-Communists obscures a broader search for political community[10] in Viet-Nam, the concomitant of the modernisation process, which was set in motion as a result of the colonial experience.

Traditional Viet-Nam was a society composed of autarchic villages loosely administered by the Imperial Court in Hue. According to French sociologist Paul Mus:[11]

> The typical village of Viet Nam is enclosed within a thick wall of bamboo and thorny plants; the villagers used to live behind a kind of screen of bamboo, or perhaps it was more like living within the magic ring of a fairy tale. Supplying their needs from the surrounding fields, they kept to themselves behind their common protection, away from strangers, away even, from the State. For instance, when it came to taxes (there, as elsewhere, the State's chief concern) they still presented a united front. They paid their taxes as a group, and the community was recognizable. The villages dominated the landscape; they were the backbone of the nation. Yet each preserved an internal autonomy and autarky, with an economy based on local consumption. Before the Europeans arrived, the Chinese carried on what commerce there was.
>
> The traditional Vietnamese state was conventionalized in accordance with Confucian political thought; it was withdrawn behind a wall of Chinese characters. It was authoritarian, but it preserved a ritualistic distance between itself and its subjects. At the same time it intervened directly in village life by regulating the agricultural calendar and by imposing, through its rituals, attitudes and standards of deportment upon the group and the individual. By its right of inspection of village affairs the State guaranteed conformity to the models provided by Chinese tradition; the codifications of the Le dynasty, in the fifteenth century, are an outstanding example.
>
> The traditional Vietnamese state kept its budgetary requirements to a minimum by governing through powers of verification and eventual repression, but not execution. The

responsibility for detailed implementation remained with the villages. The state was a coordinator, not an executive. Its object was to prevent the smaller communities from going astray, and its chief 'ministers' (the word does not have its European meaning) were a kind of high tribunal sitting in judgement upon lapses from the Confucian model. Therefore, the State recruited its personnel for all but the humblest positions from the literati; whose learning consisted entirely of Confucius, the classics, and their commentators.

As a result of the corrosive features of French colonialism, the traditional dynastic state was weakened, while the autarchy of local villages was undermined. Vietnamese society in Mus' memorable expression, was 'thrown off-balance'. Attempts by the scholars to rally around the Emperor failed, as did their resort to armed resistance against the French. Villages lost their autonomy as local society was atomised under the impact of French colonial administration. In brief, the transformation of the Vietnamese 'great tradition' was set in motion.[12] Vietnamese scholars, like their Chinese counterparts, faced with the humiliation of colonial conquest, began searching for non-traditional solutions to their dilemma.

Why had the Court proved so easy a prey? What features of French society accounted for its success? How could Viet-Nam recover its independence? There were more questions than answers as Vietnamese scholars looked to China, Japan and the Soviet Union for solutions. Eventually reformism within the context of French political institutions yielded to revolutionary activisim. The pace of developments quickened in the early decades of the 20th century.[13]

The year 1930 marked a decisive turning point. Early in the year the Viet Nam Quoc Dan Dang (Vietnamese Nationalist Party), a party modelled on the Chinese Kuo Min Tang, rose in unsuccessful revolt. The defeat of the VNQDD marked the end of purely anti-colonialist nationalism as a force capable of overthrowing the French. That same year, Ho Chi Minh unified the various communist organisations in Viet-Nam into a single Communist Party. Although Party cadres were unsuccessful in their attempts to establish revolutionary soviets in central Viet-Nam during 1930–31, the Party survived the political suppression which followed. With the advent of the Popular Front government in France, which permitted renewed political activity in Indochina, the Party grew in strength. Thereafter the strands of anti-colonialism, Vietnamese nationalism, revolutionary modernisation, and Marxism-Leninism were combined in one organisation, the Communist Party, which now assumed centre stage.

The Communist Party's rise to dominance was greatly facilitated by the events of World War II. French Indochina was in no position to resist the might of Japan, as France itself was under the heel of the Nazis. The colonial regime, like its Vichy counterpart, collaborated with the occupying forces. This action ensured that both Japanese fascism and French colonialism would become the objects of the wartime resistance movement. In 1941, Ho Chi Minh's Communist Party organised a broad national front known as the League for the Independence of Viet Nam (Viet-Nam Doc Lap Dong Minh Hoi) with precisely these objectives. A minuscule military force was established, which later served as the core from which other units would spring.

Inevitably, as the tides of war in the Pacific turned against Tokyo, Japanese leaders in Indochina became suspicious of the French administration. After evidence began to accumulate that certain elements among the French community might belatedly take to arms, the Japanese launched a pre-emptive *coup de main.* On March 5, 1945 the Japanese disarmed French forces and imprisoned them, thus accomplishing what decades of revolutionary activism had been unable to achieve: the overthrow of the colonial regime. This dramatic event, coupled with the obvious decline of Japanese military power elsewhere, led Ho Chi Minh and his colleagues to the inescapable conclusion that it was necessary to plan to seize power. The aim, of course, would be to secure recognition from the Allied Powers while presenting France with a *fait accompli.*

While the Vietnamese revolutionaries were drafting their plans, the startling news of Japan's unconditional surrender reached them. They immediately declared the formation of a provisional government and ordered the commencement of a country-wide general insurrection. The events which followed, since named the August Revolution, witnessed the seizure of power in Hanoi, Hue and Saigon by Vietnamese nationalists. Emperor Bao Dai, belatedly installed by the Japanese at the head of an 'independent' Viet-Nam, abdicated. On September 2, 1945 Ho Chi Minh declared Viet-Nam independent under the name of the Democratic Republic of Viet-Nam (DRVN). The DRVN government in fact included an amalgam of nationalist groups among whom the Indochinese Communist Party and its Viet Minh Front were undoubtedly the strongest and most cohesive.

It is a moot question as to what form this government would have taken, for external forces once again decisively intervened in Vietnamese domestic affairs. As a result of the Potsdam Conference, the Allies decided to effect the surrender of Japanese forces in Indochina by dividing the country at the 16th parallel and by assigning the tasks to the Chinese Nationalists and Britain, repectively. The Chinese army's occupation of the north brought in its

wake the return to Viet-Nam of a variety of political groups who
had spent the war in exile. In the south, British General Gracey
refused to deal with the Vietnamese authorities. He released the
imprisoned French and permitted them to re-establish their rule.
Thus, the ultimate aims of the August Revolution were thwarted.
The Allied powers neither prevented the French from returning to
Viet-Nam nor did they grant recognition to the DRVN.

As a result of negotiations between the French, Vietnamese and
Chinese, the latter withdrew from northern Viet-Nam. French
troops were permitted to return. It was also agreed that they would
be progressively withdrawn over a five-year period and that a
referendum would be held in the south to determine whether it
would opt to join an independent Viet-Nam. However, the anti-
colonial nationalist camp began to break up. Extremists condemned
Ho Chi Minh for not taking to arms. Anti-Communists split with
Communists. Politicians out of the centre of power intrigued to
undermine those in power. Politico-religious sects in the south
consolidated their power on a territorial basis, creating 'states
within a state'. Members of the bureaucracy, and pro-French
groups, sought to side with the colonial authorities. Monarchists
hankered for a return of the Emperor. Nationalist political parties
attempted to entrench themselves in local areas. The disunity of the
nationalist camp and the shift in the balance of forces as France re-
established its pre-war presence made the grant of complete
Vietnamese independence remote. Tensions on either side, which
built up in a series of incidents in late 1946, finally exploded
into open warfare. Ho Chi Minh and his government and Party
colleagues took to the mountains and began an eight-year-long
protracted resistance against the French.

The return of the French to Viet-Nam and the start of the
Resistance War postponed the resolution of the conflict among
Vietnamese groups as to which form the modernisation of Vietnamese political institutions should take. Nevertheless, this process of
modernisation was an important undercurrent of the larger conflict
between Communist-led anti-colonial nationalism on the one hand
and the forces of French colonialism and anti-Communist nationalism on the other. During the Resistance War, a radical transformation occurred in areas of the countryside under the domination of
the Communist Pary.[14]

Through the Viet Minh and Lien Viet fronts, as well as the
People's Army of Viet-Nam (PAVN) and the administrative
structure of the DRVN government, Viet-Nam's political institutions were modernised and the 'imbalance' in village society
restored. Not only was village self-sufficiency recreated within the
framework of larger 'liberated zones', but the superstructure of
central control was once again reimposed. These developments

occurred, with varying intensity, throughout all the regions of Viet-Nam.

In short, the Communist Party mobilised millions of rural folk into modern organisations with specific social, political and economic goals. A new leadership hierarchy was created in the villages. These intervening organisations, coupled with the introduction of revolutionary values, proved to be self-sustaining in the face of external stress. A new 'Vietnamese political community' was created which replaced the decimated vestiges of the traditional dynastic state.

The end of the Resistance War did not mark the conclusion of the process of political development and modernisation set in motion by the colonial experience. The 1954 Geneva Agreements, despite their references to a political settlement, merely brought about a ceasefire and the withdrawal of the French Expeditionary Corps. With the departure of the French, the colonial political model ceased to exist as a viable option. The French exit set the stage for a resumption of domestic conflict. In the south, the State of Viet-Nam failed to control vast sections of the countryside. These regions were either run as warlord fiefs by sect generals, or were administered by the Communist Party as 'liberated areas'. In the urban centres, the main support base of the State of Viet-Nam, political division reigned similarly. On the one hand were the forces of republicanism led by Ngo Dinh Diem; on the other were a variety of forces, some pro-French, others pro-monarchist, opposed to Diem. By May 1955, the urban conflict had been resolved in favour of Diem, who then turned his energies to expanding administrative control throughout the countryside of south Viet-Nam.

The overall situation has been succinctly summarised by John McAlister:[15]

> By 1954, after seven years of revolutionary conflict, two competitor governments emerged: The Democratic Republic of Viet-Nam in Hanoi and the Republic of Viet-Nam in Saigon. Each claimed to be the sole legitimate government for all the Vietnamese people, yet each controlled about half the territory of the country. When these two governments withdrew into separate territories divided at the 17th parallel by the Geneva Conference of 1954 the Western powers expected them to act like separate nation-states, instead of adversaries in a revolutionary war. But neither government did. Nor has either of them denied that 'reunification' is its ultimate goal . . .
>
> The war now raging in Viet-Nam is a continuation of the pattern of conflict launched during the First Indochina War; it is not a war being fought between two separate nations, but a revolutionary struggle within one nation. More conspicuously than in wars between nations, revolutionary war is, in the

words of Clausewitz, a 'continuation of politics by other means'. It is a competition between two or more governments, each of which wants to become the sole legitimate government of a people. In wars between nations, political objectives are usually sought by destroying the military power of an adversary, but in revolutionary wars, political goals are sought more directly. The focus of conflict is to eliminate the political structure of an opponent and replace it with a political structure of one's own.

The origins of the Viet-Nam War are firmly rooted in the process of revolutionary change and modernisation ignited by the colonial experience throughout Viet-Nam. Immediately following the partitioning of Viet-Nam in 1954, the leadership of the Viet-Nam Workers' Party (VWP), as the Party was then known, redefined the objectives of the Communist revolution from defeating French colonialism, to consolidation and socialist transition in the north and the carrying out of a national democratic revolution in the south. These twin objectives reflected the territorial division of Viet-Nam. Although both aims were interrelated, the VWP accorded priority to the former.

By early 1959, the VWP decided the time was at hand to devote increased resources to the tasks of the national democratic revolution. The Party also decided to shift its tactics, giving increased weight to armed struggle. This change in emphasis occurred simultaneously with renewed emphasis on political struggle. In brief, the Resistance model was modified and reapplied to suit the new circumstances. Military force would now provide a shield behind which base areas and 'liberated zones' could be built. The embryonic revolutionary society that had survived over the previous six difficult years was to be built up and expanded, challenging the authority and legitimacy of the RVN. From the point of view of the Party, which was not a mass organisation, the creation of a new national united front was necessary to mobilise the people for the new stage ahead.

The VWP's policy on unification and national liberation during the 1954–60 period underwent several important changes. Four sets of factors influenced the policy-making process: the effects of the international environment on the VWP's Central Committee; the interaction between the Central Committee and its subordinate Nam Bo Regional Committee; the effects of the anti-Communist policies of the Diem regime on the Party's southern organisation; and the impact of the pace of northern social, economic and political development. In other words, the VWP's political system must be seen as functioning and interacting simultaneously with both domestic and international systems.

The VWP's reactions to these diverse factors were authoritatively considered by regular plenary sessions of the VWP's Central Committee. During the period July 1954 to September 1960 (when the VWP convened its 3rd National Congress), 13 plenums were held—numbers 6 to 18. Each of these meetings assessed 'the successes and shortcomings' in the implementation of policy since the previous Central Committee meeting.

The methodology adopted in this book is to review the policy process at each Party plenum in order to assess the relative weight of domestic and international factors in shaping policy on the question of national liberation. This framework enables us to place domestic Vietnamese developments into a large and comprehensive framework. What emerges is a picture of the VWP as a complex organisation with competing priorities, reacting to and coping with both domestic and external pressures.[16] Success was never complete and policy had to be modified continually. Errors, mistakes and failures occurred—sometimes these were due to timidity, poor implementation or bad organisation; at other times, external factors intervened to frustrate the VWP in the pursuit of its objectives. For example, in 1955 the DRVN found little support from either the USSR or China when it sought their assistance to implement the political terms of the Final Declaration of the Geneva Conference, which called for consultations to decide on elections to be held no later than July 1956.

In 1956, the shock waves of Khrushchev's denunciation of Stalin threatened the unity of the socialist bloc, while the DRVN confronted the consequences of serious errors committed during the course of land reform, dissension by sections of the intelligentsia, and violent disturbances in one of its districts. Plans for quick unification of the country were shelved while longer-range strategies were devised. In the south the RVN went from strength to strength, seriously challenging the authority of the VWP underground in its base areas. Leaders of the Communist underground in the south, most notably Le Duan (First Secretary, then Secretary-General of the Party from 1960 to 1986) advocated an early resumption of armed struggle, a policy at odds with the Central Committee.

In 1957, the DRVN completed its program of economic recovery in the north; the following year it embarked on a program of socialist construction under its first three-year plan, funded by increased aid from the Soviet Union. At the same time, Chinese foreign policy veered to the left, following the November 1957 Moscow Conference of Communist Parties and the onset of the Sino-Soviet dispute. These twin developments enabled Party officials to sanction a step-up in armed conflict in the south. The key decision was taken in January 1959 at the 15th plenum of the VWP's Central Commitee. At that time, the Party's underground was struggling to survive and was desperate for the go-ahead to resume armed struggle. Permission was granted. After a year of 'concerted uprisings' against the authority of the RVN, conditions were considered ripe for the establishment of the NFLSVN and an increased effort to topple the Diem government.

Although the origins of the Second Indochina War may be found in the complex interplay of events during the 1954–60 period they cannot be precisely dated because the so-called 'Second Indochina War' was not a war in the conventional meaning of the word. It was part and parcel of the much larger historial process set in train by the impact of French colonialism: the revolutionary transformation of an agrarian Third World society.

SEMANTICS

The debate on the origins of the NFLSVN and the causes of the Viet-Nam War were obviously influenced by the passions of the day and the political viewpoints of the individuals concerned. The protagonists attempted to fit highly complex and often ambiguous developments into clear-cut 'black and white' categories. Neither viewpoint, however, satisfactorily came to grips with a fundamental semantic problem which bedevils all discussion of contemporary Vietnamese politics: what is really meant by the terms 'North Vietnamese', 'South Vietnamese' and 'Viet Cong'?

A unique set of historical circumstances, spanning a period of over 1000 years, and still being investigated and debated by scholars today, has given the Vietnamese people a sense of national identity—nationhood—that has withstood the centrifugal forces of civil war and peasant rebellion and the centripetal forces of repeated foreign invasion. It was a coherent, unified Vietnamese kingdom, with a sense of its own nationhood, that confronted the might of French colonial expansion in the mid-19th century.

As the result of conquest and French colonial policy, the kingdom of Viet-Nam was divided into three administrative regions: Cochin China (roughly corresponding to the Mekong Delta area in the south or Nam Bo), Annam (roughly the territory between the 11th and 20th parallels in the centre) and Tonkin (roughly the Red River Delta area in the north). Tonkin and Annam were governed as protectorates; Cochin China had the status of a directly ruled colony. While French colonial conquest had the effect of shattering Vietnam's political unity, it did not succeed in shattering the Vietnamese people's sense of their own common identity.

This is not to say, however, that there were no regional differences among the Vietnamese people. Indeed, the diverse pattern of settlement created during the prolonged migration southward, from the tenth to seventeenth centuries, resulted in differences of dialect and village social organisation among the Vietnamese. Yet while the authority of the central Court was occasionally threatened by revolt, especially in the 19th century, the aim of the rebels was usually to create a new order, not to secede from the Vietnamese kingdom.

The French colonial experience intensified traditional regional variations, particularly in the south. There, new patterns of landholdings were created as a result of French efforts to open up the delta. As the south was the first territory to come under French administration, it experienced the impact of French culture and civilisation over a more prolonged period than the other two regions. Nevertheless, it would be an exaggeration to claim that as a result of French colonialism a separate 'South Vietnamese' nationality had emerged. Clearly the political divisions which arose in Viet-Nam after World War II were not north–south differences, but differences within the Vietnamese body politic based on different political values and beliefs.

In 1954, the decision was made to partition Viet-Nam at the 17th parallel, in preference to the so-called 'leopard spot' solution, which would have seen opposing forces concentrated into the areas they controlled on the ground. The partitioning of Viet-Nam, which was protested by representatives of the State of Viet-Nam at the time, was supposed to have been temporary and solely to enable the regroupment of opposing military forces. According to the Final Declaration of the Geneva Conference: 'The Conference recognizes that the essential purpose of the agreement relating to Vietnam is to settle military questions with a view to ending hostilities and that the military demarcation line is provisional and should not in any way be interpreted as constituting a political or territorial boundary.'[5]

As history has recorded, the 'military demarcation line' became in fact a political boundary for nearly two decades. This boundary, it should be noted, cut across regional and political loyalties. After partition, however, it became commonplace in the Western media to refer to Vietnamese living to the north and south of the demarcation line as 'North Vietnamese' and 'South Vietnamese' respectively. These terms are somewhat misleading as they combine two distinct meanings—region of birth and political affiliation. This distinction is often blurred in usage. The use of the terms 'North Vietnamese' and 'South Vietnamese' also glosses over the existence of a third region—central Viet-Nam (Trung Bo).

The confusion in the use of these terms is illustrated in the cases of Ngo Dinh Diem and Vo Nguyen Giap. Both were born in Quang Binh province, in an area later located north of the demarcation line. Giap is referred to in Western writing as a 'North Vietnamese' while Diem is universally referred to as a 'South Vietnamese'. After 1954–55, those who lived north of the 17th parallel were called 'North Vietnamese', while central Vietnamese who lived to the south of the dividing line, or who regrouped, were called 'South Vietnamese'.

The terms 'North Vietnamese' and 'South Vietnamese' are equally misleading when used to describe a person's political affiliation. As commonly used in Western writing on Viet-Nam, by 'North Vietnamese' is suggested a person who is loyal to the Viet-Nam Communist Party and the government in Hanoi; similarly, by 'South Vietnamese' is suggested a person who is both anti-Communist and loyal to government in Saigon. Unfortunately the latter term ignores the fact that, of an estimated 10 million people living south of the 17th parallel at the time of partition, as many as 3 million persons resided in so-called liberated areas, that is areas under the control of the DRVN's war-time administrative structure.[6] These central Vietnamese and southerners were later termed 'Viet Cong' to distinguish them from genuine 'South Vietnamese' who were supposedly loyal to the Republic of Viet-Nam.

The use of the term 'South Vietnamese', as opposed to 'Viet Cong', explicitly combines region of birth and political affiliation. Implicitly, it suggests the notion of the legitimacy of the Republic of Viet-Nam.[7]

A country is the whole territory of a nation. A nation is a stable, historically developed community of people with a territory, economic life, distinctive culture and language in common. A state is the governmental structure of an inhabited country which has domestic legitimacy, international recognition and sovereignty. 'South Viet-Nam' in its geographical sense is part of the territory of the Vietnamese nation. In usage it is sometimes held to be synonymous with the Republic of Viet-Nam. This is misleading, as the RVN government did not exercise control over the entire territory of South Viet-Nam at the time it was proclaimed. The RVN in fact lacked domestic legitimacy and had only limited international recognition. Its sovereignty was likewise a matter of dispute. In the period 1954–60, the concept of a 'South Vietnamese nationality' was only tenable by those who chose to ignore the facts.

'Viet Cong', a contraction from the Vietnamese *Viet Nam Cong San*, means 'Vietnamese Communist'. It was coined in the mid-1950s to replace the expression 'Viet Minh'. Viet Minh in turn is a contraction of the Vietnamese Viet Nam Doc Lap Dong Minh Hoi—League for the Independence of Viet Nam. The Viet Minh was founded in 1941 as a broad national united front, led by the Indochinese Communist Party (ICP), with the twin objectives of opposing Japanese fascism and French colonialism. Although the Viet Minh was officially renamed and enlarged as the League for the

National Union of Viet-Nam (Hoi Lien Hiep Quoc Dan Viet Nam) in March 1951, it remained a popular term denoting anti-French Vietnamese nationalists. Such expressions as the 'Viet Minh army' or the 'Viet Minh government' blurred the existence of three distinct organisations: a party (the Communist Party), an army (People's Army of Viet-Nam) and a government (the Democratic Republic of Viet-Nam). Not all members of the Viet Minh were Communist Party officials.

In the mid- to late 1950s the term Viet Cong was used routinely in the 'South Vietnamese' press[8] to refer to DRVN government (that is 'North Vietnamese') officials, party cadres and their supporters (but not to members of the Communist Party in South Viet-Nam). Later, when the insurgency in the south picked up, the Diem government sought to undermine the prestige of the Viet Minh by referring instead to members of the wartime resistance who did not rally to the RVN as 'Viet Cong'. Viet Cong in its new usage referred only to southerners, while DRVN officials, Viet-Nam Workers' Party cadres, and members of the People's Army of Viet-Nam in the north were now dubbed 'North Vietnamese'. Both terms gained popular acceptance in the West, thus reinforcing the view that the war in Viet-Nam was solely a case of North Vietnamese aggression directed against the independent state of 'South Viet-Nam'. During the years prior to the formation of the NFLSVN, the majority of the domestic opponents to the Diem regime were non-Communists to whom the appellation 'Viet Cong' was totally inappropriate. Jean Lacouture[9] has written for example:

> But the various national and religious forces that had been only wartime allies for the Vietnamese Communists did not consider themselves bound by these [Geneva] agreements and refused to bow before the commitments taken in the name of the guerillas by the Marxist leaders, or to yield to the authority of the new chief of government in Saigon, Ngo Dinh Diem. Soon the Ngo family's 'witch hunting' policy no longer left open to the growing number of its opponents any alternatives other than prison, exile, or the guerilla forces. Soon future president [Phan Khac] Suu was in jail, all the former government chiefs were in exile, and many people who wanted primarily to escape the pursuit of Diem's police or Nhu's 'Republican Youth' were in the guerilla forces. From then on the Saigon authorities called every dissatisfied person a communist or a Viet Cong.

To overcome these semantic problems, the following conventions have been adopted: 'North Viet-Nam' and 'South Viet-Nam' are used solely as geographical expressions for the territories created by the partitioning of Viet-Nam in 1954. They are not used as synonyms for the terms DRVN and RVN, respectively. When it is necessary to refer to a person's place of birth, the expressions northerner, centrist and southerner are used. The terms 'North Vietnamese' and 'South Vietnamese' are not used to indicate a person's nationality or political loyalties. Instead, political allegiances will be identified as precisely as possible, as the following examples illustrate: 'DRVN official' and 'VWP cadre' will be used instead of 'North Vietnamese official' and 'North Vietnamese cadre.' The term 'RVN official' will be used in place of 'South Vietnamese official'; similarly the expression 'RVN government' will be used in place of 'South Vietnamese government' or 'GVN' (Government of Viet-Nam).

1

Regroupment and reorientation

JULY 1954–MARCH 1955

THE GENEVA CONFERENCE

The First Indochinese War was brought to an end as a result of the Geneva Conference of 1954. Four of the Great Powers to attend —Britain, China, France and the Soviet Union—separately reached the conclusion that a ceasefire in Indochina would serve their own interests. Britain wished to see a resolution of the conflict lest any continuation spill over and affect its position in Malaya, where it was facing a local Communist-led insurgency. The government of France, facing a population increasingly disenchanted with the 'dirty war', was at the end of its electoral tether. The Soviet Union and China shared a common fear that the war in Indochina would escalate, particularly as the United States appeared to be tottering on the brink of intervention. The Soviet Union also may have hoped to link a settlement in Indochina with negotiations over Europe, an area of greater strategic concern. China too had other reasons for wishing to see peace restored; at this time it was turning inward, concerned with a new five-year plan of economic construction. In brief, a constellation of powers on the international scene, each for their own reasons, was simultaneously moving in a direction favourable for peace in Indochina.

For their part, both the Soviet Union and China brought pressure to bear on the leaders of the Democratic Republic of Viet-Nam to agree to negotiations with the French.[1] Undoubtedly the two allies wished to encourage the momentum gained as a result of the

1

armistice in Korea (July 1953). In November 1953, Ho Chi Minh
signalled a change in his government's view on the matter.[2]

At the Geneva Conference on Indochina, after the initial political
broadsides had been exchanged, it was agreed to separate political
from military matters and to leave the resolution of the latter to
confidential talks between representatives of the French and
People's Army of Viet-Nam (PAVN) High Commands. During the
course of the conference the French government of Joseph Laniel
fell. The new Premier, Pierre Mendes-France, set a self-imposed
deadline of 30 days for an agreement, failing which he would then
resign. In such a case, he hinted, he would recommend conscription
to the National Assembly.

Representatives of the State of Viet-Nam were effectively frozen
out of the secret talks held by the various parties. By the time they
learned that partition had been seriously discussed, it was too late.
When they raised objections and an alternate proposal, they were
ignored.

Both the Soviet Foreign Minister, Molotov, and his Chinese
counterpart, Chou En-lai, intervened decisively at various stages of
the conference to keep up the progress. Chou effectively pressured
Pham Van Dong, the DRVN Foreign Minister, into dropping his
demand that the Khmer and Lao resistance forces be given separate
recognition. Molotov selected the two-year timetable for holding
reunification elections.

There were basically two solutions mooted for a settlement of the
conflict. The idea of a coalition government, with Communist
representation, was quickly discarded. Thereafter attention turned
to the idea of military regroupment. Here also two major proposals
received attention: regroupment into enclaves, the so-called 'leopard spot' solution and regroupment into zones, in other words
partition. Both sides eventually favoured partition. As a result of
staff talks held by Western military officials, it was decided that a
demarcation line across central Viet-Nam at roughly 17°30′ north
would be militarily defensible. The DRVN representatives, on the
other hand, were anxious to secure a unified territory, adjacent to
China, with its own port and capital. It was clear from gestures
made by Ta Quang Buu, representative of the PAVN High
Command, at a secret military session held on June 10, 1954 with
M. de Brebisson, his French counterpart, that the DRVN was
considering a line drawn at about the 16th parallel.[3] The French
considered the 18th parallel more appropriate. During the course of
late June and early July, Pham Van Dong pressed for the 13th, 14th
and 16th parallels. It was only on July 20, the deadline set by
Mendes-France, that Molotov intervened and chose the 17th
parallel—a compromise between the two. At the same time, he
dashed DRVN hopes for early elections by suggesting a delay of two

years (until July 1956). On May 7, 1954 on the very eve of the Indo-china phase of the Geneva Conference, the French garrison at Dien Bien Phu surrendered after a 55-day siege. The question of why the Communists would make such a generous settlement with the defeated French can be partly answered with reference to external pressures.

PAVN forces were exhausted from what turned out to be a pyrrhic victory at Dien Bien Phu.[4] War-weariness, coupled with the possibility of American military intervention, persuaded DRVN and VWP (Viet-Nam Workers' Party) officials that the negotiating table would be a more profitable arena at that point than continued military struggle. Although France had suffered a crushing psychological blow and military defeat at Dien Bien Phu, France still retained a powerful expeditionary corps, supplemented by a growing National Army of the State of Viet-Nam.

According to Janos Radvanyi,[5] a Hungarian diplomat who visited Hanoi in April 1959, Vo Nguyen Giap told him that:

> [t]he battle of Dien Bien Phu . . . was the last desperate exertion of the Viet Minh army. Its forces were on the verge of complete exhaustion. The supply of rice was running out. Apathy had spread among the populace to such an extent that it was difficult to draft new fighters. Years of jungle warfare had sent morale in the fighting units to the depths.

A similar view is provided by Nikita Khrushchev in his memoirs:[6]

> Before the Geneva Conference there was a preparatory meeting in Moscow. China was represented by Chou En-lai and Vietnam by President Ho Chi Minh and Prime Minister Pham Van Dong. We worked out the position we would take in Geneva, basing it on the situation in Vietnam. The situation was very grave. The resistance movement in Vietnam was on the brink of collapse. The partisans were counting on the Geneva Conference to produce a cease-fire agreement which would enable them to hold on to the conquests which they had won in the struggle of the Vietnamese people against the French occupation. Hanoi was securely in the hands of the French. If you looked at a map on which our own demands for a settlement were marked out, you'd see that North Vietnam was pockmarked with enclaves which had been captured and occupied by the French.

Authoritative DRVN sources have confirmed also that there was a problem with morale at Dien Bien Phu. A commentary on that famous battle published in Hanoi revealed,[7] for example:

> This second phase was thus characterized by long and extreme-ly bitter fighting. We had to solve arduous tactical and technical problems, to overcome fatigue and weariness, to meet

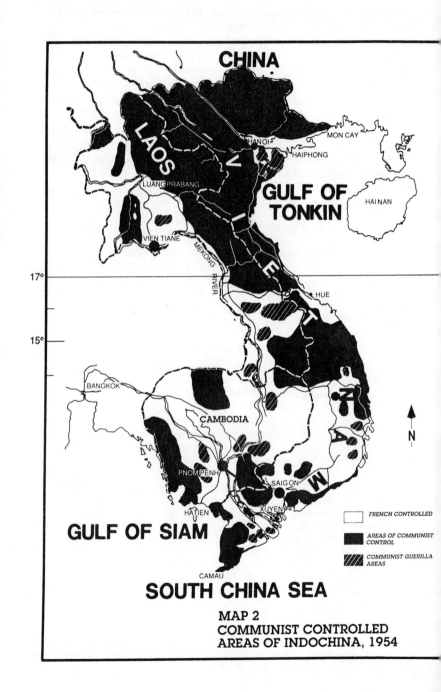

MAP 2
COMMUNIST CONTROLLED
AREAS OF INDOCHINA, 1954

extremely hard fighting conditions, living week after week in trenches and under-ground shelters. Sometimes, our positions would be flooded with rain, supplies would be insufficient, and as fighting was carried on uninterruptedly, losses had to be compensated for by reinforcements, and units had to be reorganized. Under those conditions, political work played an important role in maintaining the morale of the troops, for among certain cadres and men, negative tendencies had appeared: fear of losses, privations and fatigue; or complacency, underestimation of the enemy and impatience to gain a quick victory. Before starting the offensive which was to end this second phase, the Central Military Committee, on order from the Political Bureau, launched a campaign for 'moral [sic] mobilization' and 'ideological rectification' among the cadres and Party members.

It seems reasonable to conclude that war weariness, exhaustion after Dien Bien Phu, the risks of prolonged fighting, perhaps most importantly the possibility of American military intervention, and external pressures from the Soviet Union and China all played a part in the VWP–DRVN decision to seek a negotiated end to the war. A more difficult question, however, is whether or not the 17th parallel represented an accurate dividing line between the two contending forces. There can be no question that PAVN military and DRVN political strength were greater in the north and centre than in the south.

Any demarcation line drawn north of the 13th parallel across Viet-Nam would have cut across areas under the control of the VWP and its subordinate organisations. According to American sources:[8]

> During June and July [1954], according to CIA maps, Viet Minh forces held down the larger portion of Annam (excepting the major port cities) and significant pockets in the Cochin-china delta. Their consequent claims to all the territory north of a line running northwest from the 13th to the 14th parallel (from Tuy Hoa on the coast through Pleiku to the Cambodian border) was far more in keeping with the actual military situation than the French demand for location of the partition line at the 18th parallel.

However, as an account published later in Hanoi indicates,[9] the 18th parallel marked the divide between the 'two parts of Viet Nam':

> North of the 18th parallel which cut the 4th Interzone into two parts, the French troops only maintained their control over the Red River delta which was considered to correspond roughly to the 3rd Interzone, and in the Tay Bac Interzone (or Northwest), over the system of strong points at Na San and Lai Chau town

which they had to evacuate in August and December 1953 respectively. The greater part of Bac Bo remained under the people's power. It formed, with the three northern provinces of the 4th Interzone, an immense free territory encircling the occupied zone. Contrary to the North, the South, making up about three-fifths of the country's area, presented a carved-up aspect, with occupied and free zones interlacing one another.

As a result of the provisions of the Geneva Accords, PAVN military forces located below the 17th parallel were to withdraw into one of four regroupment zones and, over a 300-day period, transfer to the north. Regardless of whether or not the 17th parallel was an accurate guide to the balance of forces on the ground, it did serve its purpose as a military demarcation line.

The political provisions of the Geneva Agreements were much more ambiguous. The vital clauses setting forth details on elections, for example, were included in the unsigned Final Declaration.[10] The key provisions were contained in point 7, which read:

The Conference declares that, so far as Vietnam is concerned . . . In order to ensure that sufficient progress in the restoration of peace has been made, and that all the necessary conditions obtain for free expression of the national will, general elections shall be held in July 1956 under the supervision of an international commission composed of representatives of the Member States of the International Supervisory Commission, referred to in the agreement on the cessation of hostilities. Consultations will be held on this subject between the competent representative authorities of the two zones from July 20, 1955 onward.

There is some evidence that Pham Van Dong and his colleagues did not expect elections to take place. P.J. Honey[11] asserts, for example, that: 'Pham Van Dong, immediately after signing the Geneva Agreements on Indo-China under Soviet Union pressure, remarked to some non-Communist Vietnamese friends staying at his villa that the national elections envisaged by the agreements would never take place'. In a subsequent account[12] Honey states:

The worthlessness of this concession [i.e. a definite date for elections] can be seen in a remark made by the Communist North Vietnam (DRV) Prime Minister, Pham Van Dong, to one of my Vietnamese friends immediately after the signing of the agreements. When asked which side he thought would win the elections, Dong replied, 'You know as well as I do that there won't be any elections.'

Jeffrey Race[13] cites an interview he conducted with Vo Van An, a high-ranking Party cadre who later defected, to confirm this view: '[a]ccording to An, higher level cadres (province and above) were certain that general elections would never take place, although this was not discussed at lower levels to maintain morale and so as not to conflict with the Party's public stance that the Geneva Accords were a great victory for the Party.'

According to Seymour Topping,[14] a correspondent working for Associated Press in Geneva at that time: 'The Vietminh [DRVN] no doubt had every reason to believe, as did Chou En-lai and Molotov, that all of Vietnam would fall to them within two years. In this sense, the Vietminh leadership was satisfied, although members of their delegation complained privately to me that they had been cheated and expressed doubt that the national elections would be held in 1956.'

In light of Topping's remarks, and the vociferous campaign subsequently waged by the DRVN authorities to hold elections, it seems reasonable to conclude that the DRVN, despite whatever misgivings it might have expressed in private and to its own cadres, favoured elections as the means of unifying Viet-Nam. Pham Van Dong and other members of his delegation were undoubtedly gravely upset that elections had been scheduled for two years instead of within six months, a time scale they had favoured. At that time, some DRVN officials still held out hope that France would honour its commitments.

The overall view of the situation was summarised by a directive issued by the Central Committee of the VWP,[15] which was acquired by the French in November 1954:

> peace is concluded to procure advantages for us, not for the purpose of ceasing the struggle. Peace as such is not unconditional. We love peace and do not want war which causes bloodshed, but we are resolved to maintain our fundamental point of view which is independence, unity, democracy and peace. If the political struggle does not permit us to accomplish this essential aim, we are resolved to continue the war to support our just cause and to achieve total victory.

THE 6TH PLENUM (JULY 1954)

The decision by VWP leaders in 1953 to seek a negotiated end to the war was not without controversy. General Vo Nguyen Giap, PAVN Commander-in-Chief, apparently argued heatedly for pushing the siege at Dien Bien Phu to a successful conclusion as a prerequisite for any political bargaining.[16] Many staff officers refused to accept the rumours of an impending settlement at Geneva until addressed by Ho Chi Minh himself at a specially convened meeting held in June 1954.[17]

Nevertheless the VWP met in mid-July at the 6th plenary session of the Central Committee to review progress at Geneva and to approve the outline of the settlement whose basic provisions had already emerged. There is every likelihood that the self-imposed deadline set for July 20 by Premier Mendes-France weighed heavily on the deliberations. A failure to secure an agreement at this time may very well have meant a resumption of the fighting, with the possibility of American military intervention.

The tenor of Ho Chi Minh's speech to this Party gathering suggests that disagreement was rife.[18] Some, no doubt recalling the unsatisfactory agreements negotiated with the French in 1946, wanted to continue the fight. Others, reflecting on the destruction and war-weariness of the population, appeared eager to make concessions in order to secure peace. Ho's remarks touched on both points of view, but his extended comments on 'leftist deviation' suggest that the hawks were the more powerful group.

Ho argued that the very convening of the Berlin and Geneva conferences 'is in itself a victory for our side and a defeat for the imperialists'. He attributed this success to the divided nature of the capitalist camp caused by contradictions between the US on the one hand, and France and Britain on the other. In brief, the US was opposed to peace in Viet-Nam and was doing everything in its power to sabotage the Geneva Conference, even to the extent of proposing 'joint action' in Indochina. It had become, in Ho's words, 'the main enemy of world peace'.

Ho then argued for a change in policy towards the French:

> Our policy must change in consequence: formerly we confis-cated the French imperialists' properties; now, as negotiations are going on, we may, in accordance with the principle of equality and mutual benefit, allow French economic and cultural interests to be preserved in Indochina. Negotiations entail reasonable mutual concessions. Formerly we said we would drive out and wipe out all French aggressive forces; now, in the talks held, we have demanded and the French have accepted, that a date be set for the withdrawal of their troops. In the past, our aim was to wipe out the puppet administration and army with a view to national reunification; now we practise a policy of leniency and seek reunification of the country through nation-wide elections.

Ho's mention of elections was made five days before Molotov settled the issue by choosing a two-year time frame. Neither, or so it seems, was Ho aware that the 17th parallel would be picked as the military demarcation line. Nevertheless, as the following quotation reveals, Ho and the VWP were already committed to partition. In Ho's words:

> If you want peace you must end the war, if you want to end the war then you must obtain a cease-fire. If you want a cease-fire

then you must readjust [*dieu chinh*] zones, which is to say, the enemy's army must concentrate in one area, so as to be able to withdraw gradually [from the country], while our army concentrates in another area. We must obtain a very large territory where we would have sufficient means for building, consolidating, and developing our forces for the purpose of influencing other regions, and thereby bring about reunification [of the country]. Readjustment of zones is not partition; it is a temporary affair leading to reunification.

Ho then went on to talk about the various problems that would arise as a result of partition. He also expounded on the need to create new policies, especially in the north, where the Party would be given control of cities. Ho concluded this part by warning those present against the following ideological errors:

Leftist deviation. Some people, intoxicated with our repeated victories, want to fight on at all costs, to a finish; they see only the trees, not the whole forest; with their attention focused on the withdrawal of the French they fail to detect their schemes, they see the French but not the Americans; they are partial to military action and make light of diplomacy. They are unaware that we are struggling in international conferences as well as on the battlefields in order to attain our goal. They will oppose the new slogans, which they deem to be rightist manifestations and to imply too many concessions. They set forth excessive conditions unacceptable to the enemy. They want quick results, unaware that the struggle for peace is a hard and complex one. Leftist deviation will cause one to be isolated, alienated from one's own people and those of the world, and suffer setbacks.

Rightist deviation on the other hand, would lead to pessimism, inaction and unprincipled concessions. It would result in lack of confidence in the people's strength and would blunt their combative spirit, causing them to lose the power to endure hardships and to aspire only to a quiet and easy life.

The Central Committee also heard a report by Ho on his talks with Chou En-lai held during July 3–5, 1954. Chou appraised Ho of the talks he had held in Berne with Mendes-France on June 23 as well as his conversations with Nehru in India and U Nu in Burma, held en route to the Sino-Vietnamese border. Chou and Mendes-France reached agreement on certain issues relating to Laos and Cambodia; on Viet-Nam they both agreed that military issues should have priority over political ones. Both men raised the issue of regroupment zones. Mendes-France suggested the possibility of a 'horizontal' cut while Chou recommended bilateral talks between the DRVN delegation and France on the issue.[19]

Chou's trip to India was his first to a non-Communist Asian country. While in Delhi he promised Nehru that he would persuade the DRVN to withdraw its forces from Cambodia and Laos and grant recognition to both kingdoms. In their final communique both leaders agreed to conduct their future relations on the basis of the five principles of peaceful coexistence and expressed the hope that these principles would be applied 'to the solution of the problems in Indochina'.

According to one writer, '(t)he importance of this historic meeting cannot be exaggerated. It helped Chou later to persuade Ho Chi Minh to withdraw from Laos and Cambodia by pointing out that Indian and Asian opinion would be adverse toward the Vietminh's [DRVN's] aggressive moves and continuation of the conflict'.[20] Later Chou would nominate India as chairman of the tripartite International Commission for Supervision and Control (ICC), a body set up to oversee the implementation of the Geneva Agreements in Indochina.

A marked change in the DRVN's views on where to draw the demarcation line was evident after the Chou–Ho talks. According to an American account[21] these changes resulted from Chinese pressure:

> This Viet Minh [DRVN] position [on demarcation] underwent a drastic change by the middle of July; and the change can be traced to a meeting between Chou En-lai and Ho Chi Minh at Nanning near the China-Vietnam border. According to CIA reports, Chou applied pressure on Ho to accept a partition line much farther to the North, probably the 17th or 18th parallel. Pham Van Dong's subsequent compromise position indicating a willingness of the Viet Minh to discuss partition at the 16th parallel seems to have originated in the talks between Chou and Ho.

Ten days separated the end of the Chou–Ho talks and Ho's speech before the 6th Plenum of the Central Committee. The VWP Politburo met immediately after the talks. It discussed the various implications of the cross-cutting pressures being brought to bear and reviewed the situation on the ground before agreeing to accept partition at or near the 17th parallel.

According to a later Party account of this meeting:[22]

> The [sixth] session unanimously agreed with the Politburo on the decision to negotiate in order to reestablish peace in Indochina on the basis of French recognition of the independence, sovereignty, unity and territorial integrity of Viet-Nam. The Conference decided 'to direct the struggle against the U.S. imperialists and the French warmongers and, relying on the success already achieved, to struggle to realize peace in Indochina, to smash the schemes of the U.S. imperialists to prolong and expand the unity and independence, and to achieve democracy throughout the country'.

THE AFTERMATH OF THE GENEVA CONFERENCE

In the post-Geneva period most Western observers believed that the Lao Dong Party was so strong politically that it would dominate the scheduled electoral contest. French and American intelligence sources estimated Communist control to range between 60 and 90 per cent of the population in areas outside of sect control. This would mean a rural strength of approximately 2.1 to 3.6 million persons out of a total population of some 10 million living below the 17th parallel at that time.[23].

It took the VWP nearly two months to work out the details of its program for the south. This delay was due to three factors: dissension in the Party over both the principles of the peace settlement and the fine details eventually agreed to; a deep suspicion over American intentions immediately after the Geneva Conference; and problems in communicating and coordinating action with the leaders in Nam Bo. It was not until the third week of September that the Politburo assembled and approved the basic resolutions which would guide policy in the year ahead.[24]

In the meantime, on July 25 the Central Committee held another meeting. Despite whatever reservations were held, the public announcements presented a united front. An editorial in the Party's newspaper, *Nhan Dan* (July 25, 1954), declared that the Geneva Conference constituted a 'brilliant success'. A joint enlarged session of the Lien Viet Front and the Viet-Nam Peace Committee was convened to give its full support and approval for the agreements. A plenary session of the National Assembly's Standing Committee did likewise.

The immediate policy tasks in the new period were listed in both the *Nhan Dan* editorial and in an Appeal by the Party on the same date. The editorial stated that the main task of the revolutionary movement was: 'struggle to consolidate the peace we have won, faithfully and rapidly implement the provisions of the armistice agreement, and go forward to the settlement of the Indochinese political issues, so as to fully regain our national rights, that is— complete unity, independence, and democracy.'

The Appeal declared: 'The patriotic struggle of our people has entered a new phase. The phase of armed struggle is now being replaced by the phase of political struggle. However, like the armed fighting, the political struggle will certainly be long and hard before reaching complete victory.'

During the course of the First Indochina War, coordination of Lao Dong Party policy throughout the length of Viet-Nam was usually difficult. In part this reflected regional differences in the country, as well as the geographical configuration of Viet-Nam. In

1951 an attempt was made to remedy this situation by creating a special Central Committee Directorate for Southern Viet-Nam (*Trung Uong Cuc Mien Nam*). This directorate was staffed by members of the Lao Dong Party's Central Committee and served as its forward echelon. Its precise location, if there was one, was thought to be somewhere in the U Minh forest area of the Ca Mau peninsula.

It was this directorate which implemented Party policy in the south after the Geneva Agreements were signed. It was charged with implementing a ceasefire in central Viet-Nam on August 1, 1954 and in southern Viet-Nam on August 11, 1954. In each region regroupment of military forces was to take place within 15 days of the ceasefire into specified provisional assembly areas. These were: Binh Dinh and Quang Ngai provinces, Ham Tan–Xuyen Moc, the Plain of Reeds and in Ca Mau province. After this initial regroupment a final regroupment of PAVN forces north of the 17th parallel was to occur within 300 days. A similar procedure was to be followed by the French Union Forces which would result in their regroupment south of the 17th parallel. A demilitarized zone would then separate the two sides.

In the period from July 20 until a meeting of the Political Bureau in late September, the Central Committee Directorate for Southern Viet-Nam was told to exercise extreme vigilance until the ceasefires went into effect, and then to regroup into the provisional assembly areas and await further instructions. No doubt French actions were being studied with care, especially in the north, and American intentions were being closely scrutinised during this critical period.

Demonstrations were organised to welcome the restoration of peace.[25] Although reported as early as July, they did not really take shape until August 1 when they occurred simultaneously in Hue, Da Nang and Saigon-Cholon.[26] The demonstrations were suppressed in both Da Nang, where one person was reportedly killed and two wounded, and Saigon-Cholon, where police fired into a crowd, wounding several people. The demonstration in Saigon-Cholon occurred ten days before the ceasefire came into effect and thus its suppression was predictable. Reports at that time said the August demonstration welcoming the Geneva Agreements was called as a riposte to an earlier gathering on July 18 protesting partition.

Perhaps as many as 5000 were mobilized for the August 1 event. The significance of these events is that in the aftermath of the police shootings a Movement for the Defence of the Peace and the Geneva Agreements was organised in Saigon-Cholon, and branches were soon established in Hue and Da Lat. In brief the Party's underground was now beginning to flex its political muscles.[27]

THE POLITBURO MEETING OF SEPTEMBER 1954

From 5–7 September the Political Bureau of the Lao Dong Party held an important meeting which adopted a long-range policy aimed at synchronising Party policies internationally, in the north and in the south, so as to bring about the implementation of the Geneva Agreements, as the Party interpreted its provisions.

The September Politburo meeting occurred after the initial regroupment into provisional assembly areas and prior to the start of the final regroupment into the northern regroupment zone. It also occurred after an eight-nation conference in Manila had formed the Southeast Asia Treaty Organisation. Finally, it took place at the height of a political crisis in Saigon between the newly appointed Premier, Ngo Dinh Diem, and the Chief of Staff of the Army, General Nguyen Van Hinh. Each of these events was to shape the final conference resolution.

According to a Communist policy document written at this time,[28] the Lao Dong Party Politburo still adhered to Zhdanov's 'two camp theory' in which the world was seen as divided into two blocs, one composed of the forces of peace led by the Soviet Union, and the other composed of the forces of war, led by the American imperialists. The VWP proclaimed the DRVN a part of the former.

In the Politburo's view, the balance of forces was tipped in favour of the Soviet-led bloc for peace, while the bloc led by the American imperialists was entering a period of increased isolation. In these circumstances, there was a danger that American imperialism would resort to aggression in order to forestall further decline. The purpose of SEATO, and other military alliances, was to assist in the encirclement of the USSR and China. The Politburo also argued that the imperialist bloc was enmeshed in difficulties because of competition among the capitalist powers which took the form of Franco-American rivalry for dominance in Indochina.

In contrast, the VWP Politburo held that the Soviet-led bloc of peace was entering a period of ascendancy, as an increasing number of people were enlisted in a broad anti-imperialist front. With regard to Indochina, the Geneva Conference was seen as evidence for the view that '[a]ny international conflict could be resolved by negotiations' in a manner favourable to the forces of peace.

However, peace could only be maintained if it were defended properly against the aggressive schemes of the American imperialists. As *Nhan Dan* reported on March 3, 1955, the Politburo resolved: 'to achieve agrarian reform, restore and increase production and strengthen the people's army so as to consolidate northern Vietnam'. In other words, the north was to constitute the foundation for the building of socialism. This in itself would protect the peace and influence the political struggle in the south. This was explained by a Central Committee directive: 'The results which we have acquired, and the progress which we will make in the task of reconstruction will constitute [the] firm initial base. . . on which the reconstruction of the entire country will be based after the general elections. The results will be effective enough to incite [sic] the population of the South to struggle in favor of the application of the Geneva Agreements. . .'[29]

Lao Dong Party policy for the south was aimed at carrying out the Geneva Agreements, and reorganising and reorientating the Party and its united front in the new period, so that the political provisions of the Geneva Agreements would be implemented and the general elections scheduled for 1956 would be held. Party policy was to be carried out on three fronts—internationally, in the north, and in the south—and was to be integrated in such a way that each front would reinforce the others, and the combination of all three would lead the Lao Dong Party towards victory. This was spelled out by the Politburo in a resolution[30] issued after its September meeting:

> the general task of our Party is: to unite and lead the people in the struggle for the implementation of the armistice agreement, forestalling and overthrowing all schemes to undermine this agreement so as to consolidate peace; to strive to complete the land reform, restore and increase production, step up the build-up of the people's army to strengthen the North; to maintain and step up the political struggle of the Southern people, with a view to consolidating peace, achieving reunification, complet-ing independence and democracy in the whole country.

The Central Committee Directorate in the south was accordingly charged with two broad areas of responsibility: implementing the Geneva Agreements, and reorganizing the Party and its mass organisation, the Lien Viet Front, to win the forthcoming elections. The implementation of the Geneva Agreement was seen as a two-step process: carrying out the military provisions and then carrying out the political provisions. The first step was to be initiated during the 300-day regroupment period. The second step was to commence immediately with a political struggle movement demanding consul-tations between 'the competent authorities of the two zones' to begin planning for the 1956 general elections.

Party reorganisation had one main purpose: to prepare for a period of clandestine activity in which formerly 'liberated areas' were to be reoccupied by the State of Viet-Nam and French authorities. This meant that different policies would have to be designed for areas of varying degrees of Party control such as base areas, areas of contested control and 'enemy controlled' areas.

The Lien Viet Front, although not formally disbanded until

September, 1955, and the village-based committees of resistance
and administration, were also slated for reorganisation. The Lien
Viet Front's functional constituents, the national salvation associations, were disbanded. Rural members were channelled into work
exchange teams, mutual assistance associations, social welfare
groups, or into organisations for farmers and women. The program
of reorganisation was begun during the initial period of regroupment into provisional assembly areas and continued until February,
1955 when most of the officials connected with the Central Committee Directorate for Southern Viet-Nam went north during the
final phase of regroupment.

REORGANISATION IN THE SOUTH

At the time of the ceasefire in 1954, the Lao Dong Party had a
southern membership of some 60 000. After reorganisation this
number was reduced to 15 000 by 1955.[31] Most members were
retired from active service and returned to their native villages. An
unknown percentage regrouped to the north. Others, after review,
had their Party membership cancelled and were struck off the rolls.

During this period of paring down membership numbers, a
variety of reorientation courses were held to assist in the transition
from war to peace.[32] Members attended study courses on such
topics as 'the significance of the victory achieved at Geneva', 'the
new Party line in an era of peace', and 'on the immediate tasks'. The
content of each course differed according to the position of the
Party in each 'area and the expected future role of the member
concerned. Party members who retained their active status were
assigned to lead the political struggle movement.

In the countryside the Party and its youth groups were to go
underground and lead a clandestine existence. Certain self-defence
units and specialised hit squads were to become covert as well. The
Lien Viet Front was disbanded as it had outlived its usefulness. The
Party intended to replace it with another united front with a much
wider appeal, which would embrace former enemies and collabor-
ators. The new front, however, was to be organised over a period of
time, cautiously, step-by-step. In the interim, the Party chose to rely
on three types of organisations with which to wage the political
struggle: legal, semi-legal and secret groups.[33] These were to be
based in the cities as well as the countryside. Some groups were to
be *ad hoc*, while others were to be permanent.

A variety of legal and semi-legal organisations in the rural areas
were to provide a concentric ring of influence around the Party's
covert core. Included in these categories were associations for
farmers, women, war veterans, students, and rubber plantation

workers; labour exchange teams; mutual assistance groups; village self-defence organisations; and a number of single issue groups such as committees to protect the moral life of the people, to propagate the national language, to promote mass education, and committees to protect the interests of prisoners and internees organised at village level.

Party activities in towns and cities were promoted and intensified in the post-ceasefire period, but for obvious reasons had to be conducted in a clandestine matter. In this area the Party directed its energies at infiltrating previously existing legal and semi-legal groups, and where the purpose suited, setting up its own front associations. Groups targeted by the Party included trade unions, student associations, women's groups, various Chinese associations, ward committees to assist war refugees, athletics clubs, fire brigades, ancestor worship cults, and such single issue groups as the Movement for the Defence of the Peace and the Geneva Agreements, the Movement to Prevent the Decay of the National Culture, and the Movement to Aid the Victims of the Fighting (formed during the Binh Xuyen crisis).

In carrying out its political struggle movement, the party attempted to influence, if not direct, the actions of each of these groups into one of two channels, either for 'the defence of the peace' or for 'social welfare'. The 'defence of the peace' category included agitating for the implementation of the political clauses in the Geneva Agreements on such issues as democratic liberties, holding consultations with the north, normalising north–south relations, conducting general elections, and protesting reprisals and other acts of 'terrorism' against former members of the resistance.

Public action in 'defence of the peace' was to be based on the Geneva Agreements and great effort was made by the Party in the reorientation programs to instruct cadres how to file petitions and engage in other forms of peaceful protest. The aim was to bring pressure to bear on the International Control Commission, the mixed commissions and the commands of the French Union Forces and the Army of the State of Viet-Nam to intervene in situations the Party felt detrimental to its interests.

In urban areas, the Party sought to use the political struggle movement as a vehicle for advancing its own influence in a previously 'denied' area. The political struggle movement in the rural areas was also designed to defend the political rights and welfare of the people, as achieved by the Party during the First Indochina War and as enumerated in the Geneva Agreements, in the face of 'enemy' (State of Viet-Nam) encroachment into areas previously governed by the Party. In this regard, the political struggle movement focused on so-called 'social welfare slogans' related to the following themes:[34] protesting the return of landlords, unemployment, and poor refugee camp conditions; demanding a reduction in rents and interest rates, improved living conditions, and an increase in the number of schools; resisting piracy, theft, corvee labour, conscription and the expulsion of people from their homes (squatters), and guaranteeing the lives and property of the people from government action; encouraging desertion from the Army, and supporting workers' demands. Actions which threatened the 'social welfare' of the people were to be met by organised protests to the village council of notables, chiefs of military posts, and provincial authorities.

The above should highlight the fact that the Lao Dong Party saw the political struggle movement as being essentially defensive and operating mainly on the local level. One key document, issued for the guidance of provincial level authorities by the Eastern Interzone committee, dealt with the crucial questions of self-defence and village control.[35] The Party recognised that 'security of the people's lives and possessions' was essential if the political struggle objectives were to be obtained. Self-defence groups would have to be built up from small groups into larger ones. The Party suggested that youths, war veterans and former Party security men be organised for this purpose, initially at least, so that their efforts could be directed against bandits.

Party policy towards the village councils and notables underwent a change. It was recognised that the war-time policy of neutralising them was no longer appropriate. According to the new policy:[36] 'the activity of these organisations is in accord with the Geneva Agreement, for we are convinced that during the next two years, until the general elections, it is necessary to have an administrative machine to provisionally arrange the affairs of the country which is occupied by the enemy. Such a machine is indispensable for the South Vietnam zone.'

In areas where the police and council of notables had already been neutralised the revolutionary movement's organisation structure was to remain intact. In areas where the 'enemy' planned to install new councils, the Party was to gain control over them by secretly introducing its own sympathisers. It was not intended to use the Party's administrative cadres, but to rely on its supporters from among the farmers, poor peasants, even the rich peasantry and the landowning classes if necessary, and as a last resort, even former notables. This tactic was designed to protect the Party from direct exposure to security officials of the State of Viet-Nam.

REGROUPMENT AND REORIENTATION

After the September 1954 meeting the Political Bureau's resolution was transmitted to its directorate in the south, which in turn issued

Table 1.1   Estimates of military and civilian personnel regrouped to the north, 1954–55

Provisional Assembly Area	Soldiers	Civilians	Total
Ham Tan – Xuyen Moc	10 700	5 300	16 000
Plain of Reeds	13 500	6 500	20 000
Ca Mau province	20 000	9 900	29 900
Binh Dinh – Quang Ngai	42 700	21 300	64 000
Total	86 900	43 000	129 900

Source: B.S.N. Murti, *Vietnam Divided*, p. 224

detailed directives for its implementation. Regroupment to the north proceeded apace. Withdrawal from the Ham Tan–Xuyen Moc area was completed before the deadline. The first instalment of troop regroupment from Binh Dinh–Quang Ngai was completed on schedule. Despite a series of minor incidents, observers concluded[37] that the relative smoothness of the regroupment was evidence that the Lao Dong Party was fulfilling its obligations.

At the end of October, regroupment from the Plain of Reeds and the second instalment from Binh Dinh–Quang Ngai also was carried out without incident. In February Ca Mau was evacuated, thus leaving only one provisional assembly area left south of the demarcation line, Binh Dinh–Quang Ngai. There the third and final instalment was scheduled for completion by May 19, 1955.

During the withdrawal of military forces into the provisional assembly areas, preparations were also undertaken to decide who was to regroup north and who was to remain. Similar decisions had to be made concerning equipment. Much of it was stored in caches. Table 1.1 sets out the figures by provisional assembly area. These figures reveal that Communist military regroupees to the north outnumbered their civilian counterparts by two to one. The civilian figures include Party members, administrative cadres, security service personnel, technical specialists, highlanders, former prisoners, their families, and children.

Prior to regroupment, PAVN strength in the south was estimated to have been as high as 100 000 men.[38] Around 90 000 were regrouped north. Those remaining were demobbed or were retained in secret military units dispersed in base areas such as Ca Mau, Go Cong, the That Son (Seven Mountains) region along the Cambodian border, the Plain of Reeds, the highlands of central Viet-Nam, or near the border of the northern regroupment zone. Estimates by US, French and State of Viet-Nam intelligence organisations for the 1954–1960 period placed Communist armed strength in the south in the 5000 to 10 000 range, of which no more than 2000 were ever considered active.[39]

The bulk of the war-time administrators, from regional level downward, remained as there was no provision in the Geneva Agreements requiring their regroupment. Both Party and non-Party cadres were reclassified, retrained and given new assignments. Party members who were known were dispersed to other areas where they would act as 'single-contact members'. Their tasks would be to organise new cells and participate in the various organisations to be used in the political struggle movement. Party cadres who were not well-known remained in place, where they were reorganised into small three-man cells. Their tasks were to carry out Party policy covertly. Most cadres at the village level were instructed to obtain 'legal status', avoid arrest and take up legitimate occupations until they were contacted.

Other cadres were directed to move to the cities and obtain 'legal status'. This they did by obtaining identity cards and registering for the census. Efforts were made to penetrate the government administration even further. And in central Viet-Nam there seems to have been a policy for cadres to turn themselves in, obtain clearance, and then work secretly for the Party.[40] These people, as well as the covert penetration agents, were to form the base of the urban struggle movement which was to take shape.

One result of this reorientation was that the organisation of the revolutionary movement was rendered—momentarily at least—less efficient. In addition, there seems to have been a drifting away of some of the members and cadres of mass organisations who became inactive. These were people who responded to the ceasefire by returning to their home villages to begin the task of starting up normal, productive lives. Others voluntarily rallied to the State of Viet-Nam when National Army troops moved into their areas after withdrawal of PAVN units.

THE COMMENCEMENT OF POLITICAL STRUGGLE

Because of the phased nature of the regroupment process, the Party's reorientation program was undertaken at a different rate in each of the provisional assembly areas. It was the Party's intention during this period to fashion a clandestine organisation that would be able to survive the imposition of the opposing administration. Since, in some areas, Party control stretched back for eight or nine years, the Party felt confident of success because they had the people's support. Any attempt to root out the Party and destroy its organisation would be resolutely protested, not only in local demonstrations, but in appeals to the various mobile teams assigned to the ICC and to PAVN officers assigned to the mixed commissions.

The first major attempt to use the Geneva Agreements as the legal basis for political struggle is illustrated by the case of the Movement for the Defence of the Peace and the Geneva Agreements (otherwise known as the Saigon-Cholon Peace Committee). This organisation was established in the aftermath of a demonstration held in Saigon-Cholon on August 1 by a group of left-wing intellectuals and students. Branches of the peace movement were soon established in Hue and Da Lat, while in rural areas, the Party took the initiative in forming various village-level peace committees as nominal affiliates. Covert Party agents were associated with this movement from its inception, using its semi-legal status to publicise alleged violations of the Geneva Agreements.[41]

Members of the peace movement provoked a scuffle on the occasion of the visit to Saigon of Prime Minister Nehru, when they passed out leaflets supporting peaceful coexistence. This incident was followed by a demonstration called to protest the arrival of President Eisenhower's special representative to Viet-Nam, General J. Lawton Collins. Criticism of the US relationship touched a raw nerve with the Diem government and it moved swiftly to repress the group.

The arrest of three protesters in late October 1954 was followed on November 11 by the round-up of the entire eight-member Executive Committee as well as 23 ordinary members. In December, and in March of the following year, a further 29 arrests were carried out in Saigon. The Hue branch of the Movement for the Defence of the Peace was struck twice, once in March and again in April, 1955 while simultaneous raids were also carried out in Da Lat.

These arrests immediately provoked protests by DRVN authorities.[42] Pham Hung, chief of the PAVN High Command delegation in southern Viet-Nam, sent a letter dated November 26 to the command of the French Union Forces, denouncing the arrests of October and November. General Van Tien Dung raised the matter at the November 29, 1954 meeting of the Joint Commission, where he accused the French of not carrying out their responsibilities under the Geneva Agreements.

Protest statements, demonstrations and the like were quickly mounted in the north. Their aim was to capture international attention and thus bring pressure to bear on the French to stop the arrests and secure the release of those jailed. On November 2, 1954 for example, the Viet-Nam Committee for the Defence of World Peace sent a note to the World Committee for the Defence of Peace protesting the violations of the 'democratic rights' of the members of the Saigon-Cholon Peace Committee and demanding their release.[43] On November 27 a number of groups including the Viet-Nam Committee for the Defence of World Peace, the Viet-Nam General Confederation of Labour, the Peasants' National Liaison

Bureau, the Viet-Nam Women's Union and the Committee for the Protection of Vietnamese Children staged a public protest over the suppression of the Movement for the Defence of the Peace.[44]

In April, 1955 the Diem government dramatically announced that several of the leaders of the peace movement had been transferred to Hai Phong in the north, where they would be given the choice of returning to the south or of remaining when the city was turned over to Communist control. In May, when the final deadline for regroupment was reached, the PAVN delegation to the Joint Military Commission requested information on the whereabouts of the 'peace partisans' who had been deported to the north. The French promised to supply the information after making enquiries. The matter then faded in importance as it was overtaken by more dramatic events. Nonetheless, this pattern of protest was to be repeated over and over again as a response to reports of alleged violations of the Geneva Agreements by the French and State of Viet-Nam authorities.

POLITICAL INSTABILITY: DIEM AND THE SECTS

Of greater importance to the Lao Dong Party at this time was the instability of the political situation in southern Viet-Nam and the likelihood that the State of Viet-Nam would collapse as a result of domestic challenges to its authority. The State of Viet-Nam at this time was a dubious concept in political and legal terms. In the period immediately following the Geneva conference, the French controlled its Army and exercised other responsibilities of government normally the prerogatives of a sovereign state.[45] In 1954–55, the State of Vietnam was rent by the open hostility between Premier Ngo Dinh Diem and Chief of State, Bao Dai. Bao Dai loyalists, centred around the Army's chief of staff, continually threatened to overturn the government in a coup.

The State of Viet-Nam was beset by a plethora of other challenges. For example, while France and the US tried hard on a government-to-government level to fashion a common approach to the Diem government, political and military representatives of both governments followed their own inclinations and dabbled in local politics by backing opposing groups. Diem's position in Saigon was insecure, as armed elements of the Binh Xuyen sect held sway in nearby Cholon. In addition to all this, there were two large sect groups, the Cao Dai and the Hoa Hao, which ran, literally, 'states within a state'. Each of the sects, in turn, was subdivided into particular war lord factions.

When the Lao Dong Party met in September 1954, Premier Diem was facing his first grave crisis: a challenge to his authority by the Chief of Staff of the Army, General Nguyen Van Hinh. This was eventually resolved in the Premier's favour in early December when the general was summoned by Bao Dai to France. Prior to the resolution of this crisis, however, at least one plot to overthrow Diem was thwarted.[46]

The Diem–Hinh confrontation was also marked by the intervention of Bao Dai, who attempted to obtain sect backing for a new government. His gambit was to use the leader of the Binh Xuyen, Le Van Vien, in his approach to other sect leaders. This move failed when Diem enlarged his Cabinet with precisely these men. The key appointments to the second Cabinet formed on September 24 were Nguyen Thanh Phuong of the Cao Dai and Tran Van Soai of the Hoa Hao as ministers of state without portfolio. Additional appointees from the Cao Dai and the Hoa Hao filled other vacancies.

In the following months sporadic fighting broke out in the countryside between elements of Ba Cut's Hoa Hao forces and Cao Dai units.[47] The scramble to gain control of recently evacuated DRVN territory in the Plain of Reeds was at issue. The same problem also brought Ba Cut's units into conflict with the Army. The matter intensified in December, 1954 when reports revealed that fighting was taking place between Hoa Hao units, between Ba Cut's forces and Cao Dai units, and between the National Army and Ba Cut. The fighting continued into January and during the following month shifted location as the Army and Ba Cut's forces squared off to determine who would first 'liberate' the Ca Mau area after the final withdrawal of PAVN units. As it turned out, these were only the beginning rounds of a fight which was to last well into 1957.

At the same time Ngo Dinh Diem succeeded in playing on the factionalism of his opponents who, in mid-September, had managed to provide a facade of unity. American support for Diem, even over French objections, proved decisive. On December 31, 1954, the US government announced that it would no longer give aid to Viet-Nam via the French as was customary, but as of the New Year would mount direct aid to the State of Viet-Nam.[48] This move undercut the French, who had used the 'power of the purse' to encourage policies to their liking. This shift in American policy also touched directly upon the vital issue of the subsidies that had been provided by the French to the sect armies. The Diem government now found its position considerably strengthened in relation to the sects.

Thus, it was a combination of American support and monetary inducements which helped Diem to split the sect ranks.[49] In January, 1955 Nguyen Van Hue, Tran Van Soai's Hoa Hao Chief of

Staff, rallied to the State of Viet-Nam and promised to integrate a force of 3500 men loyal to him into the Army. He was followed by another Hoa Hao officer, Major Nguyen Day, who brought with him 1500 soldiers. On February 13, two days after the French subsidies officially ended, a Cao Dai leader, Trinh Minh The, entered Saigon and proclaimed his support for the Diem government. He was followed ten days later by Nguyen Giac Ngo, a Hoa Hao leader.

Meanwhile Diem had been slowly preparing the next move in his quest to gain control over the entire governmental apparatus that was nominally headed by him. His target this time was the Binh Xuyen sect, which controlled the police, security, gambling and vice operations in Saigon-Cholon. Although the showdown came in late March, it had been preceded by other events which made an armed clash highly likely. The head of the Binh Xuyen, Le Van Vien (Bay Vien) had been conspiring openly since at least August, 1954 to either bring down the Diem government or to 'kick Diem upstairs' into a figurehead position.[50] In late November a brief Army–Binh Xuyen clash foreshadowed the events of March, 1955 as Diem deliberately attempted to undermine the Binh Xuyen's financial position.

In early 1955 Diem moved to close down the Binh Xuyen-operated brothels and to cancel their gambling concessions. Then, in order to strengthen his military position in Saigon, Diem began to transfer units loyal to him, including Nung soldiers, from central Viet-Nam to Saigon. During the third week of February, 1955 the Binh Xuyen attempted to counter this gambit by bringing together the various sect factions for discussions on united action. In attendance were Nguyen Thanh Phuong, Pham Cong Tac and Trinh Minh The of the Cao Dai and Tran Van Soai, Lam Thanh Nguyen and Ba Cut of the Hoa Hao. On March 3 these men announced the formation of a united front, a mutual non-aggression pact and concerted opposition to the Diem government (of which several of them were nominal Cabinet members).[51] Pham Cong Tac, the spiritual head of the Cao Dai, was named leader.

On March 21 the tri-sect united front issued an ultimatum to Diem, calling on him to form a new government of national union and to carry out certain reforms. An intense five-day period of negotiation followed in which both France and America became involved. Diem succeeded in getting Trinh Minh The to switch his loyalty, and then prepared to attack. On March 28 he ordered Army units to dislodge the Binh Xuyen from the police and security headquarters buildings in Saigon. Fighting broke out on the evening of March 29–30, plunging South Viet-Nam into a period of domestic crisis and political instability.

CONCLUSION

The Lao Dong Party, which led the eight-year war of resistance against the French and their indigenous allies, decided in July, 1954 to cease armed struggle as the main method of achieving its objectives and to shift to political struggle. This decision was made in response to both external pressures and as a result of weighing domestic strengths and weaknesses. Externally, the DRVN found that its allies, the USSR and China, were both moving towards a limited detente with the West and for reasons of their own wished to see an end to the First Indochinese War. Second, opposition to the war from within France had created a favourable climate for striking an advantageous bargain. The PAVN victory at Dien Bien Phu was calculated to strike the French solar plexus and knock out its will to fight. Finally, the ever-present threat of American military intervention hung over the Lao Dong Party leaders.

On the domestic scene the Party itself realised that it was not strong enough to win the complete independence it had been fighting for. Its forces and strength lay in the north, not the south. But having observed this, the Party also realised that it had certain assets: a well-organised political administration in the villages, a disciplined party and a popular program. The Party weighed the balance of forces and concluded that it was better to opt for a political settlement, secure half of the country and get the French out than to continue fighting. Therefore, they signed agreements with the French at Geneva, bringing to an end the First Indochina War.

In September, 1954 the Party held a major Political Bureau Conference, where delegates took stock of the situation and decided on a long-range policy synchronised with the various deadlines and provisions in the Geneva Agreements. Since Viet-Nam was to be partitioned, Party policy would have to be adjusted to the peculiarities of each region. In the north the Party would fulfil its obligations during the period of French regroupment and withdrawal. A similar policy was to be pursued in the south; but new provisions had to be made for those personnel not slated for final regroupment. The Party directed that those who remained must prepare for a situation in which the 'enemy' would shortly become the administration. Party cadres were directed to reorganise and prepare to function covertly. Most mass organisations associated with the Lien Viet Front were either dissolved or reorganised.

By early 1955 leaders of the Viet-Nam Workers' Party could be reasonably satisfied with the implementation of the Geneva Agreements. A ceasefire had been effectively implemented, thus bringing peace to Viet-Nam. The anticipated American military intervention did not eventuate. Reorganisation of the Party's apparatus in

Nam Bo as well as the regroupment of military forces had been executed effectively. Within the space of two months the final military withdrawals from central Viet-Nam would be completed, simultaneously with the withdrawal of French troops from the north.

The completion of the major military provisions of the Geneva Agreements (ICC control and supervision of military personnel and equipment would continue) signalled a shift in attention to political matters. High on the Party's list of priorities was the north–south consultative talks to determine the modalities of the elections. The current political instability in the south came as no surprise to Party leaders. They probably felt that Diem would fall, leaving in his wake a succession of weak governments. Perhaps a group of pro-DRVN politicians would take office and smooth the process of unification.[52] If not, then perhaps France would have to play a stronger role. Either way the Party stood to benefit.

However, there were some dark clouds on the horizon. American influence in the south was growing rapidly. Aid was now channelled to the State of Viet-Nam, by-passing the French. On November 17, 1954 J. Lawton Collins, a special representative of US President Eisenhower with the rank of ambassador, announced at a Saigon press conference that 'an American mission will soon take charge of instructing the Vietnam Army in accordance with special American methods which have proved effective in Korea, Greece, Turkey and other parts of the world'.[53] Although the State of Viet-Nam was not a signatory to the Manila Pact, it had been placed under SEATO's protective umbrella in a separate protocol. The growth in American influence was at the expense of France, whom the DRVN leaders held responsible for implementing the Geneva Agreements.

2

Political struggle under the Geneva Agreements

MARCH–AUGUST 1955

The Central Committee of the Lao Dong Party held its 7th Plenum from March 3–12, 1955. Although the discussions of this meeting have not yet been published in detail, speeches delivered to the 4th Session of the DRVN National Assembly by leading Party officials offer a good guide to Lao Dong Party policy at this stage. Prior to the plenum, the Party's top echelon in the south regrouped to the north and the Central Committee's directorate for this region was deactivated. Communist military forces remained in only one area of the south, the Binh Dinh and Quang Ngai regroupment zone.

In January, a National Congress of the Lien Viet Front was convened in Hanoi. This was the largest congress since 1951, when the Viet Minh Front was merged with the Lien Viet Front. There can be no doubt as to the purpose of this congress, for one theme runs through the major reports and speeches delivered there. Typical was an editorial in the Party paper, *Nhan Dan* (January 7, 1955), which appeared on the first day:

> Today, confronted by the new situation, the Lien Viet National Committee decided to meet in order to review what has been done, the policy written, the program of the Front, acknowledge the new situation, the new missions, and deal with the very important problem of widening and strengthening the National United Front, so as to unite and consolidate the forces of the people in order to struggle for peace, independence, and the democratization of the country.

26

In the 'new situation', enlarging the front had top priority. According to the final communique: 'the National United Front must still extend and strengthen itself. Therefore it must issue new regulations better fitting the present situation'.[1] The front was to be based on the worker–peasant alliance with the aim of struggling for north–south consultations among other goals. An organising committee was set up in order to form a new front composed of all the classes, parties, groups and religions in the north and south. A congress issued a special message 'to the compatriots of the South' which raised the possibility that Viet-Nam might remain permanently divided unless the people in both zones united to strengthen the National United Front to 'struggle for the coming general elections'.[2]

These two events, the deactivation of the Central Committee Directorate for Southern Viet-Nam and the call for a national congress to revitalise the Lien Viet Front, provide the necessary backdrop to the 7th Plenum.

THE 7TH PLENUM (MARCH 1955)

In March, 1955 the Central Committee of the Lao Dong Party set forth the following tasks:[3]

- Continue to implement the Geneva Agreements and fight for their strict observance by other parties.
- Consolidate the North in all respects.
- Keep up and step up political movement of the South Vietnamese people.
- Broaden and strengthen the National United Front throughout the country.
- Intensify diplomatic activities and enlist the support and sympathy of the world's peoples.

The 7th Plenum had to consider the full range of problems that were beginning to emerge in trying to establish a DRVN administration in the north. Energy and resources that might have been devoted to dealing with southern problems, now had to be turned to deal with two major problems north of the 17th parallel: security and economic self-sufficiency.

The massive movement of refugees to the south brought with it mixed blessings for Hanoi's new leaders. On the one hand, it freed them from potential dissidents, decreased the number of mouths to feed and made available more land for redistribution. On the other hand, the massive flow of people to the south carried with it certain security problems, it disrupted agricultural production, it depleted the DRVN of certain skilled manpower, and it caused grave embarrassment internationally. Security problems were also troublesome and suppression of minor guerrilla activities required a diversion of resources. Enemy psychological warfare activities caused concern. Therefore, on the eve of final regroupment, there was some doubt as to the Lao Dong Party's ability successfully to meet all the crisis points at once.

Ho Chi Minh touched on this problem in his opening speech[4] to the 7th Plenum, when he listed four major goals for the Party, the Army and the people:

1. Continue to rigorously apply the Geneva Agreements, to consolidate peace, and to continue to struggle in order to realize unification of the country by free elections.
2. Consolidate the north from all points of view and, at the same time, maintain and energetically develop our work in the south.
3. Consolidate and enlarge the basis of the Unified National Front throughout the country.
4. Perfect the direction, complete the instruction of the members of the Central Committee, perfect the organization and the methods of work, raise the spirit of organization and of discipline, and perfect the revolutionary education of all officers and members of the Party.

On March 20, 1955 Pham Van Dong delivered a report to the 4th Session of the DRVN National Assembly in which he dealt at length with the 'present situation and tasks'. Since Dong was both a vice premier and Political Bureau member it is reasonable to conclude not only that the speech was authoritative, but that it reflected the views of the recent Party plenum. Dong dealt with three policy areas: the international situation, problems of economic recovery in the north, and the development of a broader national united front for both zones.[5]

Dong's analysis of the world situation repeated the major tenets of the September Politburo resolution: the front of peace led by the USSR was clearly stronger than the front of the imperialists and was growing stronger each day. In discussing the Southeast Asian region, Dong focused on SEATO and American designs to oust the French in order to convert Viet-Nam into a US colony. SEATO was seen as a possible springboard for an attack on China. In Dong's view, the aim of American policy was: 'to prejudice the re-establishment of normal relations between the north and south . . .' In other words, tensions were emerging in Southeast Asia which carried the potential to disrupt the larger, more favourable peace forces. Therefore, concluded Dong, '[t]he present enemies of our people are the American imperialists, the French colonialists, saboteurs of the agreements, and their lackeys, the Ngo Dinh Diem band.'

Dong then proceeded to present a statement of foreign policy

goals. First, the DRVN would further strengthen friendly relations
with the People's Republic of China, the USSR and the people's
democracies. Second, with respect to Laos and Cambodia, the
DRVN was 'ready to establish normal relations. . . on the basis of
the five principles contained in the Sino-Indian and Sino-Burmese
joint declarations.' Third, Dong acclaimed the forthcoming Afro-
Asian Conference to be held at Bandung in Indonesia. Fourth, with
regard to France, Dong stated: 'the government of the Democratic
Republic of Vietnam is preoccupied with maintaining economic
and cultural relations with France on the principle of equality and
community of reciprocal interests.'

The most significant portion of Dong's report was his analysis of
developments in the north. Dong stressed several times that the
mobilisation of the masses for the reduction of land rent and the application of the agrarian reform was considered the foundation of
all reconstruction policy. Elsewhere in his report, Dong discussed
the enormous agricultural problems confronting the DRVN leaders
as they tried to rebuild their war-damaged economy. Dong mentioned, in particular, the destroyed irrigation, communication
and transport systems which forced the Party 'to make exceptional
efforts to surmount the difficulties.'

In light of these problems, the Central Committee took the
decision to accord priority to consolidating the north, over the
carrying out of the political struggle in the south. The priorities were
justified by Dong in this way.[6]

The north becomes the basis of the Democratic Republic of
Vietnam. To strengthen the north is to strengthen the principal
bases (sic) which will decide the victory of the present struggle
for national liberation, the foundation of which is the struggle
to strengthen peace and national unification.

To strengthen the north we must do everything necessary on
the political, economic, cultural and military planes. It is a
question of developing the application of the agrarian reform
and realizing the economic and cultural recovery, in order to
improve the material and moral conditions of the people, to
progressively make the country advance toward industrializa-
tion; in order to strengthen the national defence, to defend
peace and the Fatherland, to strengthen the Government of the
Democratic Republic and to give significance to all its diplomatic actions.

In so doing we will strengthen the north, but we must also pay
attention to the south and take into consideration the aspirations of the compatriots of the south, so that they may
understand the necessity of positively participating with full
confidence in the common struggle of all our people.

In order to undertake mass mobilisation for rent reduction and to
carry out agrarian reform 'a single and central direction' was

necessary. The Party, according to Dong, must enhance its discipline and authority over 'the cadres charged with internal and external policy'.

Party policy in the south, stated Dong, would be based on the strict implementation of the Geneva Agreements 'which aim at consolidating peace, unifying the country, and perfecting independence and democracy.' Therefore, to achieve these aims the struggle in the south needed to be co-ordinated with the struggle in the north.

In both the north and the south, the basis of the Party's power would be a national united front. Its policies would be directed at creating: 'a large movement in favour of peace and unity, free general elections, a political conference between the governments of the two zones, the re-establishment of normal relations between the north and south and in favour of the plans of the National Assembly and the Government of the Democratic Republic of Vietnam concerning these problems.'

Vo Nguyen Giap also delivered a report[7] to the National Assembly in March, 1955. Though its scope was much narrower than Pham Van Dong's report, it did contain some significant revelations about Lao Dong Party policy at this juncture. Giap, like Dong, was a full member of the Political Bureau and it is reasonable to assume his words were an accurate reflection of Central Committee thinking.

General Giap addressed himself to a review of the implementation of the Geneva Agreements over the previous eight months, and to the likely developments in the future. According to Giap, the Agreements constituted a 'great victory' for the people of Viet-Nam because the international community recognised the 'sovereignty, independence and territorial unity' of Viet-Nam. The Agreements ended the war, provided a set timetable for the withdrawal of the French, and made provision for a political settlement by means of general elections to be held in 1956.

Giap's second point was that the main military provisions had been carried out satisfactorily: 'during the last eight months we have always correctly and strictly applied all clauses of the Geneva accords: the adversary, on his side, has also respected certain of these clauses.' Among the points of contention, according to Giap, was the question of prisoners still held by the other side.

Far more serious were the efforts of the American imperialists to violate the Geneva Agreements. Giap specifically mentioned SEATO and its extension of protection to Indochina as a 'cynical violation' which threatened the 'security and peace in Southeast Asia'. The Americans, Giap argued, were preparing for a war with China. The French were guilty of collusion with the Americans. Here Giap cited as examples the Ely–Collins cooperation in Saigon, meetings of officials of both countries, and France's participation in SEATO.

Certain articles of the Geneva Agreements protecting individuals against reprisal and guaranteeing their democratic liberties were being violated, according to Giap. He accused the Diem regime of conducting a policy of terrorism against former Resistance veterans. According to his figures, 'since the cease-fire up to Jan. 31, 1955, the adversary committed 2321 acts of terrorism and massacre.'

General Giap then turned his attention to the north and explained what had happened there. He concentrated his remarks on discussing the refugee flow to the south and the problem of security. Regarding refugees, Giap stated that they were either tricked or forced into regrouping to the south, where they were compelled to become soldiers in Diem's army or 'coolies on the rubber plantations'.

Giap then exposed the activities of 'reactionaries in the service of the Diem government' who used propaganda to distort 'the spirit of our policy' and who sowed panic among Catholic compatriots. Giap listed the following as examples of false propaganda:

- God has gone to the south.
- Catholics will be excommunicated if they stay in the north.
- Those who go to the south will be given ricefields, buffaloes, and will lead a happy life.
- Those who stay in the north will be exterminated by American atomic bombs.

Giap concluded this section by stating what had become a keystone of DRVN policy: even though the Americans had replaced the French militarily and political, it was '[t]he French authorities who were signatories to these accords and [who] are also responsible for it'.

Giap's conclusions reiterated previous policy and added some new features. First, developments in Cambodia and Laos were linked to developments in Viet-Nam. That is, with the implementation of the Geneva Agreements would come 'a solid base' for the opening of favourable relations among the three nations of Indochina. Second, DRVN policy towards the Agreements remained unchanged: 'We are continuing to respect and apply the signed agreements; we are resolved to struggle to demand that the adversary respect and apply the agreements'. Third, 'struggle' against the saboteurs of the Geneva Agreements was the only response Giap saw the DRVN making if America and the Diem government continued to violate the Agreements.

Lao Dong Party statements were never clear on this point, and in this instance General Giap proved no exception: 'With the struggle in favor of the application of the agreements, the struggle for the consolidation of peace and the development of unity remains intimately bound. The general elections will only take place when peace is consolidated. The struggle for the carrying out of unity will contribute largely to the consolidation of peace.'

In the final section of his report General Giap stressed the use of the 'legal' status of the Geneva Agreements as a base on which to launch this struggle. He claimed that for the political struggle movement to be successful the people must first be educated in how to denounce violations. Second, a broad front consisting of the supporters of peace, unity, independence and democracy must be formed. Third, PAVN must continue to respect the Agreements by regrouping the remaining troops in Binh Dinh–Quang Ngai provinces. Fourth, the clauses of the agreement relating to freedom of movement should be respected. Fifth, the struggle movement should protest coercive measures, restrictions of movement, acts of terrorism, distinctions in the treatment of people based on political belief and violation of democratic freedoms. Finally, Giap stated: 'We must prepare to negotiate with the adversary with regard to the general elections. To favor these negotiations our Government and the compatriots of the two zones must join their efforts in order to re-establish and increase economic, cultural and social relations.'

Although official Party histories provide no further details as to the decisions taken at the 7th Plenum, the speeches by Pham Van Dong and Vo Nguyen Giap can be taken as accurate reflections of Party thinking. We have mentioned earlier how the Party hoped to integrate policy on three levels (on the international scene, in the north and in the south) to achieve maximum impact. The 7th Plenum met just before the final regroupment of military forces. General Giap reported in his speech that the regroupment would be carried out as far as the PAVN was concerned. This event, then, marks the divide between the two-step process of implementing the Geneva Agreements; step one was focused on military details, while step two would be concerned with political affairs. Partition was to occur in May and be followed in July, supposedly, by consultations between the 'competent authorities' in the two zones.

Lao Dong Party policy at this point continued to reflect the long-range assessment drafted the previous September (1954). It also addressed itself to some new tasks, two features of which are striking: first, the DRVN was going to start a 'diplomatic offensive' among its allies and neighbours, and second, agrarian reform was going to be given top priority in the north. The south was to rely on its own resources in developing the clandestine network of Party members and in carrying out a political struggle movement emphasising slogans related to the implementation of the Geneva Agreements (namely, a call for consultations, a call for normalisation of relations, and protest at reprisals, terrorism and violations of democratic freedom). In March of 1955 at the time of the 7th Plenum there was still no reason to believe that any other policy would yield better results. In fact, the south was on the verge of anarchy. No real efforts had been undertaken yet by the State of Viet-Nam authorities to destroy the clandestine organisation of the Lao Dong Party. Overall, in March 1955, the situation looked favourable.

FOREIGN POLICY INITIATIVES

At this point in the narrative it is imperative to discuss three foreign policy events: the DRVN's attendance at Bandung (April 1955), the DRVN's attempts to open consultations with the authorities in the south (June 1955), and the trip abroad to China and the USSR by a DRVN government delegation headed by President Ho Chi Minh (June–July 1955).

In the post-Geneva period the DRVN came into being—at least as a 'State' accorded de facto recognition by other members of the international community. As a member of the 'front of peace' the DRVN soon exchanged diplomatic representatives with a majority of socialist nations. Beginning in October, 1954 the People's Republic of China (PRC), the USSR, Poland, Czechoslovakia, the German Democratic Republic, Hungary, Mongolia, North Korea, Rumania, and Bulgaria all opened embassies in Hanoi. Coincidentally with this, a series of trade and other agreements were signed and various cultural, educational, and political delegations were exchanged.

Both Nehru and U Nu paid courtesy calls to Hanoi en route to the PRC. In November 1954, a group of Indonesian diplomats spent a week touring the DRVN making soundings in advance of the Bandung Conference. It was the Bandung Conference, however, which provided the DRVN with the opportunity to make its foreign policy and views on the Geneva Agreements known to a wide body of nations. The DRVN delegation to Bandung, led by Pham Van Dong, stopped in India and Burma en route.

Dong's stay in India was marked by the release of a joint communique which stressed the 'importance of free elections and the achievement of unity of Viet Nam as provided for by the Geneva Agreements', as 'an important contribution, not only to unity and peace in Viet-Nam, but also Indo-China as a whole and in Southeast Asia.'[8] The DRVN's reception at Bandung was a marked success. According to SarDesai:[9]

At the Bandung Conference, Nehru had largely ignored the delegation from South Vietnam, whereas the DRV delegation, led by Pham Van Dong, had received sympathetic attention from the conference's sponsors, the Colombo powers, particularly India. The conference had passed a resolution recommending the admission of several countries, among them Laos, Cambodia and a 'unified Vietnam', to the United Nations.

The high point of the Conference, from the DRVN's point of view, came when Nehru and Chou En Lai sponsored a joint declaration by the Royal Lao Government and the DRVN. The State of Viet-Nam officials refused to take part, thus increasing their diplomatic isolation. Laos and the DRVN agreed to establish harmonious and good neighbourly relations on the basis of the five principles of peaceful coexistence. The DRVN stated that a political settlement between the Lao government and Pathet Lao was the internal affair of Laos. This latter point harked back to the Nehru–Dong joint statement in which the DRVN first accepted the five principles of peaceful coexistence.

The DRVN also made several attempts to encourage normal relations with the south. For example, on January 28, 1955 the DRVN Postal and Telegraphic Service addressed a memorandum to its counterpart in the south suggesting they reach agreement by March 1 on details which would allow the exchange of postal cards between the two zones. After a month's wait with no reply, DRVN Postal and Telegraphic Service sent a second memorandum to its counterpart suggesting the same exchange as before, and recalling its original memorandum. This time a reply was received and the two services negotiated an agreement in April which permitted, as of May 1955, the exchange of family postal cards.[10]

After the 7th Plenum the theme of encouraging north–south relations was given increasing emphasis in the party-controlled press, particularly as the July 20, 1955 date for the commencement of consultations approached. During the month of May, for example, the official DRVN media carried three major reports raising the normalisation issue. Thus it came as no surprise when, on June 6, 1955, Pham Van Dong undertook a major initiative on this matter.[11] After pointing out that the 300-day period for military regroupment had ended, Dong said the time had arrived to implement the political provisions. He invited the State of Viet-Nam to join with the DRVN in holding a consultative conference.

The issue of elections in Vietnam was also raised by India. On June 23, Nehru and Bulganin issued a joint declaration which strongly urged 'that where elections are to be held as a preliminary to a political settlement the efforts of the Governments concerned should be directed to the full implementation of the provisions of the agreements.'[12] Another joint statement, this time between India and Poland, declared: '[i]t is essential for the sake of peace not only in Indo China but in the Far East generally and the world that the Geneva agreements should be fully implemented by the parties concerned and the elections held as provided for therein.'[13]

In the midst of these pressures, the Ngo Dinh Diem government rejected Pham Van Dong's invitation, declaring: 'we did not sign the Geneva Agreements. We are not bound in any way by these agreements, signed against the will of the Vietnamese people.'[14] Diem went on to state that his government did 'not reject the principle of free elections' but that they could only be meaningful if they were 'absolutely free'. On July 19, the eve of the deadline set for consultations, the DRVN issued yet another plea:[15]

The Government of the Democratic Republic of Vietnam proposes that you appoint your representatives and that they and ours hold the consultative conference from July 20, 1955 onwards as provided for by the Geneva Agreements at a place agreeable to both sides on Vietnamese territory in order to discuss the problem of unification of our country by means of free, general elections all over Vietnam.

The following day, a government-sponsored mob ransacked two Saigon hotels housing ICC members, thus underscoring Diem's rejection of Hanoi's bid.

At this point it is necessary to retrace our steps and consider briefly the third major foreign policy event of this period, Ho Chi Minh's first trip as head of state to China and the Soviet Union in June and July, 1955.[16] This trip preceded a conference of the Big Four and was perhaps timed to influence its deliberations. Quite clearly Ho Chi Minh sought Chinese and Soviet backing for the DRVN's policy on consultations. The composition of Ho's delegation indicated that Ho was also seeking reconstruction aid. Ho's itinerary took him to China first (June 27 to July 7), to Mongolia and to the Soviet Union (July 12–18).

Ho's trip, almost as if by way of compensation, was a great success in terms of the amount of aid he received—aid vitally necessary for Viet-Nam's recovery and later planned industrialisation. In China, the DRVN delegation received news of a grant of 800 million Chinese yuan ($US 200 million) to be applied towards the repair of damaged roads (Nam Quan to Hanoi and Lai Chau to Hai Phong), bridges, railway lines (Lao Ky to Hanoi) and airfields, and the reconstruction of some 18 projects including the important Nam Dinh cotton mill. The Chinese also announced a manpower exchange whereby Chinese technical personnel would serve in Viet-Nam and Vietnamese workers would serve as apprentices in Chinese industrial enterprises. The final DRVN–PRC joint communique also hinted at future expansion in trade relations.

In Moscow, the Soviet government announced a non-refundable (free credit) grant of 400 million roubles ($US 100 million) to assist in the reconstruction of 23 industrial and public service enterprises (including engineering plants and textiles) and the development of Viet-Nam's tin and phosphate resources. Separate technical and trade agreements worth 200 million roubles ($US 50 million) were also negotiated. Included among them was finance for a three-cornered deal by which the USSR supplied certain goods to Burma in exchange for Burmese rice which was then shipped to Viet-Nam.[17] Finally, the Soviets also agreed to exchange personnel with Viet-Nam.

Ho Chi Minh secured *pro forma* endorsement from China and the Soviet Union for the DRVN's policy on consultations. However, it is doubtful if Soviet and Chinese endorsements went far enough. For example, Bulganin was reported as remarking to the press at a reception for Ho Chi Minh that the DRVN was 'partly a member of our family of democratic nations' and that it would become a full member only after unification and the accomplishment of 'other great tasks'.[18]

In evaluating Ho's trip to the USSR, one must place it in the context of the day, as Allan Cameron reminds us:[19]

> If the Soviet Union was displaying less than total enthusiasm for the character of the DRV as a Socialist state and for the problem of reunification, the North Vietnamese (i.e. DRVN) themselves were obviously less than enthusiastic about establishing the closest of all possible ties with the Soviet Union. Relations were, of course, correct, but the North Vietnamese chose to show their displeasure, or distrust, of the Soviets by maintaining relations on a formal government to government basis while de-emphasizing party ties. That policy was clearly demonstrated during July and August 1955 when a high level DRV delegation visited both China and the Soviet Union. Although headed by Ho Chi Minh and including Truong Chinh, then General Secretary of the VWP, the delegation was carefully described by the Vietnamese as well as by the Chinese and Russians as 'the Government delegation of the Democratic Republic of Vietnam'. The visits were correct in form, but the Soviet reception for Ho Chi Minh did not compare in warmth to that accorded to Prime Minister Nehru of India during his visit in June. The joint communiques issued in Peking and Moscow at the conclusion of the visits made no mention of party relations. Neither communique indicated that the Vietnamese had won staunch support from these Communist brothers on the issue of reunification, but differences in wording indicated that there was somewhat more success in Peking than in Moscow.

In the event, the subject of Indochina was never placed on the agenda of the Big Four conference. Private discussions did take place between Eden and Molotov, but these were prompted more by the anti-International Control Commission riots in Saigon than by Ho's special influence with Moscow. When Molotov raised the question of reconvening a meeting of the 1954 Geneva Conference members at these private talks, Eden politely turned him down. According to *The Economist*,[20] the Soviet Foreign Minister was 'unexpectedly amiable' in accepting this.

At the conclusion of the Big Four conference, Molotov slipped in a mention of the Indochina problem for the record. He stated:[21]

> The Soviet delegation regrets that further attention was not given to the problems of Asia and the Far East at our conference. Among others, such questions as the restoration of the legal rights of the Chinese People's Republic in the United Nations organisation, the regulation of the situation in the Formosa region on the basis of the recognition of the indisputable rights of the Chinese people, the execution of the Geneva agreements on Indochina and other problems will not tolerate postponement.

These remarks were aimed more at China than the DRVN. China had been left out of the Big Four meeting and would shortly pursue a policy of trying to convene an Asian Geneva-type conference. But the fact that 'peaceful coexistence' was the order of the day, and that Sino-American ambassadorial talks were about to open, meant that the DRVN was left out in the cold. The best hint of this came in remarks made by Ho Chi Minh immediately on his return to Hanoi. Ho drew attention to the American plot to partition Viet-Nam and called on the Vietnamese to maintain their 'fighting spirit' and vigilance against these moves. He then thanked China and the Soviet Union for their 'generous and disinterested' aid, before concluding, 'just like during the resistance, our line at present must be, first and foremost, to rely upon ourselves whereas the help from friendly countries must come second.'[22]

INSTABILITY IN THE SOUTH

It was also during the period from March to August, 1955 that political developments in southern Viet-Nam entered their most confused state. During this time all the forces operating against the stability of the new Diem regime were given full play. From out of the chaos and violence Diem emerged triumphant, with the sect problem reduced to mere dissidence, with control over the Army restored, and with Bao Dai deposed. This new measure of strength permitted Diem to proclaim a republic, to nominate himself as its first president, and to turn his energies towards eradicating the influence of the Lao Dong Party organisation and its supporters from the south.

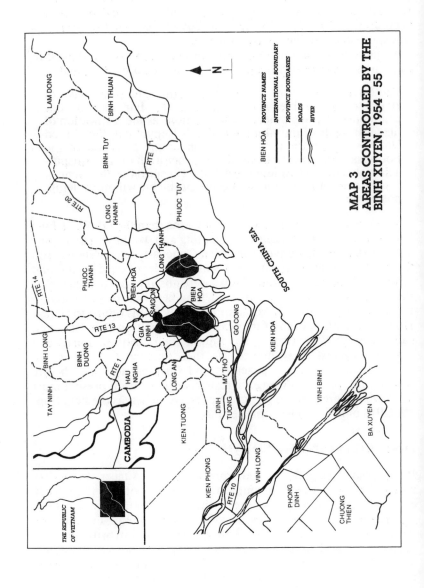

MAP 3
AREAS CONTROLLED BY THE
BINH XUYEN, 1954 - 55

During the final days of March, Diem attempted to muscle the Binh Xuyen out of Saigon. They resisted and imposed an intermittent food blockade on the capital. Eventually armed clashes occurred and it was only due to French intervention that a limited ceasefire was obtained at all. The shaky truce finally broke down at the end of April when the Army launched a concerted drive against the Binh Xuyen. Fighting now reached full force in the streets of Saigon. In the end, the Binh Xuyen were roundly beaten.[23] During the months of July and August, 1955 they went into death throes with a spate of terror bombings in Saigon. Thereafter their units were pursued into the countryside where they scattered. In October, the Binh Xuyen insurgency collapsed when its leader Bay Vien fled to Paris.

The tri-sect United Front against Diem proved similarly ineffective. The majority of the Cao Dai rallied to Diem and units loyal to Trinh Minh. They were quickly employed in the expulsion of the Binh Xuyen from Saigon. The Hoa Hao under Ba Cut provided minimal support for their allies. Despite rumors of Binh Xuyen–Hoa Hao coordination, nothing materialised. Other Hoa Hao factions rallied to the Diem government.

While the Binh Xuyen crisis unfolded, Army operations against Ba Cut and Tran Van Soai continued in the southwest region of the Mekong Delta. In June, 1955, after Hoa Hao forces mounted low level attacks against several delta towns, the National Army launched a series of sweeping operations which forced the Hoa Hao from their home territory and drove them into the hills along the Cambodian border in the That Son–Rach Gia sector. After a momentary lull, a resurgence of fighting occurred in October, when Ba Cut's forces probed the Tri Ton area. This proved to be their last major offensive, and although sporadic raids were conducted as late as March and April of the following year, Ba Cut's units were a spent force.

A third insurgency also broke out during this period. It involved ultra-nationalists operating in central Vietnam.[24] At the turn of the year, the Dai Viet party rallied some 1000 deserters from the national guard and established a maquis in the area where Quang Tri and Thua Thien provinces join Laos. There they set up headquarters near the town of Ba Lang. It came under prompt attack by the National Army and the defenders were forced to flee. In March, the Army launched another successful attack against a suspected Dai Viet base area. This pattern of attack and pursuit was repeated until August 1955 when Army units effectively overcame the Dai Viet forces.

The political situation in Saigon was equally chaotic in late April–early May as pro- and anti-Bao Dai forces clashed head on.[25] These events were precipitated on April 30 when Diem convened a meeting of 200 persons representing 18 political groups in a thinly disguised attempt to depose the Chief of State by dubious legal means. This gathering styled itself the 'General Assembly of Democratic and Revolutionary Forces of the Nation.' Its lengthy debate over a platform calling for the formation of a republic, support for Diem in his struggle against the sects, opposition to French colonialism and the withdrawal of French military forces frustrated extremist elements, who formed a breakaway Revolutionary Committee.[26] Members of this group stormed out of the general assembly and marched to Independence Palace to place their demands directly before the Premier.

The actions of the Revolutionary Committee coincided with an attempted takeover of the military by General Nguyen Van Vy, a Bao Dai loyalist.[27] Supporters of the Revolutionary Committee, outraged by this, seized General Vy and humiliated him in public by forcing him to recant. This in turn provoked General Vy's supporters into action. They threatened to assault the committee with armed force unless Vy was released. The Revolutionary Committee capitulated.

On May 1, 1955 the crisis peaked. General Vy, now freed, once again declared himself head of the Army and ordered units of the Imperial Guard to fly in from Da Lat to bolster his authority. It was at this moment that General Ely, the French representative, chose to intervene. French troops were ordered into the streets of Saigon to deter armed clashes between the opposing camps.[28] This action proved decisive. In the political manoeuvring that followed, Diem secured the support of key military figures and General Vy's grab for power was brought to an end. The Army then moved against the Binh Xuyen and after the fighting described earlier, dislodged them from their positions in Cholon.

The Lao Dong Party was unable to take full advantage of these quickly moving events. At the height of the Binh Xuyen crisis the party set up a committee for the relief of the victims of the fighting, which catered to the needs of an urban population whose homes had been destroyed.[29] In the countryside, due to the turmoil in the cities, the Party's base areas were left untouched. The Party cadres proceeded unmolested to reorganise and strengthen their secret organisation and legal and semi-legal groups. In July, on the eve of the deadline for consultations, strikes were called in various southern cities to underscore DRVN's policy initiatives calling for a consultative conference and the normalisation of north–south relations.

THE 8TH PLENUM (AUGUST 1955)

The 8th Party Plenum was convened from August 13 to 20, 1955. According to the final communique, it 'examined the situation, reviewed the implementation of the resolution adopted by the Seventh Conference . . . and laid down new tasks for the entire party and people in the days to come.'[30]

The world situation was seen as becoming 'to some extent less tense' although causes of international tension were present, especially in Indochina. There, according to the communique, the American imperialists were pushing their plans to wreck the peace. The domestic scene was marked by the 'great success of the national liberation struggle' which had led to the complete liberation of North Viet-Nam. This situation created 'a firm basis for the entire Vietnamese people to struggle for achieving a peaceful, unified, independent, democratic and prosperous Vietnam'.

The 8th Plenum received a report on Ho Chi Minh's recent visits abroad. The communique noted that 'a good result' was obtained because the friendship of the peoples of these countries had been tightened, the prestige of the DRVN heightened and further cooperation 'in all spheres' promoted as a result of the trip. Soviet and Chinese economic assistance would enable the DRVN to 'create new favourable conditions for its economic and cultural rehabilitation'. Further, the Party stated that the USSR and PRC had adopted views similar to itself concerning the situation in Indochina. Both the Soviet Union and China verbally supported the DRVN's political struggle to 'consolidate peace, achieve unity, and ensure complete independence and democracy throughout the country'.

By way of contrast, the situation in the south was grim. There the American imperialists had stepped up their interference, encouraging 'their agents' to oppose the Geneva Agreements, to flatly refuse consultations, to commit provocations against the ICC, to carry out a policy of terrorism and reprisals, and to abolish all democratic freedoms. The aim of the US was to turn South Viet-Nam into a US military base. Finally, as a result of American actions 'the French have shunned its responsibility and refused to implement strictly the Geneva Agreements.'

The following decisions regarding the Party's immediate tasks were taken by the 8th Plenum:[31]

- The United States was re-designated the 'concrete and immediate enemy' of Viet-Nam.
- A broad National United Front was to be set up 'with an appropriate policy' to oppose the American imperialists and to consolidate the peace and unify the country. Preventing 'the resumption of war in Indochina' was given priority.
- The continuation of the struggle to open consultations with the authorities in South Viet-Nam was reaffirmed.
- The consolidation of the DRVN through agrarian reform and economic rehabilitation was reiterated.

- The ideological leadership of the Lao Dong Party was to be further strengthened.

These decisions, it must be emphasised, were reached after reviewing the situation internationally, in the north, and in the south. It should be clear from the plenum's communique that the Party realised only too well the significance of the fact that the deadline for holding consultations had come and gone. On the one hand, the DRVN had received only limited support from its allies. Both China and the USSR were unwilling or unable to do much more for the DRVN on this matter than to issue statements regretting the situation. On the other hand, the Diem government had indicated quite clearly that elections would not be held unless the DRVN could guarantee that they would be free. Despite assurances that the matter could be discussed, Diem never consulted with the north. France had been supplanted by the United States and its government was to state that it could no longer be held responsible for implementing the Geneva Agreements. The US stepped up its support for Diem both economically and militarily.

The situation in the DRVN was still far from stable. The Party reaffirmed that priority should be given to the consolidation of its power in the north so as to create the basis for its efforts to reunify Viet-Nam. Towards this end the Party began preparing its cadres for the tasks ahead — carrying out agrarian reform and reorganising and modernising the PAVN.

The chaotic situation in the south was decidedly to the Party's advantage. To be sure, the official news media deplored Diem's actions against the sects because they turned Vietnamese against Vietnamese.[32] Lao Dong Party control of the Revolutionary Committee, although alleged, was never proven.[33] It seems probable in fact that the Party was taken by surprise at the outpouring of pro-republican sentiment. Covert agents appear to have reacted to rather than directed the events of early May. In fact, the impression created by police and intelligence reports covering the months following the 7th Plenum is one of a low-level, patient building up of both the Party and its allied organisations. Indeed, in June one report revealed that Party cells in Saigon were concentrating on police, administrative and military affairs.[34]

Prior to July 20, 1955, the Party's underground concentrated its attention on political struggle activities that would reinforce and echo Ho's calls for north–south consultations. On July 1 the Standing Committee of the Lien Viet Front in Nam Bo issued an appeal to the people demanding general elections.[35] This was followed by a demonstration on July 3 in which about 100 persons were arrested. Leaflets appeared calling for a general strike on July 10. Demonstrations in Saigon and My Tho were followed by similar actions in Hue and Da Nang. On July 20, the movement reached its peak as the Party mobilised people in the area around Saigon to demand consultations. These actions continued until the end of the month and then faded out.

In August, 1955 after the 8th Plenum, a directive was passed down from the Central Committee to its lower echelons instructing them to direct their attacks at 'My Diem'.[36] The intention was to bring about Diem's isolation in the eyes of the people so that a 'less dangerous' administration would be in power to consult with the DRVN over elections. Shortly thereafter Communist-instigated strikes among transport workers broke out in Da Nang, Hoi An, Vinh Diem and Hue. Included in the workers' demands were calls for consultations with the DRVN. These activities were planned to coincide with a scheduled visit of Ngo Dinh Diem to central Viet-Nam. Leaflets also appeared in the delta towns of Chau Doc, Rach Gia, Bac Lieu and Ben Tre with the same message.

The major preoccupation of the 8th Plenum was to set up a new national united front to lead the consolidation of the north and the political struggle in the south, given the clear indication that it was unlikely that the Geneva Agreements would be implemented within the time frame envisaged in July 1954.

CONCLUSION

The time from the end of the Geneva Conference until the 8th Plenum (August 1955) may be divided into two periods. Party activity during the first period (July–September 1954) was characterised by the implementation of the cease-fire and regroupment provisions of the Geneva Agreements. On most other matters the Party seems to have adopted a 'wait and see' attitude. During the second period (September 1954–August 1955) the Party discharged its responsibilities under the Geneva Agreements to regroup military forces, and then moved on several fronts to bring about the consultative conference with representatives of 'the competent authorities' in the south.

There were three features of this drive to secure agreement on consultations: diplomatic activity, direct approaches to the government in Saigon and a low-level political struggle movement. The DRVN made some important gains on the international front. Nehru of India and U Nu of Burma paid brief visits to Hanoi. These were reciprocated by Pham Van Dong, who called in at New Delhi and Rangoon en route to the Bandung Conference. Nehru's stance in favour of elections in Viet-Nam surely must have pleased DRVN leaders. No doubt they welcomed all statements endorsing the prompt carrying out of the political provisions of the Geneva Agreements, whose implementation they saw as to their own advantage.

DRVN approaches to the Soviet Union and China, however, were disappointing. Ho Chi Minh's visits to Peking and Moscow during the summer of 1955 must have played an important role in convincing Party officials that unification would come about primarily on the basis of their own efforts. Relations with France were of a similar bitter-sweet quality. Initially prospects looked bright, as Paris dispatched Jean Sainteny to Hanoi to iron out problems connected with the considerable French economic interests in the North.[37] However Sainteny's efforts were undermined by opposition within the Mendes-French government, as well as by outright American hostility. By December 1954 an exasperated Pham Van Dong was moved to remark to a specially convened press conference:[38] 'France must choose between Washington and Hanoi and only the latter choice will enable her to retain political and economic positions in the Pacific. But France is veering in the direction of Washington. She went to Manila to sign a pact of aggression. France is hesitating. But a policy must be based on stable foundations. One cannot indulge in acrobatics forever.'

The DRVN's approaches to the State of Viet-Nam were made initially through semi-governmental bodies. However, the most important initiative was Pham Van Dong's June 6, 1955 public request to the Diem government. No doubt Diem's refusal was anticipated. In such circumstances the DRVN could only hope that its diplomacy, combined with pressure from within South Viet-Nam itself, would modify this stance. At this time, there remained the likelihood that the Diem government might collapse.

The political struggle movement in the south got off to a low-key beginning with the Movement for the Defence of Peace. Diem's prompt repression of the movement must have served notice to the Party's leaders in the underground to move cautiously. The Party's fixation with demonstrations and the like in favour of consultations seems curiously disembodied from the major events of this period. There is no evidence that the Party sought to exploit and profit from the Hinh affair or the Binh Xuyen crisis. Initially, at least, these events must have been viewed as elements of a self-fulfilling prophecy as the 'internal contradictions' among the government, Army, revolutionary committees and sects in South Viet-Nam worked themselves out.

One explanation of the Party's aloofness might be found in its efforts to restructure the Lien Viet Front into an organisation suitable for political struggle under the terms of the Geneva Agreements. A preparatory committee was set up in January, 1955 to work out the details of modifying the program, platform, and membership. Later in the year, when it became clear that consultations were not going to be held on schedule, the new goals and objectives of the front took on added importance.

The period after May 1955 witnessed the transformation of the VWP from an underground organisation into a political party in control of all of Viet-Nam north of the 17th parallel. Almost at once the VWP was confronted with the staggering task of running an economy damaged by years of war. Goods were scarce, inflation rampant and famine threatened. Bui Cong Trung, the secretary general of the DRVN's Economic and Financial Commission, recalled years later:[39] 'Without the 207,000 tons of rice which we received from the fraternal socialist countries (173,000 tons of rice from the USSR, and 32,500 tons from China) at the end of 1954 and in 1955 and 1956, then we could not have stabilized the prices which continued to increase greatly, especially in 1955.'

In a separate publication[40] Trung acknowledged:

The Soviet Union supplied us with 170,000 tons of refined rice. . .; the Chinese People's Republic furnished us with . . .rice; other countries—the German Democratic Republic, Czechoslovakia, Hungary, Bulgaria, Albania, Rumania and Mongolia have extended their assistance in the past and continue to assist us by supplying drugs, fabrics, industrial goods, rice and cattle. All this allowed us to liquidate famine and epidemics, to make a considerable improvement in the public health system and to strike a crushing blow at the speculators, who sharply raised prices on all the most important commodities.

Several important tasks immediately confronted Party leaders as they absorbed the 'newly liberated areas' into the DRVN governmental structure. Increased numbers of administrative and technical cadres had to be recruited and trained. Public order and security had to be established throughout the territory. Rail lines and other parts of the transport and communications network had to be repaired.

One of the most far-reaching decisions taken at this time concerned extending the provisions of the 1953 land reform laws to areas until recently under French control. In practice this meant reducing rent and transferring ownership, through land redistribution. At that time village affairs were still dominated by the landlords, even in areas under the control of the resistance government. Thus the Party's decision to move ahead with a program differentiated along class lines immediately provoked confrontation. Accordingly a 'movement to suppress counter-revolutionaries' (on the face of it a public security measure) was combined with the land reform campaign. Within a year, when things got out of hand, the Party would acknowledge the error of this decision; but in the final quarter of 1955 this combination seemed an expedient way of handling two problems simultaneously.

3

The Fatherland Front and renewed political struggle

SEPTEMBER 1955–APRIL 1956

Immediately after the Party's 8th Plenum, a National Congress of the Lien Viet Front was convened in Hanoi from 5–10 September, 1955. Senior officials presented reports on such topics as land rent reduction, the economy, the implementation of the Geneva Agreements, and united front strategy. After deliberation, the congress announced the formation of a new front, the Fatherland Front.

The manifesto[1] of the Fatherland Front declared that because of the 'intensified intervention of the US imperialists in Indochina, the implementation of the Geneva Agreements is being hindered and the peace, unity, independence and democracy of our country are being threatened.' Therefore, the Fatherland Front was being formed in this 'new phase' for the purpose of fulfilling three major tasks:

1. To struggle for the strict implementation of the Geneva Agreements and for the consolidation of peace and the achievement of national unification.
2. To consolidate North Viet-Nam from every point of view; at the same time uphold and push forward the patriotic movement of our compatriots in the South.
3. To widen and consolidate the National United Front throughout the country; to gain the ever more active endorsement and support from peace-loving people all over the world.

According to its manifesto, the Fatherland Front was to include as members 'the organisations and individuals affiliated with the former Lien Viet Front, and those who have not yet joined the Lien Viet Front who belong... to different social strata and have different political affiliations.' In particular, this passage referred to all citizens 'no matter which side they supported in the past—who now favour peace, unification, independence, and democracy...'

The front's platform[2] called for country-wide general elections to establish a national assembly, which in turn would have responsibility for appointing a central coalition government. The details of the reunification process were left to future negotiations between the two zones. In the interim, each zone was permitted 'to issue local laws suited to the characteristics of [each] region'. In other words, the manifesto and platform of the Fatherland Front represented a major attempt by the VWP to overcome the effects of partition by offering a conciliatory approach to the problem of reunification. Implicit in the platform was the view that reunification was a complex process which would take time to accomplish.

Additional insights into the Party's policy on reunification and united front strategy were provided by Pham Van Dong, who delivered a major report[3] on the subject to the 5th Session of the DRVN's National Assembly (September 15–20, 1955). Dong highlighted his letter of August 17 to the co-chairman of the 1954 Geneva Conference in which he urged the co-chairmen 'to take all necessary measures' to ensure that the political provisions of the Geneva Agreements were carried out. Specifically Dong called for consultations between the two zones.

Dong also acknowledged that 'in the Northern and the Southern Zones of Vietnam there exist two different political regimes' but, he argued, these differences could be overcome by creating a 'bloc of nation-wide unity ... the broadest ever seen in our history'. This bloc would consist of: 'various nationalities, social classes and strata, political parties, religious bodies, and all patriotic Vietnamese citizens who desire to see the country become peaceful, united, independent and democratic. This nation-wide united bloc would embrace both the North and the South with all the differences between the two zones.'

Dong concluded by raising the spectre of renewed fighting if a political solution were not attempted:

At present two roads lie before the authorities in South Vietnam: either the authorities in South Vietnam will act in accordance with the aspirations of the people and respond to the proposal of the government of the Democratic Republic of Vietnam and agree to open a consultative conference; then the government of the Democratic Republic of Vietnam will readily examine and discuss with the authorities in South Vietnam all the issues raised by them in a spirit of understanding and conciliation so as to come to agreement for the sake of the supreme interests of the Fatherland and the people. Or the authorities in Vietnam, bent on following the U.S. imperialists, will continue to wreck the Geneva Agreements, reject the holding of consultations and general elections, unscrupulously sell out the country, and serve as henchmen of the imperialists in an attempt to partition the country and prepare for the resumption of war. The first road is a glorious one. The second road is a road full of crimes and would surely lead the authorities in South Vietnam to bitter failure.

Over the following months, the VWP prepared the northern zone for the crucial fifth phase of mobilisation for land reform, launched an international diplomatic offensive to reconvene the Geneva Conference, and attempted to rally support in the south around the program of the Fatherland Front.

DIEM MOVES AGAINST HIS OPPOSITION (AUGUST–OCTOBER 1955)

While the DRVN was fashioning new united front policies to deal with agrarian reform and reunification, the State of Viet-Nam, under the premiership of Ngo Dinh Diem, was directing its energies at eliminating all challenges to its authority. Military operations were launched against the sects and former PAVN regroupment areas. Political measures were adopted to undercut the influence of pro-Bao Dai loyalists; while harsh security measures were directed at rooting out suspected Communists.

In September–October, 1955 the Diem regime gave priority to eliminating a Binh Xuyen force which had sought refuge in the Rung Sat area after having been pushed out of Saigon-Cholon the previous May. The campaign was named Operation Hoang Dieu and was under the command of Duong Van Minh. After a month of fighting, the Binh Xuyen was much reduced and forced to break down into smaller units and disperse.

Simultaneously, Diem moved against the Cao Dai.[4] In early October, 1955 General Nguyen Thanh Phuong disarmed the 300-man papal guard at the Cao Dai centre in Tay Ninh and placed Pope Pham Cong Tac and his family under house arrest. Elsewhere, troops raided the centre of the Cao Dai Minh Chon Dau sect in Ca Mau province.

Operations against various Hoa Hao units fell off during August and September, following a successful National Army drive described in the previous chapter. Diemist forces took advantage of this momentary lull in western Nam Bo to withdraw and participate in an American-inspired training program.

On the political front, Ngo Dinh Diem moved against Bao Dai

and his supporters. On October 9 he announced that a nation-wide referendum would be held on October 23, at which the voters of South Viet-Nam would be asked to depose the former Emperor and name Diem chief of state. It was clearly understood that a vote in favour of Diem would result in the formation of a republic with its own constitution and national assembly.

Diem also directed his energies at traditional areas of Communist strength.

National Army forces conducted two major operations to occupy the temporary regrouping zones used by PAVN forces.[5] This was paralleled by a campaign to eliminate the Communists' political organisation. In July–August, 1955, for example, Phase 1 of an experimental anti-Communist denunciation campaign was launched in central Viet-Nam during which 'responsible organs' of government were created at all levels and staffed by recently trained pro-Diem cadres. The anti-Communist suppression campaign was particularly severe in Tay Ninh where one defector reported that 50 per cent of his provincial Party committee had been eliminated.[6] Another source, quoting figures supplied to the ICC by the PAVN High Command, alleged that by early July, 482 persons had been killed, 149 disappeared, 692 wounded and 9100 imprisoned as a result of the anti-Communist campaign.[7] The initial stage was followed by Phase 2 (September 1–October 20, 1955) during which 'anti-subversion committees and units' were set up within the military and among the civilian population. However, it was only in Phase 3 (October 21, 1955–May 20, 1956) that real pressure was brought to bear on the Communists' political organisation.

Clearly Diem's October 23 referendum presented a challenge aimed at undermining simultaneously the sects' and Communists' claim to legitimacy. The creation of a republic with its own constitution and national assembly would undermine the sects' claim to be operating under the orders of the legitimate head of state. Similarly, the creation of a Republic of Viet-Nam would set back the VWP's reunification plans as outlined by Pham Van Dong.

PARTY–SECT COOPERATION (AUGUST–OCTOBER 1955)

After the July, 1955 deadline for the commencement of consultations had passed, Party leaders in the south began to face a mood of pessimism on the part of the rank and file. During the ensuing months they attempted to counter this by educational efforts, and by re-emphasis on the political struggle movement to demand consultations and the holding of general elections.[8] During August and September, for example, demonstrations were instigated in the towns of Hue, Da Nang and Hoi An in central Viet-Nam. In the

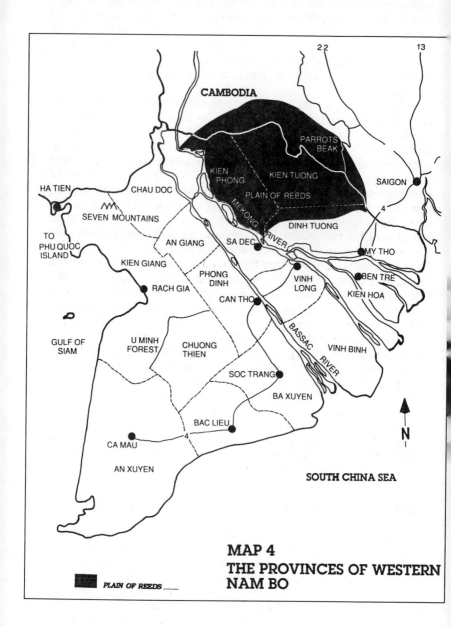

MAP 4
THE PROVINCES OF WESTERN NAM BO

Delta provinces of Chau Doc, Rach Gia, Bac Lieu, Sa Dec, Vinh Long and Ben Tre, support was voiced for north–south consultations and general elections. These efforts, which did not attract mass support, appeared desultory and half-hearted.

The deliberations of the 8th Plenum and the decision to form a new front represented the party's response to this malaise. Obviously the front's call for the inclusion of persons 'not yet members' of the Lien Viet was directed at dissident sect elements and other non-Communist but anti-Diem personalities. In broadest terms the VWP decided to form an alliance with its former enemies, the armed forces of the religious sects, in an attempt to undermine the Diem government.

In early August, Van Tien Dung, a PAVN colonel-general and former chief of the Viet Minh delegation to the ICC in Saigon secretly entered the U Minh maquis in Ca Mau province to confer with members of the Nam Bo Regional Committee.[9] At the same time, 'communist circles' were quoted to the effect that the Diem regime could be toppled by using 'militants now in the South' and that no outright invasion across the 17th parallel was contemplated.[10] A VWP directive issued to its subordinate echelons at this time stressed that united front actions directed at weakening the Diem regime would enhance the prospects for peace and eventual reunification.[11]

The purpose of Dung's visit was to forge a united front between stay-behind Communist forces and the dissident sects. In late August, Dung presided over a ceremony in U Minh where two Communist companies had been assembled. Shortly after, reports confirmed that 'Viet Minh infiltration . . . into the sectarian armies, hitherto relatively free of Communist influence' had begun.[12] In September, according to another report, '[t]he Hoa Hao and the Binh Xuyen have suffered military defeats but they are not destroyed. The remnants are tending to join up with the Viet Minh in the South to form a conglomerate underground opposition to Diem.'[13]

In October 1955, after the 8th Plenum, the Party Central Committee instructed the Nam Bo Regional Committee as follows:[14]

> We must clearly understand that the groups that are now opposing Diem, such as the Hoa Hao, the Binh Xuyen, and the Cao Dai in Nam Bo, the Dai Viet Party in Quang Tri, and the Nationalist Party (Quoc Dan Dang) in Quang Nam are doing so for their own benefit and status, but that they also oppose us and that all of them have committed cruel acts against the people. But they are now opposing Diem, so we must win them over by fully exploiting the contradictions . . . In winning them over and cooperating with them we must principally endeavor to win over the infrastructure, while also establishing

ties with and win over the upper-echelon groups that can be
won over or with whom we can establish ties. We must not win
over or establish ties with the chieftains, who have committed
many crimes against the people.

At the same time, SVN intelligence agents reported the dispatch
south of numerous small groups who were to become involved with
the sects in political, military, propaganda, intelligence and cultural
affairs.[15] There can be no doubt that this intensified activity,
minuscule by later standards, was directly related to the formation
of and efforts to enlist anti-Diem dissidents in a new united front.
For example, one political delegation sent from the north was
charged specifically with forming an anti-Diem and anti-American
movement.[16] A military delegation was charged with maintaining a
base area in eastern Nam Bo with a view towards assisting future infiltration into South Viet-Nam via Laos and Cambodia. A third
group of 55 trained cadres was dispersed upon arrival in the south
to reinforce the inter-province committees in eastern, central and
western Nam Bo.[17] A general staff for overseeing operations in
western Nam Bo was also set up.[18]

The pace of party–sect cooperation then quickened. On October
10, 1955 Ba Cut announced the formation of a 'National Liberation
Front of Viet-Nam' (Mat Tran Quoc Gia Giai Phong Viet-Nam)
composed of elements of his Hoa Hao forces and 'Viet Minh
resistance veterans'.[19] Ba Cut explained his cooperation with
communists in this way:

> Following the ceasefire between the Viet Minh and the French,
> many people in the Viet Minh ranks did not want to regroup in
> the North. Most of them stayed in the South because of their
> attachment to their native villages and families . . . Because of
> the terrorism of Ngo Dinh Diem which has lasted for more
> than a year, nearly 30 000 compatriots were either arrested, im-
> prisoned or deported. We are for the union of all people without
> discrimination with regard to political tendencies or religion.
> We appeal to the compatriots to forget all their personal
> interests. We are ready to protect all the combatants and cadres
> who formerly participated in the resistance, and who want to
> achieve the independence and unification of Vietnam. For ten
> years, despite differences in our political tendencies, we have
> been united in the desire to liberate the country.

The Nam Bo Regional Committee convened a conference in a
remote area of Ca Mau province from October 15–17 to discuss the
formation of a united front with representatives from the Hoa
Hao.[20] Tran Van Soai and Ba Cut attended. This meeting approved
plans proposed by the Party's Nam Bo Committee to establish a
joint Viet Minh – Hoa Hao political–military command for the

Dong Thap Muoi region (Plaine des Joncs). At the same time, the Party pledged to contribute one regiment for joint operations against Diemist forces, to be raised from veterans in Viet-Nam and Cambodia. The unit was to be commanded by Muoi Tri, a person with extensive dealings with the sects.[21]

These joint forces then turned their attention to disrupting Diem's October 23, 1955 referendum. The battlefield lull which had settled over western Nam Bo following the Hoa Hao–National Army confrontations of May–July was now shattered by a 'counter-offensive' initated by Ba Cut's forces. Fighting broke out in the Tri Ton area where the provinces of Long Xuyen, Chau Doc and Rach Gia abut. On voting day, widespread minor incidents directed against the referendum were reported. The worst cases occurred in Cao Lanh, Sa Dec and Ben Tre, where the Hoa Hao forces of Tran Van Soai and Ba Cut were held responsible. These actions had their effect as voter abstentions were considered 'notable' in western Nam Bo.[22]

The united front's campaign of disruption failed to stop Diem from achieving his aims. In the end Bao Dai was deposed in a refer-endum whose results were rigged.[23] On October 26, 1955, Viet-Nam became a Republic and was promptly recognised by the United States, France, Britain and some 40 additional states.

THE UNITED FRONT IN THE SOUTH
(NOVEMBER 1955–FEBRUARY 1956)

The October 23 referendum and the October 26 declaration establishing a Republic of Viet-Nam mark a watershed in the development of non-Communist politics. These events were swiftly followed by Diem's denunciation of the December 1954 Franco-Vietnamese agreement on financial and economic matters, by the recall of Vietnamese representatives from the Assembly of the French Union in Paris and by the dissolution of the Revolutionary Committee. Clearly Ngo Dinh Diem had moved quickly to elimin-ate all encumbrances on the sovereignty of the RVN and threats to his authority.

In order to further solidify his position and to demonstrate convincingly that the Republic of Viet-Nam was not bound by the political terms written into the 1954 Geneva Agreements, especially on the question of general elections, Diem took two major steps. First, on November 28 he announced by means of a presidential decree the formation of a constitutional committee on elections. Second, on January 19, 1956 Diem informed France that the continued presence of its troops on Vietnamese soil was 'incompat-ible with Viet-Nam's concept of full independence'[24]. The first step signalled the RVN's movement towards the election of a national assembly, and by extension, the drafting of a new constitution. The second step was designed to eliminate France's ability to exert pressure on the RVN to participate in talks with the DRVN on general elections.

Simultaneously with Diem's political manoeuvring, the VWP was taking steps to gird its political position. During November–December, 1955 a major effort was undertaken to enlist as many groups as possible behind the program of the Fatherland Front. One feature of this renewed effort was the return to the south of a probable several hundred regroupees.[25] These returned cadres had been thoroughly trained in the Party's new united front line and their appearance on the scene signalled a renewed emphasis on building up a popular struggle movement whose objective was to ensure north–south consultations and general elections. Accordingly a twin campaign was mounted against the RVN's Constituent Assembly elections (scheduled for March) and in favour of the July 1956 general elections.

It was not until late November, 1955 that the by-laws, program and manifesto of the Fatherland Front reached the south. The organisational structure that emerged was very different from that of the front in the north, where it was a legal mass organisation. In late December leadership of the Fatherland Front in Nam Bo was entrusted to a nine-member executive committee including Le Duan (president), Ba Cut and Tran Van Soai (vice presidents), and Huynh Tan Phat, Nguyen Van Vinh, Pham Hung, Pham Ngoc Thuan, Phan Ngoc Tue, and Tran Van Tra (members).[26]

The main purposes of the front were threefold: to struggle for the strict implementation of the Geneva Agreements; to push forward the political struggle movement in the South, and to widen and consolidate the national united front throughout Viet-Nam. For most party members, the VWP's line emphasising political struggle had been reaffirmed. For example, one Party member of the Vinh Long province Committee for Propaganda and Training has stated that the VWP's main objective at this time 'was to struggle to bring about general elections and reunite the country, by means of political action, rather than through the use of armed force.'[27]

However, beneath the veneer of the Fatherland Front's political objectives, the party also pursued its alliance with the sects, which included training and material support for their military activities. On December 3, 1955, General Tran Quang was appointed chief of 'Viet Minh' forces in Nam Bo , with the responsibility for upgrading Party-led units.[28] Accordingly, 'Viet Minh' Battalions 307, 309, 311 and 410 in eastern Nam Bo were ordered to reassemble in the Dong Thap Muoi area for reorganisation.

While these developments were in train, remnants of the Binh Xuyen which had managed to regroup in northern Bien Hoa province made contact with Party officials. According to a later account: 'Diem pursued this force to the Rung Sat. Finally it was an-nihilated. There was only one small element left. This element has always maintained contact with our forces.'[29] This group was led by Vo Van Mon (Bay Mon), a founding member of the NFLSVN.

The Party's emphasis on peaceful struggle, on the one hand, and its alliance with the various sect armed forces, on the other, can be explained in this way. During the months of August 1955 to March 1956 the countryside of southern Viet-Nam was plunged into chaos as various sect forces battled with Diemist military units and, in some cases, with each other. The major opponents of Diem's rule were the Hoa Hao forces led by Tran Van Soai and Ba Cut, as well as units of the Binh Xuyen. In addition, other units of the Hoa Hao and Cao Dai which had declared their loyalty to Diem baulked at integration or demobilisation procedures agreed to earlier. Some returned momentarily to armed dissidence. As the fighting contin-ued, organised units were broken up and scattered about the countryside. Some abandoned political objectives and took to banditry; other units sought refuge in the inaccessible Viet Minh base areas.

ARVN military action against the sects was accompanied by repressive political measures against Viet Minh veterans and the Party's organisation. During this period of rural anarchy, the RVN launched the third and most effective stage of its Anti-Communist Denunciation Campaign. This sparked spontaneous efforts at self-defence (and no doubt revenge) by resistance veterans, not all of which came under Party control. According to an account written by Ta Xuan Linh in the *Vietnam Courier* (March, 1974):

> The brutality of the Diem regime went beyond the calculations of the patriots and former resistance cadres. They were faced with a decisive choice, either to limit themselves to peaceful methods of struggle, expressed in purely political forms, and continue to be wiped out in the bloodbath of the white terror, or to combine political struggle with taking the most effective measures of self defense. The situation allowed no further hesitation and guided by their long experience in combating the oppressors, they chose the second path ...
>
> Thus, the first self-defense teams were gradually formed in the villages, grouping a dozen or score of young men in some places and from 30 to 40 in others. They stayed in their villages like the other peasants, working the fields and taking part in political struggles. They armed themselves with everything they could in order to defend the people in their work in the field or during demonstrations. The more the enemy intensi-fied its acts of terror, the more rapidly the self-defense teams grew, especially in the Mekong delta where every day a most bitter confrontation took place.

From the end of 1955 to 1956, as Diem stepped up his 'denounce the Communists' campaign, the hunt for patriots and former resistance members became fiercer. Finding it impossible to live and carry on the political struggle in the countryside the latter fled to former resistance bases such as the Plain of Reeds [southwest of Saigon], the U Minh jungle [between Bac Lieu and Rach Gia provinces on the Gulf of Thailand] or Resistance Zones D and C [north and northeast of Saigon]. Diem sent his troops after them. Cornered, they had to organize self-defense together with the local population. In their first fight for survival the Liberation Army took shape, one or two companies in strength in some places and a battalion in others.

A number of former members of the resistance who had returned to the cities to resume a normal life were also persecuted and finally had to leave. All these men rallied together, formed armed units and occupied some areas to organize resistance against the Diem forces such as Lai Thieu and Gia Dinh province, or the mountain region in Rach Gia province. First created on the local populations' own initiative, they later managed to establish contact with the people's armed forces which provided them with command.

The months from October 1955 to March 1956 mark only the beginning of this process. At this time the Party continued to implement the instructions it had received in September permitting the use of armed self-defence in coordination with the political struggle movement.[30] Various resistance base areas in Nam Bo and the central highlands were reorganised. Wartime workshops began functioning once again, producing a limited supply of mines, grenades and ammunition.[31] Buried arms caches were dug up and weapons distributed to the reactivated village self-defence groups. Trenches and other defence systems were built to protect the population. A few detachments of the so-called Tan Viet Minh (new Viet Minh) began operations with Hoa Hao units under the banner of 'Lien Minh Hoa Binh' or 'peace alliance.'[32]

Not all of the Party's activities were military in nature. There appears to have been a deliberate policy to disrupt the economic connections between Saigon and the countryside. Efforts were made to siphon off part of the tenth month rice crop before it reached the capital. Some of the rice was diverted to Cambodia where earnings from its sale were used to finance the purchase of military supplies. Smaller amounts of rice were reportedly shipped to the north,[33] which was experiencing severe shortages at that time.

Covert Party agents directed their attention to penetrating all branches of the RVN's rural administrative apparatus.[34] Specific targets included village councils and guard units, ARVN military posts in western Nam Bo, the police and security services as well as the Ministry of Information. The Party also attempted to sabotage the RVN's newly launched civic action program and refugee resettlement efforts, especially in the Cai San area of western Nam Bo. Underground Party agents in the urban areas directed their energies to propagating the program of the Fatherland Front.

Despite this rather long catalogue of Party actions, it must be stressed that they ran into difficulties and were only partly successful. In November, for example, American intelligence was privy to captured reports from Party field operatives which contained pessimistic forecasts for the future. These reports acknowledged that the struggle could be 'long, painful and complex' and that 'it is not time . . . to meet the enemy.'[35]

During January and February, 1956 the sect alliance against Diem began to suffer irreparable losses. In December, Duong Van Minh, fresh from his success against the Binh Xuyen, concentrated elements of three ARVN divisions in the Rach Gia, Long Xuyen, Chau Doc area. The operation, code named Nguyen Hue, was designed to attack the combined Hoa Hao forces of Tran Van Soai and Ba Cut. At the same time, President Diem announced a plan to resettle 100 000 northern refugees in Long Xuyen, an area regarded as a Hoa Hao stronghold. Early skirmishing between ARVN and the Hoa Hao forces soon developed into heavy fighting.

In February, Tran Van Soai buckled under this pressure and surrendered to the ARVN. Shortly after, 4600 Hoa Hao troops crossed over, following their leader.[36] Ba Cut's position was greatly weakened by these defections and his demise followed swiftly. In April, Ba Cut was captured and eventually beheaded. General Minh then declared Operation Nguyen Hue a success and western Nam Bo pacified. American intelligence analysts concurred, and in a mid-year assessment they reported 'all significant sect resistance in South Vietnam has been eliminated.'[37]

It is no wonder in the midst of all this turmoil that Le Duan (Secretary of the Regional Party Committee in the South) was reported to have lost faith with the Party's self-imposed restraints on the use of armed force. At the end of 1955 he was reported to have urged the Central Committee to overthrow forcibly the Diem government as quickly as possible.[38] At the height of the fighting in February, 1956 he once again stated his view that military action was necessary if Viet-Nam was to be reunified and that bases would have to be prepared in the Central Highlands to support such a policy.[39]

In mid-March, 1956 after the assembly elections had been held, and after the military balance turned in Diem's favour, the Nam Bo Regional Committee held a post-mortem. It was obvious that the campaign to boycott and disrupt the elections had failed. According to a document captured by RVN authorities,[40] Le Duan addressed a meeting on March 18 and was quoted as stating:

Our political struggle in the South will sometimes have to be backed up with military action in order to show the strength of the forces which won at Dien Bien Phu. With political and military activities properly carried out, we will surely defeat the enemy [Tran Trung] Dung and Diem; and the population will cooperate with us. The population ascribed the defeat of the Binh Xuyen and the Hoa Hao to military causes, but the population realized that it was because our troops had to move to the north that Diem's forces were able to occupy the west. Therefore, we should increase our forces in the South and develop military action.

The document made clear that '[a]lthough England, Russia, France, China and India are trying to arrange a second Geneva Conference to solve the problem of Vietnam . . . Military activity is considered most important in SVN now'. The Nam Bo Committee then adopted the following 14 point plan of action submitted by Duan:[41]

1. Military action should be used in support of other activities.
2. At least two support bases should be created to aid activities in Cambodia and in the Central Highlands.
3. Nam Bo and Cambodia, although separate countries, are part of the same battlefront, therefore budgetary assistance should be increased and senior cadres should be seconded to Cambodia.
4. The Highlands should be consolidated as a base.
5. The number of battalions should be increased from the present 14 to 20. One or two companies should be assigned to each district and 1 to 3 guerrilla squads to each village. Party members who are fit for guerrilla service and refuse will be expelled.
6. Village militia and self-defence groups are to be given military and political training by provincial military commanders.
7. Supplies are to be stockpiled according to the needs of local forces.
8. Consolidate the military organizations in the western interzone of Nam Bo.
9. Consolidate the military organizations in the eastern interzone of Nam Bo.
10. Consolidate the military organizations in the central interzone of Nam Bo.
11. Consolidate the leading organizations in the Saigon-Cholon special zone.
12. Consolidate the leading organizations in Cambodia.
13. Tighten relations with pro-French and anti-Diem elements to form a United National Front.
14. Strengthen the Movement for the Protection of Peace.

This new plan of action was forwarded to the VWP Central Committee with the request that the overall tactics in Nam Bo be changed to permit a more effective exploitation of the current situation. Specifically it was suggested that Party military forces be used in conjunction with (although subordinated to) a struggle movement organised around economic issues during the forthcoming rainy season (May–October/November, 1956). In response VWP leaders in the north stressed the exploitation of agrarian issues until a longer-range strategy could be worked out.[42] In approving some of the proposals of the Nam Bo Regional Committee, the Central Committee ordered that this new tactical approach should be conducted under the slogan, 'Liberate South Viet-Nam through its fields!'

In early April, 1956 senior party officials in Nam Bo convened a special conference and in light of these instructions they agreed on two propositions:

1. That the policy of using violence through the medium of the sect armed forces, initiated in September 1955, had not achieved satisfactory results.
2. From the standpoint of the DRVN's international diplomacy the situation, especially in Nam Bo, did not favour the continuance of violence.

Le Duan instructed those present on the content of the new political struggle movement with emphasis on the following political tasks:

1. Develop support in the villages for the purpose of gaining control of local administrative committees.
2. Popularize the themes of the Fatherland Front and win over the rich farmers and landowners.
3. Organise rural youth groups as the base for their recruitment into 'popular forces' as needed.

Le Duan also issued orders that secret grain storage areas should be prepared for use when food was scarce and that peasants should be urged not to sell their paddy to the Saigon government. Le Toan Tu, a senior Party cadre, was put in charge of organising the new rural struggle over the ensuing three months with the purpose of building up an 'all-out struggle for peace' by the deadline for general elections. Various intelligence organs were instructed to launch actions in the cities and towns to divert RVN security officials from the countryside. Instructions were also issued to lower echelons recommending that they abandon so-called 'illegal activities' (holding demonstrations, distributing tracts, hanging banderoles etc.) and adopt instead 'legal' methods in order to avoid attracting RVN repression. The elimination of 'wicked tyrants' was also proscribed.[43]

THE DRVN'S QUEST FOR EXTERNAL SUPPORT

On March 23, 1956 the DRVN announced that Soviet Deputy
Premier A.I. Mikoyan would soon visit Hanoi. Shortly after, it was
announced that the Politburo of the VWP had met recently to
discuss the reports on the 20th Congress of the Communist Party of
the Soviet Union by its two delegates, Truong Chinh and Le Duc
Tho, and had decided to call an enlarged conference of the Central
Committee to discuss this issue.[44] Both of these events were to have
an important impact on the deliberations of the Central Committee's 9th Plenum which convened on April 19, 1956.

Throughout 1954 and 1955 Soviet–Vietnamese state relations
could be best described as 'correct'. It was not until February 8,
1955, when Molotov delivered a foreign policy report to the
Supreme Soviet that the Democratic Republic of Viet-Nam was
listed as a member of the socialist camp. However, slogans issued
subsequently on the occasion of May Day and the October
anniversary of the Russian Revolution did not list the DRVN
among those countries 'building socialism'. Mikoyan's visit to
Hanoi in early April, 1956 marked the first visit by a senior Soviet
official to Viet-Nam. Earlier (in December 1955) Khrushchev and
Bulganin, who had made an Asian tour visiting India, Burma and
Afghanistan, failed to include the DRVN on their itinerary.

As there was no joint communique issued at the end of Mikoyan's
visit, we are forced to speculate about what items were under
discussion. The Party newspaper editorially hailed Mikoyan's visit
as 'an event of great significance'.[45] According to *Nhan Dan*,
Mikoyan's visit came at a time when 'the Vietnamese people are
endeavouring to fulfil the 1956 State Plan, to achieve agrarian
reform and push forward their political struggle for urging correct
implementation of the Geneva Agreements'. This suggests that
Vietnamese reunification and the Soviet Union's role as Geneva
Conference co-chairman were discussed. In particular, we might
speculate that the forthcoming Reading–Gromyko talks were of
particular Vietnamese interest.

It would seem likely that if the VWP delegation to the 20th
Congress of the CPSU was not fully briefed on Soviet policy in these
matters, Mikoyan took this opportunity to explain his government's
stance with respect to Vietnamese reunification. Of all the possible
issues that might have come under discussion, only this one seems
likely to have caused sufficient disagreement between the two
parties to have prevented the issuing of the customary joint
communique. We might also speculate that the failure to sign some
sort of economic–trade agreement, which was expected,[46] arose out
of Vietnamese concern not to be seen as acquiescing to the Soviets
in exchange for needed economic assistance.

By late 1955, if not earlier, Soviet indifference to the cause of Vietnamese unification must have been evident to Hanoi (Soviet May Day slogans for 1955 supported the German and Korean peoples' struggles to reunify their countries; no such mention was made of Viet-Nam). The Soviets operated on two planes: in public they provided *pro forma* support for Vietnamese reunification, in private they acquiesced in the status quo. For example, the Soviets responded in public to Pham Van Dong's August 17, 1955 note to the Geneva Conference co-chairmen by declaring:[47] ' . . . we are entitled to expect that steps will be taken to carry out the Geneva Agreements on Indochina and that a breakdown of the consultation between the representatives of the North and South Vietnam will be prevented. This is essential if the general elections are to be held within the prescribed time limit to unite the country by restoring its national unity.'

In private, when Molotov met with Macmillan and raised the matter of Diem's failure to agree to consultations, he dropped his July 1955 suggestion for a meeting of conference participants to discuss this obstruction. According to *The Economist*, Molotov now appeared quite willing to leave the matter in Macmillan's hands.[48]

Molotov and Macmillan met again at the Big Four Foreign Ministers meeting in Geneva in November 1955. By that time Diem's negative reply to Pham Van Dong's August 17 letter had been received. Molotov only raised the question of Vietnamese elections in private with Macmillan and Pinay, the French Foreign Minister. As one veteran diplomat[49] has written:

> In November 1955 as official documents when later released will evidence, Molotov bluntly dismissed the Indochina item from the agenda of the Geneva Foreign Ministers' Conference; even the United States had been willing to have the matter discussed. Diem's anti-consultation and anti-election posture was thereby assured of success, and the perception grew in Washington that, by tacit agreement of the superpowers, there were to be two Viet-Nams as there were two Koreas, two Germanys and two Chinas.

Viet-Nam followed up Dong's August 17 note with three further approaches to the Geneva Conference co-chairman (November 25, 1955; February 14 and April 9, 1956). The Soviet position remained unaltered (see discussion of the Gromyko–Reading discussions below).

Vietnamese press reports and the composition of the Soviet delegation suggest that economic issues were also on the agenda. In fact, North Viet-Nam was in very serious economic strife at that time. At the 5th Session of the National Assembly, in September 1955, Ho Chi Minh spoke bluntly[50] about the need to boost agricultural production 'to avert the danger of famine and to

provide a food reserve.' A contemporary CIA assessment observed
that 'as a result of wartime damage to irrigation facilities and an unprecedented series of floods, droughts, and insect scourges, the rice
deficit in each of the past two years (1954–55) has amounted to at
least 500 000 metric tonnes.[51] The assessment then concluded that
'imports through April 1956 consisting of token shipments from
Communist China and some 200 000 tons of Burmese rice pur-
chased by the USSR, have fallen far short of the minimum
requirements.'

One other item was probably on the agenda: the recently held
20th Congress of the CPSU, in February 1956, at which Khrushchev denounced Stalin and at which he also set forth his policy of
peaceful coexistence. Khrushchev's formulation of a policy on
peaceful coexistence was of more than passing concern to the VWP.
In his speech Khrushchev argued peaceful coexistence was 'a
fundamental principle' of Soviet policy and that in the present era
there were only two policies a nation could pursue: 'either peaceful
co-existence or the most destructive war in history. There is no
third way.'[52]

Of particular concern to Vietnamese leaders was Khrushchev's
exposition as to how revolutionaries might gain power. Khrushchev
argued that a sharp parliamentary struggle offered the best path,
although the potential for violence was ever present. To quote
Khrushchev directly:

> Leninism teaches us that the ruling classes will not surrender
> their power voluntarily. And the greater or lesser degree of
> intensity which the struggle may assume, the use or the non-use
> of violence in the transition to socialism, depends on the
> resistance of the exploiters, or whether the exploiting class itself
> resorts to violence, rather than on the proletariat.
>   In this connection the question arises of whether it is possible
> to go over to socialism by using parliamentary means.

As we now know, Khrushchev's 20th Congress speech marked the
start of the Sino-Soviet dispute. On April 5, 1956 while Mikoyan
was still in Hanoi, the Chinese, who had been silent on these issues,
published their first reaction. Viet-Nam was by now increasingly
confronted with the difficult task of pursuing its own interests, as a
junior member of the socialist camp, in the face of ideological
differences between its two major allies. The previous stormy
pattern of Soviet–Yugoslav relations served as a warning should
North Viet-Nam choose to 'go it alone'. This option was foreclosed
from the beginning as Viet-Nam needed both Soviet and Chinese
aid and diplomatic assistance in order to rehabilitate its economy
and achieve national reunification.

No doubt VWP leaders, after hearing Mikoyan's report on the
20th Congress, wondered what implications all of this bore for Viet-

Nam. In this regard it is instructive to compare the different emphases given by Mikoyan and Ho Chi Minh in their speeches before a rally in Hanoi's Ba Dinh Square on April 3.[53] Mikoyan stressed two points: the DRVN should heal the wounds of the war and develop the national economy; it should achieve the reunification of Viet-Nam by peaceful and democratic means. Ho Chi Minh, however, linked these two propositions, stressing that consolidation of the north meant laying a firm basis for the reunification struggle. Whereas Mikoyan had been mute concerning how Vietnamese reunification would occur, Ho Chi Minh stressed the implementation of the political provisions of the Geneva Agreements, and the achievement of unity in the struggle for reunification 'on the basis of the political program of the Viet-Nam Fatherland Front'.

THE 9TH PLENUM (APRIL 19–24, 1956)

An exchange of views on policy matters took place between the Nam Bo Regional Committee and VWP leaders in Hanoi during March and early April prior to the 9th Plenum. One of the key issues discussed was the Party's policy on reunification. In March, after the meeting of the Politburo, new instructions were sent south.

It is clear from remarks made by Truong Chinh[54] that there was opposition in some quarters to the present line of peaceful struggle. Le Duan and others on the Nam Bo Regional Committee were the most likely sources of this. According to Chinh:

> Our policy is to reunify the country on the basis of independence and democracy and by peaceful means. The Viet-Nam Workers' Party has, along with other political parties, mass organizations, and personalities in the Viet-Nam Fatherland Front, adopted the Front's political program 'to struggle to build up a peaceful, unified, independent, democratic, prosperous and strong Viet Nam'.
>
> However, there are some people who do not yet believe in the correctness of this political program and in the policy of peaceful reunification of the country, holding that these are illusory and reformist. The view of the 20th Congress of the Communist Party of the Soviet Union on the forms of transition to socialism in different countries, and on the possibility of preventing war in the present era, has provided us with new reasons to be confident in the correctness of the policy of the Viet-Nam Workers' Party and Fatherland Front in the struggle for national reunification.

In other words, while the VWP had decided against using their forces in the south to overthrow the Diem regime , the Party would not stop its fellow-travelling with Ba Cut's Hoa Hao forces. Obviously the VWP made a distinction between direct military action, and tacit support for armed forays by the sect forces. When it was reported that the VWP was supplying the Hoa Hao with military forces, though, DRVN spokesmen officially denied it.[55] No doubt any admission by the VWP on this matter would have to some extent legitimised the Diem regime's continued refusal to enter into consultations with the north. Party officials probably feared that too great an involvement in military activity would have provoked retaliation from either or both the ARVN and the United States.

At the beginning of April, 1956 the Voice of Viet-Nam began broadcasting in Bahnar, Jarai and Rhade.[56] These are languages spoken by three of the largest ethnic minority groupings in South Viet-Nam's Central Highlands. No doubt they were begun to assist Party cadres in their task of implementing points two and four of Le Duan's 14-point action program. VWP policy had now evolved to the point where direct military involvement was ruled out, but organisational work to consolidate the Party's military position and to prepare for armed struggle was not. Thus the option of using armed force was retained at the same time as the Party was emphasising that reunification would come about by peaceful means, by relying on the 1954 Geneva Agreement and the program of the Fatherland Front.

The VWP's 9th Plenum was an enlarged meeting of the Central Committee to which the secretaries of Hai Phong, Hanoi, and various interzonal, regional and village committees as well as 'a certain number of responsible cadres' had been invited. The main item for discussion was a report delivered by Truong Chinh on the CPSU's 20th Congress. We may speculate that Mikoyan's visit was also reported on although no mention of it has been made in any of the published materials on the plenum.

Truong Chinh was called on to relate developments at the CPSU's congress to the concrete situation in Viet-Nam, as well as to explain the Politburo's views on the matter. Truong Chinh's report[57] touched on three parameters likely to affect Party decisions: external assistance, the state of the domestic economy and national defence.

Truong Chinh noted that the DRVN enjoyed assistance in economic rehabilitation 'aimed at healing the wounds of war and raising the people's living standards' from the Soviet Union, China and other members of the socialist camp. In fact, 'the economy of the Democratic Republic of Viet-Nam is part of the economic system of the Socialist camp'. The Secretary-General's remarks on domestic economic conditions pointed out that the economy of the DRVN 'is still at a low level' and the 'living standard of our people is still very low'. He concluded that 'we must therefore endeavor

now to restore and develop agriculture, handicrafts and small
industry and to fulfil the target set by the 1956 State Plan'.

Later in his remarks, Truong Chinh hinted that some within the
Party might disavow this emphasis on agricultural and small
industry, in favour of the development of heavy industry. According to Truong Chinh, '(w)e oppose the idea of underestimating
agriculture, depreciating the restoration and development of light
industry, and hurrying up the building of heavy industry, thereby
failing to improve the well-being of the people and to create a firm
basis for the development of the national economy'.

Truong Chinh's remarks on national defence revealed a serious
concern with both internal security and the possibility of attack
from the south. On the matter of internal security the Secretary-
General stated: 'In North Viet-Nam we have the conditions to
advance toward socialism by peaceful means. But this does not
mean that we will not use force to deal with any enemies who wreck
public order and security or who carry out military interference in
North Viet-Nam.'

These remarks must be seen in light of the following. In
September 1955 it was reported that 'armed resistance' to the
DRVN's authority had broken out in Hai Phong, Nong Cong and
Hoi Xua and that bombs had been set off in Hanoi.[58] Other reports
of armed opposition to the DRVN by tribal groups in the north and
northwest were confirmed by intelligence sources at that time.[59] We
now know that US officials were involved in organising sabotage
activities in the north in the post-Geneva period.[60] Truong Chinh's
remarks indicate quite clearly that these activities were taken
seriously.

Concerning the possibility of attack on the DRVN, Truong Chinh
had this to say:

> ... our policy is to achieve national reunification through free
> nation-wide general elections. Nevertheless we cannot belittle
> the question of consolidating national defense. We do not
> neglect the fact that South Viet Nam is being taken over by the
> American imperialists. They are helping Ngo Dinh Diem to
> increase his military forces and are preparing to include South
> Viet Nam in the aggressive SEATO bloc.
>
> The Ngo Dinh Diem administration is bent on repudiating
> the Geneva Agreements, and what is more, has increasingly
> called for a 'March to the North'. That is why we must
> endeavor to consolidate our national defense and be ready to
> deal with all eventualities.

The Secretary-General's views represented a long-standing fear
on the part of the VWP leadership, extending back to the Resistance
War, that America would either attack North Viet-Nam or support

an ARVN attempt to do so. These perceptions were reinforced by South Viet-Nam's inclusion under the SEATO protective umbrella, as well as by a US training program which upgraded ARVN units to divisional size. During 1955 DRVN officials observed a parade of high-ranking American officials pass through Saigon[61] as well as a series of SEATO meetings which discussed Viet-Nam's security.

In the latter half of 1955 DRVN propaganda began to attack what it alleged was a campaign 'to march to the north' and 'to fill in the Ben Hai river' separating the two zones. ARVN Chief of Staff General Le Van Ty was reported to have made these remarks after an inspection tour of the demilitarised zone in December 1955. DRVN propagandists linked this campaign to a visit to Saigon several months earlier by a retired US Army general. Also, according to DRVN allegations, violations along the DMZ, including armed intrusions, increased rapidly at this time.[62]

The policy on reunification which emerged at the 9th Plenum represented a careful weighing of the following three factors: the DRVN as a member of the socialist camp, tied by links of economic dependency on the Soviet Union, had an obligation to respect Khrushchev's new line on peaceful coexistence; faced with serious domestic economic and security problems the VWP had to consolidate its control over the territory of the DRVN as a matter of priority; and faced with external threats to its security the DRVN had to consolidate its own capacity for self-defence and to rely on Soviet and Chinese initiatives to reduce tension in the world in general and in Indochina in particular.

According to the resolution[63] adopted by the 9th Plenum, the VWP recognised the possibility of preventing war and the possibility that Viet-Nam might be reunified by peaceful means. The party chose to underscore its own peculiar dilemma in this way:

> In light of the 20th Congress of the Communist Party of the Soviet Union, our party will take into account the new possibilities of the present revolutionary struggle. While recognizing the possibilities of preventing war, we do not forget that as long as imperialism exists the economic basis of war continues to exist. Therefore the peoples of the world must constantly reinforce their struggle for peace and remain vigilant to the plots of the warmongers.
>
> While recognizing that a number of countries have the potential to advance towards socialism by peaceful means, we must bear in mind that where the bourgeoisie still controls a powerful army and police machinery and is determined to use violence to repress the revolutionary movement, an armed struggle for power is inevitable. Therefore the proletariat must be well prepared in advance.
>
> In light of the 20th Congress of the Communist Party of the Soviet Union, our party reaffirms its confidence in the policy

of consolidating the North, and the struggle for the reunification of the country on the basis of independence and democracy by peaceful means as completely correct. However there exists in the other half of our country reactionary forces who are plotting war. Therefore we must enhance our vigilance, consolidate national defense and prepare for all eventualities.

While it might be argued that this passage merely reflected the VWP's giving lip-service to Khrushchev's ideological formulation, Ho Chi Minh, in his closing address to the 9th Plenum, linked it directly to the situation in Viet-Nam.[64] According to Ho:

While recognizing that in certain countries the road to socialism may be a peaceful one, we should be aware of this fact: in countries where the machinery of state, the armed forces, and the police of the bourgeois class are still strong, the proletarian class still has to prepare for armed struggle.
   While recognizing the possibility of reunifying Viet-Nam by peaceful means, we should always remember that our people's principal enemies are the American imperialists and their agents who still occupy half our country and are preparing for war; therefore, *we should firmly hold aloft the banner of peace and enhance our vigilance* [we should be in a position to change the form of the struggle].

CONCLUSION

The VWP's 9th Plenum recognised that the reunification of Viet-Nam would have to take place within a different time frame from that envisaged in July 1954 at the Geneva Conference. For the moment, any policy changes on this matter would have to wait for improvement in the economic and internal security of the north as well as changes in the international environment more conducive to a relaxation of tensions and peaceful settlement of outstanding issues.

The VWP did not initiate a full-scale review of reunification strategy at the 9th Plenum as other issues, such as those arising from the CPSU's 20th Congress, commanded attention. Primary emphasis continued to be placed on construction in the north; 'paying attention to the South' meant taking into consideration changes in the balance of forces there. Although the first voices of disenchantment with this emphasis were heard, the VWP resolved to continue its campaign for the reunification of the country 'by peaceful means'. Approval was also given to certain steps advocated by Le Duan that would allow a consolidation of the party's forces and which would provide a basis for 'political violence' should that ever become necessary. These steps were to be undertaken by cadres in the south using their own resources; the return of regrouped cadres was slight indeed and their main task seems to have been to apply the program of the Fatherland Front to the situation in the south. Efforts over the next three months were directed at carrying out these policies in time for maximum impact in July 1956, the deadline set for nation-wide general elections.

4

Political struggle reaffirmed
MAY–SEPTEMBER, 1956

The 9th Plenum marked a crucial moment of truth. The Party's line on reunification, set in September 1954, had been a failure. The party's organisation in the south was now ordered to conduct a holding operation until new plans could be formulated. Meanwhile attempts were made to shift the focus of Party activities from a preoccupation with the terms of the Geneva Agreements to other issues, such as working conditions and social welfare.

THE AFTERMATH OF THE 9TH PLENUM (MAY–JUNE 1956)

Following the 9th Plenum, the Party orchestrated two separate political struggle movements. The first was focused on the July electoral deadline; the second on working conditions. Even though senior Party officials now assumed that elections would not be held as scheduled, they still maintained that the Agreements formed the basis for legal political activities. It was to be expected, too, that demonstrations of popular discontent, legitimately expressed, would be heard on the international scene, thus reinforcing DRVN diplomatic moves.

The election issue was raised in May, 1956 when banners bearing slogans calling for 'consultations' and 'unification' were reported at a mammoth May Day parade in Saigon. According to a later account:[1]

A movement for North–South consultations with a view to general elections and the restoration of normal relations between the two zones was founded in Saigon in June 1956. It

reached its climax [o]n July 10, 1956, ten days before the date
for general elections provided for in the Geneva Agreements.
Strikes in factories and markets were held in support of this
movement with the participation of the great majority of the
Saigon population. The struggle continued until August in an
atmosphere of white terror practised by the Diem regime.

In July a massive effort was launched in the rural areas where
meetings, parades and demonstrations were held. Leaflets, banners,
and slogans painted on walls and houses demanding 'consultations',
'unification' and an 'end to terrorism' made their appearance. Some
village councils passed resolutions and circulated petitions, many of
which were presented to the International Control Commission.
However when all these activities are compared to the party-
initiated 'movement for better living conditions' it seems evident
that the former were mechanical protests designed to garner the
maximum propaganda effect.

Whatever revolutionary fervour was built up during this short
period was certainly dashed when the failure of the campaign
became obvious. The July 20 deadline for elections came and went,
leaving in its wake a disillusioned rank-and-file. The Party was
trapped between its commitment to the Geneva Agreements and
the knowledge that the Agreements' most crucial political provisions would not be implemented. One US government study,[2] based
on interviews with Party members, noted that the failure to hold
elections in 1956 'came as a sharp disappointment to Hanoi whose
political program for two years had been aimed at precisely the goal
of winning them . . .' It was in this context that the Party turned to
other issues in a bid to retain mass support.

In the previous chapter it was mentioned that in early April, 1956
the Party took steps to put its urban organisation into operation.
This clandestine network had been built up since the period of
regroupment when the Party assigned cadres to the cities. An
official history[3] of this period states:

> In the province capitals, district seats, Saigon and some other
> areas, we succeeded in exploiting the enemy's legal organiza-
> tions, such as worker and schoolboy unions, women's associa-
> tions, etc. Through these organizations we successfully guided
> the people to struggle, thereby gaining a number of necessary
> benefits for them and, at the same time, recruited many key
> personnel for the Revolution.

In June 1956, the Nam Bo Regional Committee held its first
conference to review the results of the political struggle movement.
The conclusions reached at this gathering were brought into accord
with the Central Committee's views. In fact, the difficulties
experienced in the conduct of political struggle were now ascribed

to the underestimation of the worth of the so-called 'social welfare slogans' and not to the failure to employ revolutionary violence. A Party review[4] of the post-Geneva political struggle movement commented on these events in this way:

> From the restoration of peace to the middle of 1956, the struggle movement stressed general elections more than social welfare. However, after corrective action the slogans [emphasizing] social welfare and democracy were given more prominence, but this was still not enough. Meanwhile conditions were favorable for the motivation of the struggle for the normalization of North-South relations, peace and national reunification ... At the start of this period the struggle movement stressed slogans demanding general elections; but when there was no hope for these elections, the struggle movement stressed social welfare, the slogans of democracy were still neglected.

The first congress also reviewed the results of Party action on social welfare issues particularly in the urban areas. During the six-week period between May and mid-June major strikes involving perhaps as many as 27 000 workers broke out in various industries:[5] the metal trades, water power, shoe trade, waterside workers and on rubber plantations (in Thu Dau Mot, Dau Tieng and Ba Ria). Besides echoing support for consultations, the major issues in all cases revolved around specific grievances related to working conditions. For example, employees of Charner and Eiffell metal companies went out on strike demanding higher wages, family allowances, sick care and other benefits as well as the abolishment of the foreman system. This urban offensive continued well into August. However, in the face of police reaction and other forms of repression, the movement collapsed. The struggle movement related to the Geneva Agreements was similarly affected. A crucial turning point was now reached as RVN forces went over to the offensive.

THE GENEVA AGREEMENTS: CONSULTATIONS AND ELECTIONS

DRVN initiatives in 1955–56 to hold electoral consultations with the 'competent authorities' in the south were unsuccessful. In all cases, the Diem government demanded that preconditions guaranteeing free elections be met. The Diem government was also extremely fearful of entering into talks lest it come under pressure to implement other provisions of the Geneva Agreements, a document the government repeatedly stressed it did not sign or agree to. Other considerations may have influenced Diem's outlook: the possibility of eroding its base of support among northern refugees; pro-Hanoi bias—in the RVN's view—in the operation of the ICC; and fear that the Party underground would manipulate the situation.

Diem also moved to restrict the pressures that France could apply. When it became clear that due to the demands of the war in Algeria, France would no longer maintain a deterrent force in Vietnam, Diem exerted pressures on the French to relinquish control over Vietnamese units still technically a part of the French Union Forces. The RVN also invoked a commitment, made by France at the conclusion of the Geneva Conference, to respect the sovereignty of the RVN and to withdraw its military forces if requested. As a result, France announced that it would dissolve its High Command by April 15, 1956.

This provoked an immediate reaction from India, chairman of the ICC. In a note dated March 23 India informed the co-chairmen:[6]

It will be recalled that a representative of the Commander-in-Chief of the French Union Forces signed the agreement pertaining to Viet-Nam and Laos, assumed responsibility for the execution of the agreement and pledged the cooperation of the Franco-Viet-Namese Command with the International Supervisory Commission to help administer it. Neither the French authorities nor the Viet-Nam authorities have made any proposals as to the manner in which the Commission could continue to supervise the Cease-fire Agreement after the withdrawal of the French High Command. Although the South Viet-Namese authorities have promised to give practical co-operation and to take over the responsibility for the security of the Commission from the 1st April onwards, they are not prepared to assume the legal obligations of the French High Command as successors of the French Power in South Viet-Nam.

In the circumstances, the Commission views with serious concern the prospect to supervise an agreement which will cease to have any legal basis since one party to the agreement—the French High Command—will have disappeared. It is clear that the Commission will be unable to hold the South Viet-Nam accountable, unless it accepts the full residuary obligations undertaken by the French High Command.

The Commission, therefore, desires that the two Co-Chairmen should consider the situation as early as possible and, in any case, before the 15th of April, 1956, with a view to resolve the legal lacuna and to enable the Commission to discharge the functions entrusted to it by the Geneva Conference on Indo-China.

Prime Minister Nehru also expressed his country's views to the Geneva Conference co-chairmen, warning them that India would not participate as chairman of the ICC unless all the Geneva

Conference participants accepted the 1954 Agreements.[7] He also advanced the argument that the State of Viet-Nam, in India's view, was the successor to France and therefore bound to undertake all the political and military responsibilities until then assumed by France.

On December 21, 1956 as a result of these developments, the co-chairmen (Britain and the USSR) addressed letters to all the conference participants and members of the ICC, requesting their views. First, France replied that although it had residual responsibilities (control of the DMZ, security for the ICC) under the provisions of the Agreements, these would end if the structure of the French High Command was altered (which is precisely what Diem had in mind to accomplish prior to July 1956). Second, France stated that it regarded its obligations as in no way exceeding those of the other conference participants who had agreed to the Final Declaration.[8]

The Communist countries, Poland, China and the USSR, all supported in varying degrees the DRVN's call for convening of a new Geneva Conference, to include the original nine participants plus the three ICC members. This approach was effectively scuttled when, after receipt of the Indian note of March 23, Britain proposed and the Soviet Union accepted, that the co-chairmen meet in London and discuss the matter. Lord Reading and Andrei Gromyko then met in late April and early May. On the eve of these talks France announced that it would dissolve its High Command in Viet-Nam.

In summary, the combination of France's withdrawal, Indian warnings, and RVN obstinancy all threatened to upset the framework of the 1954 Geneva Agreements. In these circumstances the co-chairmen, in an attempt to prevent the resumption of armed conflict, concluded that the preservation of peace in Indochina was more important than carrying out on schedule the political provisions of the 1954 Accords.[9]

INTERNATIONAL DIPLOMACY: DRVN INITIATIVES

In the wake of Soviet Deputy-Premier Mikoyan's April 1956 visit to North Viet-Nam, the VWP leaders hammered out and then initiated a diplomatic offensive designed to dramatise their commitment to the political provisions of the Geneva Agreements. There were two main aspects to this new offensive: an intense interaction with the co-chairmen, and a series of specific proposals designed to ensnare the Diem regime in bilateral consultations with the DRVN. Needless to say both approaches failed and by mid-year senior Party officials were confronted with internal dissatisfaction over the course of these policies.

Approaches to the co-chairmen

By the time of the 9th Plenum in April, 1956 the VWP leadership
had been appraised of Soviet reluctance to give more than perfunc-
tory support to the DRVN in its attempts to start consultations with
the Diem government. Therefore the results of the Reading–
Gromyko talks in London came as no surprise. In fact while the
Geneva Conference co-chairmen were still deliberating, senior
VWP leaders gave public expression to two themes that were to
come into increasing prominence. In late April, VWP Secretary-
General Truong Chinh called upon France and the RVN to respect
the Agreements, and in particular called upon the Diem regime to
'open a political consultative conference with the Government of
the Democratic Republic of Vietnam to discuss the question of free
general elections throughout the country.'[10] On May Day, Pham
Van Dong gave stress to the second theme, the reconvening of a new
Geneva Conference.[11]

On May 8, 1956 Lord Reading and Andrei Gromyko, acting in
their capacity as co-chairmen of the Geneva Conference, sent out
four letters, one each to France and the ICC, and identical letters to
the DRVN and the RVN. This led analysts at the time to conclude
that the Soviet Union was signalling its acceptance of Viet-Nam's
partition.[12]

The letter of May 8 called upon the DRVN and the RVN[13]:

> to make every effort to implement the Geneva Agreements on
> Vietnam, to prevent any future violations of the military
> provisions of these agreements, and also to ensure the imple-
> mentation of the political provisions and principles embodied
> in the final declaration of the Geneva Conference. To this end
> the authorities of both parts of Vietnam are invited to transmit
> to the cochairmen as soon as possible either jointly or separ-
> ately their views about the time required for the opening of
> consultations on the organization of nationwide elections in
> Vietnam and the time required for holding elections as a means
> of achieving the unification of Vietnam.

In short, Great Britain and more significantly the USSR had
accepted the status quo and the implied postponement of the
electoral provisions of the Geneva Agreements. A high-level US
assessment concluded:[14]

> The Soviet position, as it developed at the April-May Geneva
> co-chairmen talks, accepts maintenance of the status quo for
> the time being . . . the Soviet Union has shown no disposition
> to support the DRV's basic objective of securing control of all
> Vietnam at the risk of jeopardizing Soviet policy objectives in
> other areas or the Bloc's campaign of emphasizing 'friendship'
> and reducing tensions.

Despite the fact that the Reading–Gromyko talks were so disappointing to the DRVN there was nevertheless one ray of hope. Paragraph six of the May 8 letter stated that the co-chairmen would continue to consult: 'and if necessary in the light of the situation [in Viet-Nam] they will also discuss measures which should be taken to ensure the fulfilment of the Geneva Agreements on Vietnam, including the proposal to convene a new conference of members of the original Geneva Conference and of the states represented in the International Commission on Indochina.'

In light of this passage, Pham Van Dong addressed a letter to Ngo Dinh Diem on May 11 proposing consultations.[15] When it became obvious that this approach had been rejected, Dong wrote to the co-chairmen on June 4 strongly hinting that his government would formally request a new conference: 'if the South Viet-Nam authorities continue to reject the holding of consultations and general elections.'[16]

Two days earlier, however, Chou En-lai had stated that even though the People's Republic of China had proposed a new conference his Government would 'wait to see how recent proposals by Britain and the Soviet Union . . . worked out'.[17] In light of Chinese and Soviet attitudes the DRVN had to content itself with statements for the record. On July 13, that is one week before the scheduled election deadline, Pham Van Dong drafted another letter to the conference co-chairmen calling for the convening of a consultative conference.[18]

On July 21, 1956, the day after the election deadline, the Soviet Union approached the British government proposing that they as co-chairmen address a note to the RVN requesting that the RVN communicate without delay its considerations concerning dates for the start of consultations as well as for the holding of general elections. The following month Pham Van Dong formally placed his government's views on the record. In a letter dated August 10[19] addressed to the Geneva Conference co-chairmen he endorsed the Soviet note and called upon the co-chairmen to recommend to the RVN the dates for the convening of a consultative conference.

Approaches to the Republic of Viet-Nam

In the period from April to July, 1956 the DRVN publicly committed itself to a series of specific proposals on consultations and elections with the RVN. These statements were designed to counteract the argument that free elections were impossible in the Communist-ruled north. They had the secondary purpose of undercutting the RVN's position by offering concessions in the hopes that elements of the RVN could be won over into at least agreeing to open consultations.

On June 13, the Voice of Vietnam introduced a new item in the debate. In order to counter the view that free elections could not be held in the north it invited a delegation of 'representatives of the people, army and the administration to the North to see whether or not there is freedom there before holding general elections.' On July 6 Ho Chi Minh, no less, made an appeal to the nation[20] in which he proposed two steps to bring about national unity:

> Normal relations and freedom of travel between the two zones to be restored; facilities to be restored; facilities to be provided for contacts between various political, economic, cultural, and social organizations of the North and of the South.
>
> A consultative conference to be held between representatives of the administration of both zones to discuss the issue of free general elections for the reunification of the country, on the basis of the Geneva Agreements.

As was to be expected, the RVN refused to take up the DRVN's offers. July 20 came and went, presenting no further opportunity for the north to bring effective pressure to bear on Diem to respect the political provisions of the Geneva Agreements. As time passed RVN and US observers took the DRVN's failure to respond with a demonstration of military force as evidence that it too had accepted the status quo.

In reality VWP leaders, after reviewing their priorities and assessing the balance of forces, had concluded, in Ho Chi Minh's words[21]:

> ... our policy is: to consolidate the North and to keep in mind the South. To build a good house, we must build a strong foundation. To have a vigorous plant with green leaves, beautiful flowers and good fruit, we must take good care of it and feed the root. The North is the foundation, the root of the struggle for complete national liberation and the reunification of the country.

On July 20 *Nhan Dan* once more called for the convening of a new Geneva Conference 'in view of the present grave situation'. Two days later Ton Duc Thang, a senior VWP and DRVN official and a native of the Mekong Delta, signalled a further shift in his government's position. In recognition of the fact that north-south consultations were a long way off, Thang suggested several small steps that might be taken.[22] He renewed the call for representatives of the south to come north to discuss how 'normal economic, cultural, and social relations' could be restored. He proposed a meeting between the appropriate 'competent organizations' to negotiate a fixed ratio of currency as well as 'an exchange of raw materials and goods beneficial to the economy and people's life' in both parts of the country.

On a more personal note Thang proposed that the exchange of family post-cards, which had been agreed upon earlier, be expanded to include letters, and that northern refugees currently in the south 'whether they be army personnel or civilians' be permitted to visit the north 'to see their birthplaces, their parents, their wives and children, and their other relatives'. And, as a clear indication of his government's long range view on national unification, Thang revealed that '[t]he houses, land, and other properties left behind by these compatriots [refugees to the South] in the North are being carefully looked after by the Government and people here'.

There is some evidence that the DRVN may have offered privately to postpone the elections. Jean Lacouture has written:[23] '[i]n 1955 and 1956 the leaders of the Vietnamese People's Republic [i.e. the DRVN] made it known in Saigon, on several occasions and through several intermediaries, that they were ready to postpone the plebiscite and to appeal to a foreign arbiter.'

Dennis Bloodworth reported:[24]

Ho Chi Minh . . . has offered—on condition—to stop pressing for the unification of North and South Vietnam for the next five years, or even longer.

His conditions are that the Government of the Southern Premier, Ngo Dinh Diem, shall be replaced by one favouring economic coexistence with the Communist North, and that all American economic and military aid personnel be withdrawn from the South.

According to opposition sources in Saigon, the offer has been made to anti-Diem Nationalists and sect leaders who, in a semi-clandestine exchange of views, have stipulated that the Colombo Powers be asked to guarantee the integrity of the South under such a scheme. The Vietminh replied by agreeing to this condition.

Although Ngo Dinh Diem has been maintained firmly in power by continued and unreserved American support and the Nationalists cannot, therefore, implement this offer, the Vietminh proposal provides them with an important propaganda weapon.

There were, of course, a variety of non-government politicians who were active in maintaining contacts with all sides. The Dai Viet radio reported,[25] for example:

It is reported that political activities led by Tran Van Huu [a former SVN Premier] and Nguyen Manh Ha are being plotted in the capital of Cambodia . . . An important conference was convened in Phnom Penh on February 22–26 to discuss their attitude, possibly to form an action committee or a government in exile to be set up in the western region of South Vietnam from where it will negotiate with the Viet Minh. It is known

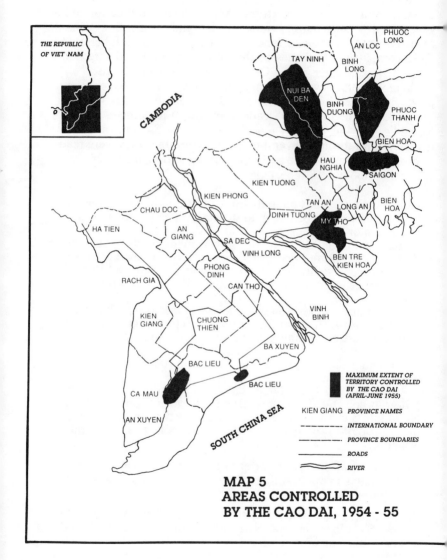

MAP 5
AREAS CONTROLLED
BY THE CAO DAI, 1954 - 55

that Huu favors relations with the Viet Minh while Nguyen Manh Ha is a well known Communist. . .These two people held this meeting with the participation of representatives of Ba Cut, Nam Lau, Bay Vien [all prominent sect leaders]. . .

The object of this semi-secret manoeuving, from the Party's view, of course, was to negotiate an acceptable arrangement with non-Communist politicians in an effort to undermine Diem's position.

In summary, DRVN attempts to bring about the implementation of the political provisions of the 1954 Geneva Agreements on schedule or at some future date, were unsuccessful on both the international and domestic levels. Externally the USSR provided minimal support for the DRVN's diplomatic efforts, preferring instead the status quo in Indochina and detente with the West. China too seemed to have accepted the indefinite partition of Vietnam when it dropped its call for a new Geneva Conference. France extricated itself from its responsibilities in Indochina and then signalled its acceptance of the prevailing political situation. Finally, India came to accept the view that peace could best be maintained by not upsetting the status quo by trying to force the question of a political settlement. All of these developments, when taken together, present a clear picture of the international system drifting into a phase of detente rendering the sharpening of tensions over the issue of Viet-Nam's unification out of the question for the DRVN's major allies.[26] In mid-1956, in short, the Democratic Republic of Viet-Nam was left without firm international support for its policy objectives.

THE SOUTH: DIEM TAKES THE OFFENSIVE

By early 1956 Diem was firmly in political control in the south, having turned back the various challenges to his regime described earlier. Nevertheless Diem pressed on with the consolidation of his power base, reducing the remaining sect forces even further until they became fugitives operating astride the border with Cambodia. With the sect dissidence reduced if not eliminated, Diem increasingly turned his attention towards those areas of rural Viet-Nam where the Party and its supporters had maintained their influence. By the end of the year the combined effects of an officially sponsored Anti-Communist Denunciation Campaign as well as various full-scale military operations had similarly reduced the Party's fortunes. It was obvious to all that the Republic of Viet-Nam had survived its painful birth and that the initiative had passed to Diem. The United States provided a full measure of support as the adolescent Republic was poised to enter what later became known as the 'miracle years'.

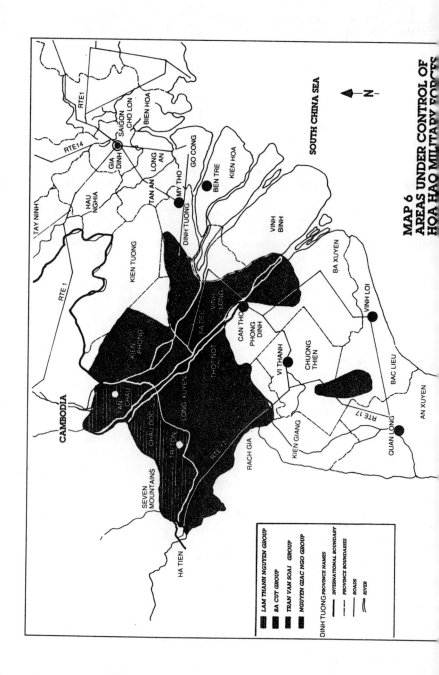

MAP 6
AREAS UNDER CONTROL OF
HOA HAO MILITARY FORCES

The sect remnants: the Hoa Hao and the Lien Minh Cao Dai

ARVN units pursued the remnants of Ba Cut's Hoa Hao forces throughout April and May.[27] It was a one-sided affair, as Ba Cut's lieutenants proved incapable of reviving the anti-Diem struggle. Increasingly these key dissident leaders surrendered or were captured. Both the Le Quang and Nguyen Hue 'regiments' disintegrated as fighting units. On May 25, Pham Cong Cam, the new Hoa Hao Chief of Staff, was killed in a skirmish in Long Xuyen province. The Hoa Hao remnants then came under Party control.

Units of the Lien Minh Cao Dai fared slightly better.[28] They managed to elude combat with ARVN forces by slipping across the border into Cambodia. ARVN units caused a diplomatic incident when they intruded into Cambodia in hot pursuit of what they termed 'Communist forces'. The Khmer government refuted these charges. The situation was resolved in August, when over 300 men of the Lien Minh Cao Dai placed themselves under the protection of the Royal Khmer government and were disarmed by the Cambodian Army. This incident marked the end of the Cao Dai dissidence.

The Anti-Communist Denunciation Campaign

In May 1956, at a conference of officials connected with the Anti-Communist Denunciation Campaign, Tran Chanh Thanh, head of the Department of Information, boasted that the ACDC had 'entirely destroyed the predominant communist influence of the previous nine years'.[29] He documented this assertion with the following figures: 94 041 Communist cadres had rallied to the RVN and 5613 cadres had surrendered. In addition, 119 954 weapons had been captured, 75 tons of documents uncovered and 707 secret arms caches unearthed.

These estimates were grossly exaggerated, as were figures provided by the Committee for the Denunciation of Communist Subversive Activities.[30] Party sources, for example, indicated that by February 1956 a total of 40 768 persons had been arrested in addition to 732 reported missing.[31] It would appear that all opponents of the Diem regime, Communist cadres and non-Party sympathisers as well as sect adherents, were included in the ACDC's tables. No doubt some of the figures were inflated by officials anxious to please (for example Phu Yen province alone accounts for over 70 per cent of all defectors). RVN claims that it had destroyed the Communist underground by mid-1956 were premature to say the least. RVN officials, if they believed their claims, grossly overestimated the effectiveness of their anti-Communist campaign because they failed to take into account the extensive nature of the

Communist underground organisation and the wide network of supporters which sustained it.

On May 20 it was announced that the Anti-Communist Denunciation Campaign would enter 'period II, stage 1' whose purpose would be 'to destroy the whole network secretly woven by the adversary which covers the whole of free Vietnam.'[32] During July attention was turned to the provinces in central Viet-Nam, especially areas of Communist strength (Quang Nam, Quang Tri and Thua Thien provinces). There a three-pronged offensive involved Army units, security service personnel and mobile propaganda teams who would work over an area, classifying the population according to their past political commitments. Anti-Communist indoctrination courses were run in which the people were subject to numerous lectures. Later anti-Communist rallies were convened in the villages at which former Communist cadres recounted their past activities and declared their support for the Diem government. Alleged Communist agents stepped forward, declaring repentance for their past misdeeds and conversion to anti-Communism. At some meetings individuals were denounced from the crowd as 'Viet-Cong', whereupon they were taken away and encouraged to repent and participate in anti-Communist denunciation sessions.

Suspected Communists were hauled off to political re-education centres where they were forced to undergo political re-training courses. Many, in fact, remained under administrative detention for up to two years. According to Tran Chanh Thanh, in the period from July 1954 to May 1956, 15 000 to 20 000 individuals, considered either Communist or pro-Communist, had been detained in political re-education centres.[33] One French observer estimated that by the end of 1956 the number of political prisoners stood at 50 000.[34]

The ACDC was accompanied by widespread abuse, including the reported execution of some suspects. Attempts by underground cadres to mobilise protest movements proved ineffectual. The anti-Communist repression was effective—many authentic Communist officials were trapped in the dragnet, alongside the innocent.

Diem also issued a variety of decrees to restrict and hinder his political opponents.[35] Ordinance No. 6 (January 1956) permitted government officials to place under arrest and detention anyone considered a danger 'to the defence of the state and public order'. Ordinance No. 47 (August 21, 1956) made it illegal to act on behalf of any organisation designated as Communist. Conviction under this decree carried with it the death penalty.

Military operations[36]

Hand in hand with 'period II, stage 1', the political side of the ACDC, went various military operations: Nguyen Hue (December

Table 4.1 Results of ARVN military operations launched against dissident forces in 1956: a comparison of Communist and non-Communist estimates

Estimates by	Arrested	Killed	Wounded	Rallied	Prisoners
Operation Nguyen Hue (December 29, 1955–May 31, 1956)					
Communist[a]	1 005	681	63	–	–
Non-Communist[b]	8 649	–	–	–	–
Operation Thoai Ngoc Hau (June 28–August 31, 1956)					
Communist[a]	2 117	441	–	–	–
Non-Communist[c]	124	106	60	147	115
Operation Truong Tan Buu (July 17–September 15, 1956)					
Communist[a]	882	102	–	–	–
Non-Communist[c]	261	24	–	174	32
Total for all three military operations					
Communist	4 004	1 224	63	–	–
RVN-estimates	9 034	130	60	321	147

Sources:[a] Vo Nguyen Giap, Memorandum presented to the ICC (March 6, 1959); and *Vietnamese Studies*, Nos 18/19, p. 70. No figures were given for 'rallied' and 'prisoner'.
[b] *The Times of Viet-Nam Weekly*, June 9, 1958. Figures for those 'arrested' include those designated 'surrendered' and 'captured'.
[c] Figures compiled from *Journal d'Extreme-Orient*.

29, 1955–May 31, 1956), Thoai Ngoc Hau (June 14, 1956–February 24, 1957) and Truong Tan Buu (July 17, 1956–February 15, 1957). In fact, each operation involved several ARVN initiatives in various regions, and at different levels of intensity. The main purpose of each operation seems to have been to seek out and destroy any military forces opposed to the Republic of Viet-Nam. In practice this meant engaging and defeating bandits, the various sect forces and their Communist allies.

In the course of these operation ARVN units entered previously sacrosanct Communist base areas, uncovering supply and ammunition caches as well as greatly disrupting the Communist organisational structure. Many cadres were forced to flee their areas of assignment, thus paralysing any attempt at a concerted response. Table 4.1 sets out conflicting estimates provided by the RVN and the DRVN on the results of these military operations.

THE *DIEU LANG* PHASE: POLITICAL STRUGGLE IN THE SOUTH (JULY–SEPTEMBER 1956)

In June, the Nam Bo Regional Committee's 1st conference thrashed out the Party's options for the period following the July election deadline.[37] It seems probable that a draft of a major policy review was initiated at this time. There is additional evidence too that

Party leaders in the north had made it clear that nothing drastic should be undertaken. For example, intelligence reports[38] stated that Party cadres in the south had received orders which stressed 'an ideology of lying low for a long time'.

The attempt to rebuild the Party and to revitalise the Party-controlled military units was carried out under the slogan 'to lie patiently in ambush, gathering one's forces, waiting to strike at the right moment [to bring about] the General Uprising to liberate southern Vietnam (*truong ky mai phuc suc tich luc luong don lay thoi co tong khoi nghia giai phong mien nam*).'[39] The main military activity engaged in by the Nam Bo Regional Committee, besides quartering and reorganising the sect remnants, was the formation of self-defence units 'aimed at countering bandits, uniting the people, maintaining order and security in the hamlets, and opposing the enemy's terrorism and robbery by the Hoa Hao and Cao Dai forces.'[40]

After the July election deadline had passed serious dissent arose within the Party's ranks. For example one Party history stated:[41]

A mood of skepticism and nonconfidence in the orientation of the struggle began to seep into the Party apparatus and among some of the masses.

Western intelligence agencies at this time likewise detected that morale was on the decline and that disagreement over policy was spreading. One group advocated a resumption of armed struggle. Another group became so disillusioned that they ceased working and became inactive. In one sense the Party was responsible as it had encouraged the belief that reunification elections would be held in mid-1956. When this deadline passed there was marked disappointment: not only had the Party built up false hopes, but it had betrayed an apparent powerlessness to effect the changes it so enthusiastically espoused. One official American government study[42] summed up this point succinctly: 'The failure of 1956 was a severe blow to the morale of the Viet Cong organization in the South. Defections were numerous. Some broke away because of disillusion with the Hanoi regime, others because they realized that there was hope for a non-Communist orientation for their country [sic], still others because they opposed a new resort to force after the long years of fighting.'

In July the Party's newspaper *Nhan Dan* published a frank editorial on divisions within the VWP over southern strategy. Perhaps the editorial was a summary of the major tendencies emerging from the Regional Committee's congress. Whatever the case, other documents indicated that Party policy towards the south, which had been authoritatively set by the Politburo in September 1954, had remained virtually unchanged for nearly two years.[43]

The *Nhan Dan* editorial[44] specifically drew attention to the Politburo's September 1954 resolution and indicated that circumstances had changed in the meantime: 'the implementation of the Geneva Agreement is encountering serious obstacles, peace is being threatened, national unification is facing big difficulties, and free general elections throughout the country cannot be materialized in July 1956.' It seems reasonable to conclude that a major policy review was underway which would be considered by the Central Committee's next scheduled plenum, the tenth.

According to the editorial, during the Resistance War:

> ... when the struggle of our people met with difficulties, there often appeared in the minds of our people and cadres many complex emotions. When the Resistance began there were many doubts. Some people were not confident of victory, others were impatient and wanted to win quickly. When the situation changed and the Resistance dragged on there were fears of long hardships. People became impatient and subjective to the point of depression. Especially in campaigns in the enemy's rear areas where guerrilla warfare was carried on under cruel conditions. With the enemy's repeated mopping-up operations and our successive losses, pessimism and lack of confidence were prevalent. Similarly, when we won big battles on our main fronts, we easily became subjective.

> A major experience, it can be said a principal experience, in ideological leadership at that time was the control of false and wrong ideas; the education and nurturing of the spirit of long resistance and the conquest of pessimism and impatience. This was a decisive condition in the firm maintenance of the struggle to gain final victory.

The editorial reviewed the present situation in which armed struggle had been replaced by political struggle. *Nhan Dan* pointed out that similar 'complex ideas and illusions' had arisen among the cadres and four tendencies had emerged:

1. There are a number of compatriots who have always been simple in their thoughts. They did not figure out all the schemes of the enemy and were therefore sure in their minds that when the two years time was over, elections would certainly be held. Subjective propaganda in a number of regions also helped breed this simplemindedness among a number of compatriots. The two years' time is over and the elections have not been realized. Hence some people have become pessimistic and disappointed.
2. There are a number of compatriots who lack confidence in the future of the struggle for national unification because they see that the enemy is daily consolidating his forces and going all out to terrorize and massacre our compatriots in South Vietnam.
3. There are a number of compatriots who believe in victory

but do not believe in peaceful methods. We must understand that the reestablishment of peace in Indochina is an
achievement for us and a defeat for the imperialist war-
mongers.

4. Then there are a number of compatriots who believe in the
final victory but are reluctant to carry on a long and hard
struggle and who are anxious to find a more effective
method of achieving national unification more quickly . . .

The editorial concluded:

More than ever before we must now intensify our tasks of
propaganda and education among the people to patiently,
deeply and widely control the above mentioned wrong ideas
and false illusions. Thus we can enhance the will to struggle in
the Party and among the people.

According to a later Party review,[15] in mid- 1956 the Nam Bo Regional Committee considered information provided by the VWP
Central Committee. Accordingly it reached the conclusion that
South Viet-Nam was becoming a colony of the American imperialists, that Diem was establishing a fascist regime and that it was the
duty of Vietnamese in Nam Bo to promote a revolutionary war
against them. The Regional Committee's plans to reorganise and
revitalise the Party's organisation were later criticised for not giving
greater emphasis to armed force. This same history, written after
the line had been changed to armed struggle, stated: 'The Regional
Party Committee was also aware of the plans of the imperialists. It
realized that the Nam Bo population had to promote a revolutionary war against them. However, it did not change its unfavorable
political policies. It continued to motivate the people to participate
in the struggles which requested negotiations and general elections.'
This approach fell victim to the RVN's Anti-Communist Denunciation Campaign, as well as the various ARVN military operations
described above. One Party member, a deputy secretary of the
western Nam Bo inter-province committee, reported that the Tay
Ninh Party province committee had 90 percent of its cells smashed
by the summer of 1956 and that a similar ratio prevailed across the
country.[46] In central Viet-Nam, he reported, the situation was
worse. The Party was now entering its 'dark period' according to
this source 'because of a lack of faith in the future and in the Party's
judgment, which had proved [to be] completely wrong'. The
situation was to grow worse over the ensuing months.

According to Colonel Woodbury, the US Army attache stationed
in Saigon at that time, the total 'Viet Minh' military strength in
southern Viet-Nam in July 1956 was 4300.[47] Colonel Woodbury's
estimate of 4300 is very close to the CIA's estimate of 'approximately 5000 [Communists] organized in skeletal and battalion
sized units'.[48] These figures suggest that intelligence analysts were

applying too narrow a definition of what constituted Communist forces during this period. Their approach ignored the various categories of paramilitary and guerrilla forces which could be mobilised in support of main force units. Years later Pentagon analysts puzzling over the rapid growth of Communist military strength in 1960–61 concluded:[49]

> The statistical picture...of an insurgent force declining in numbers from 1954 through 1959, and then mushrooming rapidly in 1960 and there-after, is obviously misleading. What U.S. intelligence focused on in the immediate aftermath of Geneva were the remnants of the Viet Minh military force [i.e. PAVN] following regroupment. These, whatever their strength, probably represented only a fraction of the numbers of former Viet Minh in active opposition to the GVN [i.e. RVN] after 1956, and apparently did not reflect the total numbers of armed dissidents from 1957 onward, nor the locally recruited political and logistic apparatus which supported the Viet Cong [i.e. Party] 'armed propaganda teams', or guerrilla bands. The phenomenal growth of the Viet Cong, given the low estimates on infiltration from North Vietnam (some 5000 through 1960), means either tha[t] the DRV cadres were extraordinarily effective in organizing and motivating rural people among whom U.S. intelligence detected little unrest through mid-1960, or that U.S. estimates were low. The latter seems probable.

The Nam Bo Regional Committee was later criticised for its failure to mobilise these forces. According to the above-cited Party review:[50]

> ... the Nam Bo Committee also decided to maintain the armed forces of the religious sects, but they did not activate any other forces. This meant that the Regional Party Committee did not thoroughly understand the role of the armed forces in the revolutionary struggle. The self-defense problem was not totally discussed because the Party did not have a clear view on the activation of many military forces ...

In mid-1956 the VWP was primarily concerned with the economic development of the north, and the problems of the southern Party organisation were accorded a lower priority. The Nam Bo Committee was given the responsibility for fashioning a new long-haul strategy to keep the Party's underground infrastructure in place so that when priorities changed there would be an effective instrument in the south to execute them.

Over the course of the next six months, the Nam Bo Regional Committee concentrated its attention on reorganising and building up its clandestine political organisation. According to a later RVN Ministry of Defence Study of this period:[51]

That was the first step in the 'attention to the South' phase. Long-range preparations consisted of planting personnel in [the Saigon government bureaucracy], setting up agencies, and in particular, reorganizing political and military forces. The short-range preparations consisted of the promulgation of resolutions, strategies and guide-lines in the armed struggle for the liberation of the South.

This extensive Party reorganisation was expressed in the Vietnamese phrase *dieu lang*. Cadres with legal status were ordered to stop functioning and either move elsewhere (*dieu*: to flee) or remain quietly in place (*lang*: to be stationary). This marked the first phase of underground activity, according to Party historians, because for the first time the administrative machinery at province and district levels was under the control of the Diem government. As the full weight of the anti-Communist campaign and the various military operations bore down on the Party, its cadres had to disperse or go into hiding. A later study recounted:[52] 'Party members gradually decreased in number. The key personnel in our organizations developed slowly. This prevented the Party from replenishing them. The remaining personnel had a large area of responsibility and much work to do. For that reason they were easily arrested or tracked down. Many Party members had to live in tunnels the year round. They only appeared at night.'

THE 10TH PLENUM (SEPTEMBER 1956)

According to the historian Ta Xuan Linh, 'the leaders in Nam Bo compiled an important document at the end of 1956 entitled *On the Revolution in the South*, (*Duong Loi Cach Mang Mien Nam*, also translated as *The Revolutionary Line in the South*).[53] Its author was Le Duan. Duan's reassessment, with policy recommendations, was passed to the Central Committee for review sometime in late 1956, probably in December.[54]

The VWP held two plenary sessions in late 1956, in September (the 10th) and in December (the 11th). While it is possible that a draft document on Nam Bo was submitted to the 10th Plenum, it is unlikely that it received detailed consideration as other, more important, issues pre-empted a full discussion. The 10th Plenum dealt with pressing problems arising from the agrarian reform movement.

It is not relevant here to review in detail the course of the agrarian reform movement conducted by the VWP since 1953.[55] We need only observe that after the partitioning of Viet-Nam the VWP was given control over land and people previously outside the Party's sphere of influence. In trying to grapple with the myriad problems in rural areas after 1954 the Party chose to compress its program for agrarian reform. The chosen instruments for this phase were

specially created agrarian reform teams, which drew their membership and authority from outside the existing local Party organisation. In November 1955 the crucial fifth wave of mass mobilisation
for agrarian reform was launched. Disastrously, as it turned out, the
Party decided to incorporate in this wave another campaign
designed to weed out spies, reactionaries, and counter-revolutionaries.

As the agrarian reform movement proceeded it was evident that
the quality of administrative cadres was sadly lacking. Errors and
mistakes were committed and numerous individuals were erron-
eously punished, imprisoned and executed. By early April 1956 the
first murmurs of dissent were heard. These protests and grievances
were acknowledged in the Party press over the ensuing few months,
but still the VWP made no major effort to rectify these mistakes. By
mid-year it was evident that serious problems had arisen, affecting
both the Party and its relations with the peasantry.

On August 17, 1956 Ho Chi Minh candidly admitted that 'some
cadres do not yet comprehend the policies and correctly cultivate
the mass line. Because the Party Central Committee and Government leadership have had substantial weaknesses ... land reform
has caused deficiencies and errors in the tasks of achieving rural
unity'.[56] Ho went on to acknowledge these errors and announced
that the Central Committee had already formulated plans to
'rectify' them. Those who had been wrongly classified would be
correctly reclassified; those who had been wrongly punished would
have their grievances attended to (dismissed cadres would be re-
instated, political rights restored, etc.). These and other errors were
also publicly discussed by Ho and other senior party officials.[57]

In late September, most likely after the VWP delegation returned
from the 8th Congress of the Chinese Communist Party (which
ended on September 27), the VWP held its 10th Plenum. The
decisions taken at this meeting were indeed momentous, for on
October 29 the VWP held an unprecedented press conference at
which it released a blunt communique reporting on the plenum's
decisions:[58]

> ... mistakes and shortcomings have been committed during
> the past period. In agrarian reform and the readjustment of
> organizations, grave mistakes have been committed. The 10th
> plenum of the Central Committee of the Vietnam Workers'
> Party has analysed the results of land reform and the readjust-
> ment of organizations and carried out a stern examination of
> the mistakes committed in these two tasks. It has found the
> causes of these mistakes and has adopted measures for correct-
> ing them.

The communique went on to enumerate mistakes committed in
the movement for rent reduction, the agrarian reform campaign

and in the readjustment of organisations. The errors were labelled 'leftist deviations', primary blame for which was attached to 'shortcomings in leadership'. Specifically:

> ... the 10th plenum of the Central Committee of the Vietnam Workers' Party 'recognizes that these mistakes are due to shortcomings in leadership.' That is why the Central Committee of the Party bears responsibility for these mistakes. The Central Committee members directly responsible for the mistakes committed in the guidance of the execution of the Party's policies have made a self-criticism of their mistakes and shortcomings before the Central Committee. The latter has taken appropriate disciplinary measures against these members.

Separate announcements[59] carried the startling news that Truong Chinh had resigned his post as VWP Secretary-General; that Ho Viet Thang, the head of the Standing Committee of the Party group on the Central Land Reform Committee, had been dismissed from the Central Committee; and that Le Van Luong, head of the Central Organisation Board (and therefore in charge of overseeing the readjustment of organisations at the local level) had been stripped of his membership in the VWP's Politburo as well as his membership on the Central Committee's Secretariat. The post of Party Secretary-General was filled by Ho Chi Minh, thus lending the full force of his popularity to the embattled VWP organisation.

According to the press conference communique,[60] three other issues were discussed at the 10th Plenum: questions of democratic practice, liberties and legality; improvement in the standard of living for workers, army personnel, cadres and civil servants; and the struggle for the reunification of Viet-Nam. Point three contains the only indication that southern affairs had been discussed. No decisions were announced. The final sections of the communique made it clear that these and other pressing issues were now the responsibility of the Politburo. Following the 10th Plenum a campaign for the rectification of errors was launched throughout northern Vietnam. It seems reasonable to conclude that if any report on Nam Bo had been presented to the 10th Plenum for action, it was now passed to the Politburo for review prior to convening the 11th Plenum.

Sometime in mid to late October the Politburo met and discussed the situation in Nam Bo. Prior to this meeting several statements on South Viet-Nam appeared in the Party-controlled press, indicating that some high-level discussions were going on. It seems likely that it was the policy review, *The Revolutionary Line in the South*, which was under consideration.

On October 31 *Nhan Dan* commented editorially, 'on reviewing the causes of these mistakes [including *inter alia* the struggle for national reunification] the [10th] plenary session of the Central Committee realized that for some time there had been a number of ideological deviations in the Party.'[61] This was the first time that the leadership dismissals were ascribed, however indirectly, to mistakes committed in carrying out the Party's reunification policies.

A conference of the Viet-Nam Fatherland Front was then called into session. It heard a report on 'the struggle for national unity' presented by Tran Cong Truong. Later—after heated discussions, according to one account[62]—the conference reached agreement on several points including the following: 'The conference noted that during these last two years the movement for Viet-Nam's unification. . .has achieved some success. Nevertheless, there have been many mistakes in the consolidation of the North and the maintenance of the struggle in the South.'[63] Accordingly the Fatherland Front adopted a number of 'concrete measures' to help restore north-south relations in all fields as well as the strengthening of 'the activities of the Action Committee of the Central Committee of the Front on behalf of Vietnam's reunification'.

In other words, the Party now acknowledged that there were defects in its policy towards the south, and made this assessment available to its principal instrument for achieving national reunification, the Fatherland Front. These public comments by Party-controlled organs foreshadowed further changes in leadership, as well as in policy towards Nam Bo. Unfortunately, from the point of view of VWP officials assigned to Nam Bo, developments in the north were once again to claim priority.

5

Policy revision

OCTOBER–DECEMBER 1956

THE LAND REFORM CAMPAIGN

During the last quarter of 1956, VWP leaders grappled with difficulties occasioned by the failure of their policy on reunification in the south, as well as with problems arising from the conduct of the land reform campaign in the north. The conundrum for party leaders was how much emphasis to place on each separate yet interrelated issue. The former was dealt with in a comprehensive policy review entitled *The Revolutionary Line in the South (Duong Loi Cach Mang Mien Nam)*, while a 'rectification of errors' campaign was instituted to alleviate grievances arising from the latter.

The policy guidance incorporated in *Duong Loi Cach Mang Mien Nam* reflected this dilemma. At the precise moment when southern strategy was being reformulated, events in the north cried out for immediate attention. Since the north's 'firm foundation' was in fact a shaky edifice at that time, the new policy for the south had to take this into account. In short, priority continued to be assigned to building up the north so that in future it would serve as a reliable base for the struggle in the south.

According to an official history,[1] the 'greatest difficulty' encountered in the north was developing its backward and war ravaged economy. The north faced a chronic shortage of foodstuffs and the possibility of famine was ever present. In order to overcome this, the party embarked on a land reform campaign as part of its attempt to rehabilitate the northern economy. The campaign was

92

conducted on an experimental basis in Communist-controlled territory in December 1953 and was applied in five phases to the remainder of northern Viet-Nam in the period from May 1954 to July 1956.

Land reform was termed a 'fundamental strategic task'. In general terms, land reform embodied all elements of rural policy designed to increase agricultural production, such as rent reduction, land redistribution, and capital and technical inputs into paddy farming.[2] Land reform teams were directed to apply a classification scheme of five categories: landlord, rich peasant, middle peasant, poor peasant and landless. Land, animals and implements were taken from landlords and rich peasants and redistributed to those at the bottom end of the scale. Landlords who had misused their socio-economic power were denounced in public for their crimes. Land reform also involved altering the local power structure so that the landless and poor and middle peasants would control the village people's committee. At the same time, the Party conducted a suppression of counter-revolutionaries campaign to detect 'spies and saboteurs' in areas recently evacuated by the French.

'By the summer of 1956', as the above history observed,[3] 'the land reform had been completed in the lowlands and midlands and a number of villages in the highlands of our north.' By that time the Party found itself confronted with a paradox: on the one hand, paddy production reached an all-time high, while on the other hand, serious errors had been committed which vitally affected the Party's organisation and prestige at the local level. Many long-serving cadres with bourgeois backgrounds were denounced; landlords and rich peasants were condemned in public trials for committing crimes, and an estimated 5000 persons were executed.[4]

These issues were considered at the VWP's 10th Plenum. Immediately afterwards, Party officials made forthright public statements about the mistakes which had been committed. The DRVN's Council of Ministers, under the chairmanship of Ho Chi Minh, immediately revoked the authority of the central and local land reform committees.[5] The special land reform tribunals were also suspended.

A crash survey of the damage was conducted. As early as late October, wrongly classified and imprisoned peasants and cadres were released. In January a full-blown campaign was launched to rectify the errors committed during the course of the land reform campaign. Peasants who had been wrongly categorised as landlords and rich peasants were now reclassified, and property wrongly expropriated was either returned, or compensation was offered.

Nevertheless, a variety of problems surfaced to hinder the rectification campaign. Tension arose between old cadres who had suffered during the land reform campaign and new cadres who led the land reform campaign and who were now expected to rectify their errors. In some cases violence broke out between the protagonists. In addition, there was some foot-dragging on the part of those who resisted the reclassification of those incorrectly punished. As late as August 20, 1957, *Nhan Dan* was moved to query why the rectification campaign was moving so slowly.

There can be no doubt that the land reform campaign achieved its prime objectives of redistributing land ownership, boosting paddy production, and breaking the control exercised by rich peasants and landlords over the rural masses.[6] This success, however, was accompanied by a great deal of turmoil. This was sufficiently serious to cause the VWP to divert its attention, for a period of several months, to rectifying the errors committed in its name.

DISTURBANCES IN QUYNH LUU DISTRICT

During the months of October–December, 1956 several disturbances occurred in North Viet-Nam in reaction to the arbitrary manner in which the land reform campaign was being conducted.[7] These disturbances were unrelated to the de-Stalinisation process then underway in Eastern Europe, which led to the Polish workers' riots in mid-year and to an uprising in Hungary in November. The main events in Vietnam were confined to a specific locality where grievances connected with abuses of the land reform campaign were particularly intense.

The most dramatic disturbances occurred in Quynh Luu district in the central province of Nghe An during the first three weeks of November. The major issue was religious discrimination against the local Catholic community, exacerbated by abuses in the conduct of the land reform campaign. The catalyst for these disturbances appears to have been the arrival in the area of an ICC Fixed Team which prompted members of the local Catholic community to petition for regroupment to the south.

During the course of implementing the land reform campaign, party cadres denounced local Catholic leaders as 'reactionaries and saboteurs'. Tensions flared and a series of violent incidents ensued.[8] On November 9, a group of villagers assembled in Cau Giat to present petitions outlining their grievances to the Canadian members of the ICC Fixed Team.[9] Attempts by the local militia to disperse the irate demonstrators proved ineffective and reinforcements were called in. Violence broke out and shots were fired. Attempts at mediation failed. Two government delegations were turned away, while a third, composed of high-level provincial Party officials, was seized.

The final showdown took place on November 13, 1956. On that

day, a crowd of several thousand persons, mainly Catholics from
the villages of Quynh Yen, Quynh Thanh, Quynh Ba and Quynh
Lam, armed with farming tools and captured weapons, marched on
the district seat of Quynh Luu. En route they were blocked by
regular troops. The confrontation turned violent when the marchers
refused to disperse. As a result, according to the official version,
several persons were killed and many more wounded.[10]

On the following day regular soldiers occupied Quynh Yen
village, the headquarters of the dissidents. Troops arrested the ring
leaders and released the local officials who had been held captive.
Within a week sufficient calm had returned for the Cau Giat market
to be reopened and the Canh Truong Cathedral was once again
holding Sunday religious services.[11] Although it was announced on
November 21 that 'order and security (had) been restored', regular
army troops were not replaced by the local militia until late
February.[12]

THE *NHAN VAN–GIAI PHAM* AFFAIR

Throughout 1955–56 members of North Viet-Nam's intellectual community—artists, journalists, lecturers, poets, musicians,
lawyers, students and writers—began to express concern about a
lack of freedom of expression in their respective fields of interest.[13]
This concern was deepened as a result of events relating to the land
reform campaign. Gradually the criticism extended to a much
wider range of issues. This concern was intensified as a result of
external factors: Khrushchev's denunciation of Stalin (February),
the Polish workers' uprising (June) and the Hundred Flowers
Campaign in China (May). During the final quarter of 1956 this
intellectual discontent found expression in a number of publications, such as *Giai Pham*, and *Nhan Van*, which printed material
highly critical of Army, Party and state officials.[14]

The seeds of discontent began to sprout prior to the CPSU's 20th
Congress and before China's 'Hundred Flowers' Movement; they
grew to maturity in company with the recognition that serious
errors had been committed in the movement for agrarian reform;
they blossomed at the same time as the disturbances in Quynh Luu
district. As a result the so-called 'revolt of the intellectuals'[15] took on
an added significance in the eyes of the VWP leadership.

According to the available evidence, intellectual dissent
coalesced in early 1956 around the Minh Duc publishing house,
which produced various critical tracts and pamphlets.[16] The first
issue of *Giai Pham* was produced in March. Soon after, the journal
was seized and one of its contributors arrested. In August *Giai
Pham* reappeared, attracting support from a considerably wider

group of intellectuals than previously.[17] A fortnight after the second issue of *Giai Pham* appeared, permission was given to publish another periodical, *Nhan Van*. It appeared that party officials were prepared for the moment to tolerate unprecedented written criticism. The third and fourth issues of *Giai Pham* were published in October and December, respectively. A further five issues of *Nhan Van* were produced. In addition to these major publications, outlets for satire and social criticism were found in various other publications such as *Dat Moi*, a student publication, and *Tram Hoa*.

In the period from August to mid-December, when new press laws were introduced, the VWP appears to have exercised tolerance in its dealings with dissident intellectuals. After mid-December this gave way to slow but calculated moves to circumscribe this brief experiment in intellectual freedom.

The crack-down in Vietnam came at least six months before the Chinese called a halt to their Hundred Flowers Movement. Quite simply, Vietnam's party leaders were unwilling to sanction criticism which raised politically sensitive issues at a time of mounting domestic unrest. In the eyes of the party ideologues, Vietnam's dissident writers were duty bound to serve as 'a tool of struggle for the people'. This they had failed to do. According to Xuan Troung:[18] '*Nhan Van* talked about the "national unification", but does it know the enemy radio station in Saigon has used its slanderous and distorting articles to attack our regime? A number of enemy papers in South Vietnam have used *Nhan Van*'s articles to defame North Vietnam, split the people, and to create doubts among the people of South Vietnam.'

Party leaders, in light of recent events in Hungary and in Quynh Luu district, must have feared the ramifications. One Party-endorsed attack on the '*Nhan Van–Giai Pham* Group' stated:[19]

> . . . they [the dissident intellectuals] took advantage of the Twentieth Congress of the Communist Party of the Soviet Union, which condemned the worship of individuals and the mistakes of Comrade Stalin. They took advantage of the disturbances in Poland and the counter-revolutionary agitation in Hungary. They took advantage of our Central Committee's uncovering of mistakes in the land reform . . . attempting to strike directly at the regime and the leadership of the Party on both the political and artistic fronts.

CHOU EN-LAI'S VISIT (NOVEMBER 1956)

On November 16, in the midst of these events, the DRVN Foreign Ministry announced that 'at the invitation of the government of the Democratic Republic of Vietnam Mr Chou En-lai, Prime Minister [Premier] of the People's Republic of China will arrive on

November 18, 1956 for a visit to Vietnam.'[20] Chou En-Lai's, visit to Viet-Nam was part of a seven-nation swing through Asia that would also encompass Cambodia, India, Burma, Pakistan, Nepal and Afghanistan. Viet-Nam was the only socialist country on the list.

Chou's arrival in Hanoi immediately followed the CCP's 2nd Plenum (8th Congress), which had heard a political report by Liu Shao-chi on the situation in Eastern Europe. It would appear that the main reason for Chou's trip was to explain China's newly formulated policy on the nature of inter-state relations within the Socialist bloc.[21] Undoubtedly Chou sought VWP understanding and approval. It would appear from speeches and the text of the joint communique issued after Chou's visit that the Chinese Premier had also come to discuss problems related to Viet-Nam's reunification under the terms of the Geneva Agreements, as well as the nature of continued PRC aid and technical assistance to the DRVN.

The Chinese formula for bloc unity in the post-Stalin era was alluded to by Chou En-lai on November 19 in a speech made on the premises of the Viet-Nam–China Association.[22] Here Chou stated that the 'friendship and cooperation' between China and Viet-Nam had been successfully based on the Five Principles of Peaceful Co-existence, as well as on the basis of 'socialism and internationalism'. A day later, in a speech given at the Chinese Embassy, Chou expanded this formula for successful bi-lateral relations to embrace the entire socialist bloc. According to the Premier, 'Socialist countries too, should observe the Five Principles of Peaceful Co-existence in their relations.'[23]

In this same speech Chou En-lai pledged that 'China would determinedly and thoroughly eradicate great-nation chauvinism, just as Chairman Mao Tse-tung has said.' The phrase 'great-nation chauvinism' refers to its usage by Mao in an address to the CCP's 8th National Congress on September 15, 1956. The phrase appeared in the section on international affairs. According to Mao:[24] 'We must never adopt a conceited attitude of great-nation chauvinism and become arrogant and complacent because of the victory of the revolution and some success in the construction of the country. Every nation, big or small, has its own strong and weak points. Even if we had achieved extremely great success, there is no reason whatsoever to feel conceited and complacent.'

The term 'great-nation chauvinism' refers to external relations in contrast to 'chauvinism' which refers to relations between ethnic groups within one country.[25] The term 'great-nation chauvinism' was also used in the PRC's November 1 endorsement of the Soviet declaration of October 30. Clearly the expression used by Mao was an oblique reference to and defence of China's support for the Gomulka regime in Poland, against Soviet pressures. As one observer has pointed out, the Chinese chose the tactic of chiding themselves against 'great-nation chauvinism' as an indirect means of criticising the Soviets.[26]

The wording of the final Sino-Vietnamese joint communique[27] indicated that China had not brought the Vietnamese around to a full endorsement of its position: 'The two prime ministers [sic] pledged that in the relations between their two countries as well as in relations between them and other countries, the Five Principles of Peaceful Co-existence would be strictly observed and mistakes due to chauvinism resolutely prevented'.

In brief the words 'great nation' (an unmistakable reference to the Soviet Union) were dropped. This changed wording must have been more acceptable to the Vietnamese, who had no compelling reason to openly support the Chinese criticism of the USSR. To the extent that Chinese specialists and/or Soviet and Eastern Europeans then serving in Viet-Nam had exhibited 'chauvinistic attitudes' towards their Vietnamese counterparts, the wording of the joint communique gave the DRVN the best of both positions.[28]

On November 21 the Chinese *People's Daily*, in another important comment on the Soviet October 30 declaration, raised the issue of 'great-nation chauvinism' and 'narrow nationalism'. According to the editorial: 'If in future relations between socialist countries the larger nations could make a greater effort to avoid 'big power chauvinism', (that is the main thing) and the smaller nations could make greater effort to avoid nationalism (that is also important), then there is no doubt that friendship and solidarity based on equality would be strengthened and continue to grow . . .'

Once again the Vietnamese staked out the middle ground on this question. In an editorial appearing in *Nhan Dan* on November 29, in obvious reference to the previous Chinese pronouncement, the VWP accepted the view that chauvinism and narrow nationalism were both problems. They once again dropped the words 'great nation' and neglected to comment on which of the two (chauvinism or narrow nationalism) was more important.

Undoubtedly of greater importance to the Vietnamese was the second item on the agenda for Chou's visit: Chinese views on the reunification of Viet-Nam. This issue was raised repeatedly during Chou En-lai's stay. The fact that several members of the Chinese delegation (Chou En-lai, Ch'iao Kuan-hua and possibly Lo Kuei-po) had attended the 1954 Geneva Conference may be evidence that discussion of this issue was anticipated.

Premier Dong broached the subject in remarks at a Presidential reception for Chou on the day after his arrival. After pointing out that the unification of Viet-Nam had met many difficulties and that the Geneva Agreements were being seriously threatened by US military intervention, he stated his belief that with the support of

'China, the Soviet Union and the world peace forces, the Vietnamese people. . . will certainly be victorious in the struggle for the just cause of realizing national unity in accordance with Geneva Accords.'[29]

By way of reply Chou outlined his country's views on this matter. According to the Chinese Premier, 'this disregard of international obligations [which meant a 'delay', in his words, in the holding of general elections] and the wrecking of the Geneva Agreements will impel the nations participating in the Geneva Conference to take up their inescapable responsibility and adopt effective, joint measures for the complete implementation of the Agreements.'[30] The question of who or what would 'impel' the Geneva Conference participants to undertake joint action was left unstated. Did the Vietnamese want China to undertake new initiatives? A partial answer may be found by referring once again to the joint DRVN–PRC communique and more importantly to the differing interpretations given by the Hanoi and Peking press.

The joint communique[31] made three points with respect to the 1954 Geneva Agreements: that their application in Cambodia and Laos had 'brought good results'; that the ICC had 'contributed towards restoring peace in Vietnam' and therefore should be permitted to carry on its work; and that the implementation of the Agreements was 'being gravely sabotaged' in Viet-Nam. The only solution suggested was 'that the countries participating in the 1954 Geneva Conference had the irrefutable responsibility to stop the development of such a situation, and that they should take effective joint measures to ensure full implementation of the Geneva Agreements'.

The differing views on the extent of Chinese support, although papered over in the joint communique, were made quite clear in the divergent editorial comment on the communique. *Nhan Dan* (November 24, 1956) raised the question of reconvening the Geneva Conference 'as proposed by Premier Chou En-lai on January 30, 1956'. As we have seen the Chinese since then had adopted a 'wait and see attitude'. *Nhan Dan* then went on to warn of 'serious results for peace and security' in Indochina and Southeast Asia if the Geneva Conference participants remained 'indifferent' to the present situation. Finally, *Nhan Dan* explicitly stated what 'effective measures' it expected conference participants to take: that the two co-chairmen, in accordance with the Soviet Union's proposal of July 21, 1956, would 'again recommend that South Vietnam communicate their views about the time requested for opening consultations on (the) organization of nationwide elections as a means of achieving the reunification of Vietnam'.

The Chinese obviously did not agree to renew their call for a new Geneva Conference, and neither did they give verbal support to

North Viet-Nam's 'warning'. According to an editorial in the *People's Daily* (November 23, 1956): 'as a party to the Geneva Conference and a neighbour of Indochina, China is very interested in the consolidation of peace in Indochina and the carrying out of the Geneva Agreements.' On this basis China was willing to join the DRVN in urging the Geneva Conference participants 'to take effective joint measures' to implement the Agreements, but nothing more.

The third and perhaps least controversial item on the PRC–DRVN agenda was the nature of Chinese assistance to Viet-Nam. Although no formal trade or other agreement was announced at this time, it seems certain from remarks made during Chou's tour that discussions had occurred, perhaps even that an agreement had been reached. On November 18 Chou En-lai pledged that 'the Chinese people will as heretofore, firmly support the national construction of the Vietnamese people.'[32] The final communique repeated this formulation after reference to the expanding nature of 'economic and cultural exchanges and contacts' and the fact that Pham Van Dong had 'clearly pointed out the importance of China's technical aid to Vietnam'. The Chinese delegation did not include any economic or technical aid specialists and it is doubtful that anything more than agreement in principle was reached on the nature of future Chinese assistance.

In summary, Chou En-lai's visit to Hanoi was intended to enable the Chinese leaders to appraise the Vietnamese leaders of how, in the Chinese view, developments in Eastern Europe affected social-ist bloc unity. No doubt Chou sought Ho Chi Minh's own opinions. Chou's visit also served as a convenient forum for consultations on matters of mutual interest such as Vietnamese unification and aid.[33]

THE 11TH PLENUM

In December 1956 the VWP Central Committee held its 11th Plenum. Two major sets of problems confronted Party leaders: how to consolidate economic progress in the North in the aftermath of disruptions caused by the conduct of the land reform campaign and secondly, what kind of strategy to devise for the south now that reunification under the terms of the Geneva Agreement seemed unlikely.

At this Plenum the Party also reviewed decisions taken three months earlier, at the 10th Plenum, regarding consolidation of the north.[34] Such a review was obviously imperative as a result of the disturbances in Quynh Luu and agitation by members of the literati. The importance of the decisions the Party faced with regard to the south was highlighted by the presentation at the Plenum of a major policy review undertaken by senior officials in Nam Bo.

The 11th Plenum was followed later in the month by the convening of the 6th Session of the DRVN's National Assembly. This session lasted for nearly a month—an unprecedented duration—from December 29, 1956 to January 25, 1957. What explains the extraordinary length of the National Assembly's 6th Session? According to the official press reports, it would seem many areas of policy were extensively discussed, reported on, and eventually approved. While the National Assembly continued to play its rubber stamp role, it also seems likely that the gravity of the issues faced by the VWP required a full and lengthy review by officials outside the circle of the Central Committee. The National Assembly provided a convenient forum for this review.[35]

At the 11th Plenum the Central Committee grappled with the complex problem of how to integrate policies for the north and south into one comprehensive strategy. According to Pham Hung:[36]

The revolutionary task which arises from the fact that our country is partitioned into two zones, demands that all policies and activities in the North be implemented with the central objective of winning over the South ... Acting in conformity with this line is advantageous to the realization of unification as well as to the consolidation of the North. Acting counter to this, either neglecting the consolidation of the North for the sake of winning over the South, or concentrating on the consolidation of the North without paying due attention to winning over the South, would bring about negative results for the revolutionary movement. The consolidation of the North and the winning over of the South are not contradictory—indeed they cannot be separated from each other.

The Party's theoretical journal *Hoc Tap* (Studies), which discussed the decisions taken by the December plenum, made it clear that given these two tasks, priority was to be given to consolidation of the north: '[t]he consolidation of the North is the key task in realizing national unification. Therefore we must not allow the winning over of the South to detract from the requirements of consolidating the North.'[37]

One other concern seems to have vexed VWP decision-makers: were the policies then being drawn up for the north and the south in fact 'revolutionary polices'? *Hoc Tap* argued: 'Speaking from the viewpoint of the entire nation, it is due to the scheming of the American imperialists and their henchmen that our country is still divided into two zones. The struggle for national reunification is clearly a revolutionary struggle, although this line [is] long and difficult.'

The very fact that VWP leaders, Pham Hung in particular, had to argue that their policies were 'revolutionary' is an indication of the nature of the problems that they faced. In the north, on the one hand, the completion of the anti-feudal task as a result of the land reform campaign did not lead immediately to collectivisation but rather to 'rectification' and 'consolidation'. In the south, on the other hand, reliance on the Geneva Agreements and the policy of peaceful struggle had clearly failed to achieve reunification. Cadres there were rebuffed in their attempts to get permission to resume armed struggle. Indeed, Party officials in Nam Bo were called upon to exercise 'close control' over cadres who violated Party policy by employing violence.[38] These restrictions led certain cadres to question whether they were to be engaged in 'revolution' or 'reformism'. In addition, other cadres chose to question the efficacy of Khrushchev's policy of so-called 'peaceful transition to socialism' in the light of the Anglo-French seizure of the Suez Canal. Again, according to *Hoc Tap*: 'the Anglo-French attack on Egypt posed the question: are the forces of peace really growing daily? Is the capacity of these forces to prevent violent conflict increasing or decreasing?'[39]

Because of these doubts, one of the objectives of the 11th Plenum was to redefine the theoretical nature of northern and southern strategies within a comprehensive revolutionary framework. This difficult task was left to Pham Hung. He reasoned that the national democratic revolution was still a nation-wide struggle, despite the fact that the north had been liberated. The objective of this struggle was to free the entire country from both imperialism and feudalism. In Hung's words.[40]

Although the present situation is more complicated than before, and although the manner of struggle is different than before, the basic nature of the question of national unification is still a matter of implementing revolutionary tasks, still a matter of continuing and completing the people's national democratic revolution throughout the entire country. Because our country is temporarily partitioned into two zones the work of completing the people's national democratic revolution is being carried out under the slogan of 'National Unification':

In other words, after an intensive review of Party policies for all of Viet-Nam, the VWP leadership attempted to overcome the growing ideological malaise within its ranks by stating in forthright and unequivocal terms its renewed commitment to Vietnamese independence by revolutionary means. National independence, however, could not be achieved immediately and cadres were enjoined to recall Ho Chi Minh's remarks made on July 22, 1954, immediately after the Geneva Conference, that the struggle for independence was a long and arduous affair.[41]

The new revolutionary strategy to emerge from the VWP's 11th Plenum had three main components: first, consolidation of the north as the base for unification; second, maintenance and development of the struggle movement in the south; and third, winning the sympathy and support of the world's peoples. Extensive public discussion was given to points one and three. Point two, concerning the south, was dealt with in a major statement, which remained confidential. It was transmitted to the Nam Bo Regional Committee for discussion and implementation, a task which appears to have been accomplished by about March 1957. From that moment on it served as the basis for Party policy in the south until late 1958.

Consolidating the north

The 'key nature' of consolidating the north was made evident at this time in numerous statements attributed to Party and government leaders. According to *Hoc Tap*[42] the VWP's present policy priorities were: 'consolidation of the North, leading it toward socialism step by step while at the same time struggling to achieve national unification on the basis of independence and democracy by peaceful means.'

Pham Hung, speaking before the National Assembly's 6th Session,[43] chose to underscore these priorities in this way:

> The task of consolidating the North is a basic one. The government's report delivered to the National Assembly's fifth session [in September 1955] clearly pointed this out: 'In order to consolidate peace and to realize national unification we must be strong. This strength is based on the unity and the struggle of all the people from North to the South. The basis of this strength is the Democratic Republic of Viet-Nam—the North. Therefore we must pay special attention to the consolidation of the North, turning it into a stable and powerful foundation for the struggle of all the people in order to consolidate peace and realize national unification, complete independence and democracy throughout the entire country.'

'Consolidating the north' was a short-hand expression for a broad range of developmental activities being undertaken at that time in the DRVN. Pham Van Dong summarised these developments under five main headings which provide an indication of the breadth encompassed in the phrase 'consolidating the North': land reform; economy and finance (agriculture, industry, small industry and handicrafts, communications, posts and telegraphs, commerce, finance and banking); cultural and social affairs (mass education, anti-illiteracy, publications, movie making, theatre, hospitals and sport); domestic affairs (public order and security, minority policy, religious freedoms); and national defence (regularisation and modernisation of the Viet-Nam People's Army).

The VWP decided to stress 'economy and finance' for the immediate future. Priorities arising from the decision were clearly spelled out in the final communique of the 11th Plenum:[44]

> The (11th plenary) session decided that the general line of economic and financial work in 1957 will be as follows: all economic and financial work must aim at encouraging an increase in production and the practice of frugality. Production should be developed under the leadership of the State-owned economy and of the State itself. In the overall national economy agricultural production will be the main task. Light industry and handicraft production are the key points at present. All economic and financial plans and policies must aim at consolidating the North while at the same time winning over the South . . .

It seems quite clear that there were impelling reasons behind this new policy emphasis. First, areas of dissatisfaction remained, despite the fact that 'good preliminary results' had been obtained in the rectification of errors campaign. According to *Hoc Tap* the 'ideological situation of various social strata' had become 'rather complex'[45]. In the countryside 'hooligans and subversive elements' were still active. In the cities both cadres and workers were dissatisfied with their 'standards of living' and were impatient over the slowness of efforts at improvement. In certain areas speculation and hoarding of goods were reported. Elsewhere, according to *Hoc Tap*, demands were made for so-called 'capitalist freedoms' which affected social life in the urban areas, adversely from the Party's point of view.

Second, the Party was affected by these developments too. *Hoc Tap* frankly admitted that organisation building within the Party was 'slow' and that friction had arisen between old and new cadres and that problems persisted in coordinating the tasks of the land reform cadres with those of the cadres engaged in the readjustment of organisations. Pham Hung acknowledged that although the interrelatedness of Party policy in the north and in the south had been expounded since 1954 it had 'not yet been fully realised in the policies, activities and in the mass organizations' in the north. He argued that further education would be necessary before people saw the relationship between consolidating the north and achieving national unification. Indeed, this problem was a two-edged one as both southern regroupees, and northerners, had to be convinced.

The Line of the Revolution in the South (Duong Loi Cach Mang Mien Nam)

'Consolidating the North' was only one prong of a three-pronged strategy designed to bring about Viet-Nam's unification. The second prong, 'maintaining and developing the struggle movement in the south', was not discussed in public in any detail. It was, however, discussed at some length in private. We know from subsequent accounts that this was a major policy review which settled for a time the arguments over north-south priorities and whether or not revolutionary violence and/or armed force should be employed at this time.

In December the Nam Bo Regional Committee met and considered the Politburo's resolution of June 1956 ('The Situation and Missions of the Revolution in the South') and Le Duan's *The Line of Revolution in the South.* The meeting concluded:[46]

> Due to the needs of the revolutionary movement in the South, to a certain extent it is necessary to have self-defense and armed propaganda forces in order to support the political struggle and eventually use those armed forces to carry out a revolution to overthrow U.S.–Diem ... The path of advance of the revolution in the South is to use a violent general uprising to win political power.[46]

The decision acknowledging that 'military activities' could now support political struggle activities was a major one. This decision was not a *carte blanche* to resume all-out guerrilla struggle, however. At the most basic level it resolved a growing dispute within the Party brought on by the evident failure of its policy of peaceful struggle, reliance on the framework of the Geneva Agreements and use of the sect forces to achieve unification. According to a captured Party history which reviewed this period:[47]

> ... after 20 July 1956, the key cadres and Party members in South Vietnam asked questions which demanded answers: 'Can we still continue to struggle to demand the implementation of (the Geneva) Agreement given the existing regime in South Vietnam? If not, then what must be done?'

This same history made it explicitly clear that a crisis had arisen over southern policy and that the decisions taken in late 1956 were momentous:

> At the end of 1956 the popularization of the volume by Comrade [Le] Duan entitled 'The South Vietnam Revolutionary Path' was of great significance because the ideological crisis was now solved ... the volume outlined a *new strategic orientation* for the South Vietnam revolution, a strategic mission in which everyone could have some confidence: It is necessary to continue the national democratic revolution in South Vietnam and it is necessary to use force to overthrow the feudalist imperialist regime in order to establish a revolutionary democratic coalition and create the conditions for the peaceful reunification of the Fatherland.

The importance of the decision to sanction the use of force should not be underestimated. The policy spelled out in *Duong Loi Cach Mang Mien Nam (The Line of the Revolution in the South)* was mainly a justification for not taking immediate, premature action. On the one hand, the restriction on the use of force had been removed; yet on the other hand, no encouragement was given to its immediate employment. In brief, force would be used at some future time, when circumstances were ripe. With that issue resolved, cadres were enjoined to build up their organisation in preparation for the future. A secret directive accompanied *Duong Loi Cach Mang Mien Nam*, which was sent to all Party members in Nam Bo operating at province level and above.[48] It authorised a limited policy of violence known as 'killing tyrants' (*tru gian*). It was kept secret so as not to cause confusion among lower level cadres who were now being instructed in organisation-building tasks.

Duong Loi Cach Mang Mien Nam is divided into two sections.[49] Section one presents the ideological and theoretical explication of the new strategy; section two provides historical argumentation justifying it. The policy document begins by noting that the Central Committee had set forth three main missions: consolidation of the north, strengthening of the movement in the south, and gaining the sympathy and support of the world's people. It then focuses almost exclusively on the second mission, which it discusses under three headings: the revolutionary movement in the south, forms of struggle for the revolutionary movement, and guidelines for the movement.

The revolutionary movement in the south

The main objective of the movement in the south, according to the policy review, was the overthrow of the US–Diem regime and that would only be possible when the situation throughout all of Viet-Nam was ripe. The revolutionary movement in the south is viewed as part of a nation-wide movement sharing national objectives, while being at the same a southern movement with its own specific objectives.

South Viet-Nam is classified as a neo-colony of the United States. Therefore, according to the document, the targets of the revolution consist of both US imperialism and Vietnamese feudalism. In any neo-colonial relationship between a foreign power and a client state certain contradictions will inevitably arise. In Viet-Nam's case four specific contradictions are enumerated:

1. The contradiction between the people's desire for peace and the warlike policies of the U.S.–Diem regime;
2. The contradiction between the people's desire for national unification and the policy of partition of the U.S.–Diem regime;

3. The contradiction between the people's desire for democratic rights and Diem's dictatorial rule;
4. The contradiction between the people's livelihood and the selfish interests of the U.S.–Diem regime.

According to the policy document, the people's just aspirations arose from these contradictions and it was the Party's duty to educate the people to a true understanding of them. In short, the workers and peasants needed to be shown by the Party how their interests were adversely affected by neo-colonialism.

Forms of struggle for the revolutionary movement

According to the policy review, in order to select the correct form of struggle three considerations had to be taken into account: the world situation, the situation and prospects within Viet-Nam, and the balance of forces between revolution and counter-revolution.

The world situation is characterised by the document as one in which the forces of neutralism (represented by India, Burma and Indonesia), as well as the strength of the socialist bloc, were increasing. These developments, it is stated, had helped to isolate the United States. In such a climate, it is argued, revolutionary ends could be achieved by peaceful means, not only in Viet-Nam but elsewhere in the world.[50]

Duong Loi Cach Mang Mien Nam also points out that the 20th Congress of the CPSU affirmed that all international conflicts could be settled by peaceful means, and revolutionary movements could develop peacefully. The document includes the standard disclaimer that this strategy might be altered if forces in power resort to repression. So far as Viet-Nam was concerned, it concludes, violence was unlikely due to the overwhelming aspirations of the Vietnamese people for peace.

Guidelines for the revolutionary movement

According to *Duong Loi Cach Mang Mien Nam*, the revolutionary movement could develop according to a peaceful line because the political force of the people was the key, not armed force. Was this possible in the face of Diemist repression? It answers affirmatively, arguing that as the Party relied on the people and was intimately bound up in supporting their aspirations, repression would be unsuccessful. The Diem regime is described as isolated and unable to rely on the support of any political force.

Difficulties in the current state of the revolutionary movement in the south are ascribed to the fact that the movement itself was underdeveloped. Two reasons are advanced to account for this, the objective difficulties encountered in changing from a strategy of armed struggle to peaceful struggle, and the subjective difficulties caused by cadres who failed to rely on the people and who failed to develop appropriate political struggle techniques.

According to *Duong Loi Cach Mang Mien Nam*, every revolutionary movement has its periods of ascendancy and decline. In order to be successful a revolutionary movement must be conducted flexibly, employing various forms of struggle. At the time, according to the document, the party's strength in Nam Bo had been depleted and its capabilities lowered, due to the repressive actions of the RVN. However, according to the analysis, if the Party's cadres continued to mingle with the people and defend their interests it would never be destroyed. 'The Party and the people are one. To destroy the Party, one would have to destroy the people,' it concludes.

Section two of *Duong Loi Cach Mang Mien Nam* reviews the history of the Party's activities since 1930 and lists five major lessons which could be drawn from that experience. The inference was that those lessons were directly applicable to the present era. These lessons were:[51]

1. *To exploit a favourable international situation it is necessary to have an internal force in being.* According to *Duong Loi Cach Mang Mien Nam*, the 1945 August Revolution would not have been successful if the Party had relied solely on favourable international conditions. The lesson was that the revolutionary movement must be built up from within as a result of organisational work over a long period of time.

2. *A revolutionary movement needs a Marxist–Leninist Party in the vanguard.* The lesson here was that the Party must be in control of the revolutionary movement at all times and not let it be captured by the bourgeois class. The Party must direct the movement against imperialism and feudalism.

3. *The worker–peasant alliance must be strong.* Under this heading, *Duong Loi Cach Mang Mien Nam* argues against class warfare. Noting that some cadres had called for land redistribution in the south, the document argues that each landlord 'must be treated as a separate case.' All elements of southern society are seen as potential allies. In urban areas, Party cadres must organise the workers around their self-interests, such as improving their living conditions.

4. *Strengthen and develop the national front.* Based on past experience, *Duong Loi Cach Mang Mien Nam* argues for the creation of a national united front composed of the worker–peasant alliance in coalition with the bourgeoisie and certain other patriotic elements, such as religious figures and sect leaders. All of these groups harbour grievances against the Diem regime and its American backers, it states.

5. *Take advantage of the contradictions in the enemy's ranks, isolate
   him and introduce agents into his ranks. Duong Loi Cach Mang
   Mien Nam* advocates dividing Diem's ranks and trying to win
   over groups and individuals who then supported the RVN. The
   aim is to isolate the 'My-Diem regime' from its subordinates,
   and to take advantage of any dissension in the countryside, in
   the military, among political parties and even within the RVN
   itself.

Section two ends with the following four-point set of conclusions:
1. the revolution should be led by a Marxist–Leninist Party based
   on the worker–peasant alliance;
2. a broad worker–peasant alliance should be created;
3. a national united front should be developed, expanded and
   consolidated; and
4. the enemy's internal contradictions needed to be exploited, the
   enemy to be isolated and the Party's forces to be introduced into
   his ranks.

In conclusion, *Duong Loi Cach Mang Mien Nam* ends on an
optimistic note, listing five reasons why the revolutionary movement would overcome its difficulties and succeed. These advan-
tages were as follows:
1. the strength of the north;
2. the patriotism of the people of the south;
3. the favourable international situation;
4. the weakness and isolation of the enemy; and
5. the use of the 1954 Geneva Agreements as a legal base.

Winning the sympathy and support of the world's peoples

The third prong of the VWP's revised strategy was concerned with
the conduct of the DRVN's foreign relations in order to bring about
the unification of Viet-Nam on the basis of the 1954 Geneva
Agreements. The phrase 'winning the sympathy and support of the
world's peoples' captured the flavour of a foreign policy orientation
that was designed to obtain external backing for the twin domestic
policies of consolidation of the north, and the strengthening and
development of the revolutionary movement in the south on the
basis of the Geneva Agreements.

Pham Van Dong, in his report to the National Assembly's 6th
Session,[52] advanced two major propositions in this regard: that
membership in the socialist camp was 'the key,' and that the
Geneva Agreements provided a legal basis for the DRVN's exter-
nalisation efforts. According to Dong, the Democratic Republic of
Viet-Nam, as a member of the socialist bloc, was bound by the spirit
of internationalism to cooperate closely with its fraternal allies in all
fields—political, economic and social. This relationship was

mutual for 'the friendship between our counry and the people's democracies is a sure guarantee of the independence and prosperity of our country and for our people's struggle to consolidate peace and achieve the reunification of our country.' The 'key' to this relationship was the further strengthening of relations with all socialist countries, and with the Soviet Union and China in particular. Dong left no doubt that the assistance of the countries of the socialist camp had made an important contribution to the consolidation of the north. In return, the DRVN gave loyal and predictable support to those issues on which the bloc was united: opposition to the Anglo-French operations in the Suez and support for Soviet intervention in Hungary. On other issues Dong steered a middle course, endorsing Soviet and Chinese policies almost equally:

> The government of the Democratic Republic of Viet-Nam fully supports the proposals of the Soviet Union to ban the testing of weapons of mass destruction, for a reduction in armaments, for the abolition of military blocs, for the dismantling of bases in foreign countries and for the signing of a treaty of collective security in Europe ... The government of the Democratic Republic of Viet-Nam supports China's proposals for the elimination of all aggressive military blocs in Asia and the signing of treaties between the countries concerned to maintain peace in the Pacific region.

With regard to his second proposition, Dong stressed the importance his government still attached to the 1954 Geneva Agreements. 'These Agreements,' he said:

> ... are a good basis for our struggle to consolidate peace and achieve national unity. We must continue to maintain throughout the legal basis of the Geneva Agreements, mobilize the people firmly throughout the country and mobilize world public opinion to urge that the South Vietnamese administration respect and implement these agreements, and urge that the countries participating in the Geneva Conference fulfil their tasks. The Geneva Agreements represent a great victory of the Vietnamese people. We must thoroughly apply these agreements in the revolutionary struggle of our people aimed at reunifying our Fatherland.

It is important to note the stress given by VWP officials to the legal basis of the Geneva Agreements. In their eyes, these agreements acknowledged the 'independence, sovereignty, unity and territorial integrity' of Viet-Nam. Any repudiation of these Agreements, in public or private, would have had the most serious consequences.

Since the DRVN was in no position to prevent the United States from aiding the Diem regime, let alone forcing the RVN's compliance with the political provisions of the Agreements, the DRVN had to be content with wringing every bit of propaganda advantage out of them. The DRVN could not bring much pressure to bear on the Soviet Union either. With respect to France, Pham Van Dong could only hint that 'economic and cultural relations' might improve if France 'as a signatory to the Geneva Agreements' fulfilled its responsibility for their implementation.

In private, and especially when confronted by criticism from those cadres who disagreed with post-Geneva strategy in Nam Bo, the VWP maintained that one of the reasons why reunification did not come about was excessive reliance on the Agreements as a means of arousing popular support.[53] The party still maintained that the Agreements were useful, for in its view many people in the south desired the normalisation of north-south relations. In this context, the political provisions of the Agreements provided a useful, but by no means exclusive, source of appeals.

Pham Hung put the issue succinctly: 'the legal basis of the Geneva Agreements is a good support enabling us to step up the political struggle, but the factor that determines victory is the strength of the unity and the spirit of struggle of all the people from the North to the South.'[54] In terms of international relations, Hung stated that 'our basic stand is that the Geneva Agreements must be respected and their implementation continued. The South Vietnamese administration is bound by the Geneva Agreements and is France's successor in implementing them'. Although Hung once again raised the issue of re-convening the Geneva conference 'to discuss measures to implement the Geneva Agreements', neither he nor other Party officials could have expected anyone to take heed.

Thus, by early 1957 the VWP had passed into the eye of the storm and in the momentary calm that followed, prepared to implement a comprehensive two-year strategy designed to bring about Viet-Nam's unification. There was no doubt that the new policies would take time, for Party and government officials continually stressed the 'long and arduous nature of the struggle.' Le Duan, the secretary of the Party's Regional Committee for Nam Bo, was recalled to the north at this time.[55] Thus, the foremost advocate of more militant policies in the south was brought into the inner circle of decision-making, the Party Politburo. From this vantage point Le Duan began to play a decisive role in overseeing the consolidation of the north and the development of the revolutionary movement in the south. Le Duan formally assumed the office of Party Secretary-General at the 3rd National Congress in September 1960. His elevation was to have a decisive impact on subsequent developments in the south.

6

Domestic policies of the Diem regime

JANUARY 1957–DECEMBER 1958

During the last quarter of 1956, while the Democratic Republic of Viet-Nam grappled with the effects of its disastrous land reform campaign, its southern counterpart, the Republic of Viet-Nam, moved aggressively to assert its control over South Viet-Nam and to suppress all manifestations of opposition to its authority. As chapter 4 detailed, in 1956 Diem moved firmly to consolidate his regime in the urban areas. Non-Communist opponents of his rule, including pro-French elements, anti-Communist nationalists and the sect forces, were suppressed or driven into the countryside. ARVN units then conducted a series of military operations designed to eliminate all organised armed resistance. On the internal security front, Diem initiated an Anti-Communist Denunciation Campaign to deal with Communist cadres and their supporters.

In 1957–58, Diem moved to consolidate his government. The armed forces were reorganised and retrained. Refugees from the north, poor peasant farmers, and suspected Communist sympathisers were relocated in highland camps or specially prepared rural settlements. At the same time, the RVN turned its attention to land reform in the Mekong Delta. This chapter reviews developments in this period and discusses their impact on southern society.

PACIFICATION OF THE COUNTRYSIDE

In mid-1956 ARVN launched two military operations designed to pacify the Nam Bo countryside and to eliminate the sect remnants and their Communist allies. Operation Truong Tan Buu focused on the eastern delta provinces, while Operation Thoai Ngoc Hau covered central and western Nam Bo. Both operations were concluded in February of the following year.

In October, 1956 Operation Truong Tan Buu stimulated the defection of some 45 soldiers, members of the Trinh Minh The regiment. This led the commander of this operation, General Mai Huu Xuan, to declare at a press conference that with defeat of the sect forces 'the battle was over'[1] and that only the Communists were capable of continuing sporadic guerrilla raids. The following month ARVN units conducted a sweep in Tan Uyen district, located in the famous Zone D base area, 'to destroy the last remnants of the Communist Viet Minh.'[2] Later the press reported that 302 'outlaws' had been arrested and 63 'rebels' had rallied to the government.[3] During August–November, ARVN units assigned to Operation Thoai Ngoc Hau moved into Ha Tien province to conduct operations against a 'Viet Minh rebel zone' in the Tra Tien plain along the Giang Thanh river and Vinh Te canal. Several arms caches were also uncovered in the nearby Trai and Giang Thanh hills.

Increasingly, the pacification of the countryside involved co-ordinated action by civil and military commanders. In Ba Ria province, for example, General Mai Huu Xuan, the commander of Operation Truong Tan Buu, initiated a new civic action program by black pyjama-clad province officials designed to counter dissident activity. In neighbouring Bien Hoa, the province chief, in conjunction with Operation Truong Tan Buu, completed a population census, established village councils, set up youth and inter-family groups, and recruited villagers into the Civil Guard. The population was also mobilised to assist the Army in repairing roads, building bridges, constructing schools and sports grounds. The Army, for its part, distributed medicine as well as anti-Communist propaganda.[4] Both Operation Truong Tan Buu and Operation Thoai Ngoc Hau provoked complaints by the PAVN High Command to the International Control Commission. According to these protests, both operations were a violation of article 14(c) of the Geneva Agreements, which prohibited reprisals against former members of the Resistance. There can be no doubt that ARVN targeted veterans of the Resistance War. General Xuan stated, in fact, that one of his main objectives was the destruction of 'the Viet-Cong organisation.'[5] The allegations made by the PAVN High Command, as set out in Table 6.1, should be taken as an upward limit of possible numbers of victims.

During the period from March 1957 to mid-1958 the Diem regime momentarily relaxed its anti-Communist drive in the countryside. The Party took advantage of this lull and moved to

Table 6.1   Results of Operation Truong Tan Buu and Thoai Ngoc Hao, July
1956—February 1957

Period	Arrested	Killed	Wounded
July–September 1956	3 016	136	68
September 1956–February 1957	1 984	300	30
TOTAL	5 000	436	98

Source: Vietnam News Agency, January 24, 1957 and May 25 1958

capitalise on the ineptitude of the RVN administration's handling
of land reform and rural resettlement. According to a former deputy
secretary of the Party's Western Nam Bo Interprovince Committee:[6]

> We can say with absolute certainly that by 1956 the Party was
> weakened . . . In 1957 the party began to recover, because of a
> number of not very intelligent actions and policies on the part
> of the [Diem] government, which the Party exploited. Among
> these actions and policies the most deserving of attention were
> Ordinances 2 and 57 of the land reform program, which
> automatically restored to the landlords who had followed the
> French all the lands granted to the peasants during the Resist-
> ance . . .

THE ANTI-COMMUNIST DENUNCIATION CAMPAIGN

In May 1956 phase one of the Anti-Communist Denunciation
Campaign was brought to a close when a conference was held in
Saigon to review the results achieved. After the conference, phase
two of the campaign was launched, with special attention devoted
to those provinces where past progress had been sluggish.[7]

The direction of the ACDC campaign was now placed in the
hands of province chiefs. As a result of an administrative reshuffle,
the duties of province chief and sector commander were merged
into a single post held by one individual. Thus the top administrative and military posts were combined, giving the new province chief
control over the provincial bureaucracy as well as the Civil Guard
and Self-Defence Corps. Increasingly the post of province chief was
filled by Army officers holding field grade rank.

The course of phase two of the ACDC has been described by a
party historian as follows:[8]

> In its second phase, the campaign switched its priority target to
> the jungle areas along the Truong Son (the Indochinese
> Cordillera) and the Central Highlands . . . By the end of 1957
> and early 1958, the central target of the 'denounce the

Communists' campaign switched to the Mekong River delta where the enemy [i.e. Diem] had only obtained poor results in the previous campaigns. Saigon sent its most efficient, most experienced agents from Central Viet Nam to the Mekong delta where in conjunction with the local reactionaries, they launched a campaign 'to wipe out the remaining Communist cadres.' i.e. patriots and former resistance cadres. The explicit goal of this campaign was to 'root out the Communists'. Dinh Tuong province (formerly My Tho) was chosen as a pilot province in the campaign which was to spread to the surrounding areas, in particular the former resistance zones . . .

This account tallies with reports made by the PAVN High Command to the ICC at this time. From June 1956 to July 1957 the High Command filed numerous complaints alleging major reprisals against Resistance veterans in the central Vietnamese provinces of Quang Tri and Quang Nam as well as Binh Dinh, Khanh Hoa, Phu Yen, Pleiku, and Thua Thien.[9]

With respect to Quang Tri, the PAVN Liaison Mission addressed 53 separate complaints to the ICC in the period from July 1954 to February 1957. These letters reported 685 cases of reprisals in violation of article 14(c) in the period from July 1954 to August 1956. These included 292 alleged killings, 534 woundings, and 5441 illegal detentions in 'concentration camps.'[10] Further accusations were laid later in the year when it was alleged that in the village of Gio Linh 150 suspects, including Resistance veterans and families of soldiers who had regrouped in 1954–55, had been arrested.[11] In January 1958 a further 32 Resistance veterans were apprehended. Prison camps were later constructed to house 52 families with Viet Minh connections.

In March 1957, Chau Di village in Quang Nam province reportedly suffered a similar fate.[12] There a provincial ACDC team in the company of local security forces compelled villagers to attend a one-month program of anti-Communist indoctrination. Afterwards a series of arrests took place involving mainly former members of the Resistance. By March 1958 perhaps a total of 700 persons had been taken away and incarcerated in the Phu Hoa prison camp.

One of the most publicised events occurred in Dai Loc district of the same province. There, according to the Saigon daily *Tu Do* (January 17th, 1958), 360 'ex-Communists' were subject to a four-month long indoctrination course. Later more than 1000 suspected Communists were confined in nine provincial re-education centres while a further 160 were imprisoned. PAVN protested to the ICC that these persons were subject to maltreatment. In another case, in Que Son district, PAVN reported that 500 Resistance veterans had been illegally detained.[13]

In the Mekong Delta, meanwhile, military and political pressure continued to be applied against the sects and Viet Minh veterans. Mass defections were reported in Ca Mau and Soc Trang in late 1956. In April 1957, as a result of ARVN sweeps along the Cambodian border, the PAVN High Command complained to the ICC that families of ex-Resistance fighters were being herded into 'concentration camps' in Bac Lieu, Chau Doc and Rach Gia.[14] Vietnam News Agency, the DRVN's official newsagency, reported that more than 30 000 people in Chau Doc's An Phu district were forced to relocate their homes away from the frontier.[15] The following year, the PAVN Liaison Mission to the ICC filed reports alleging 42 specific cases of reprisal under article 14(c) involving the killing of more than 100 persons, the wounding of another 13, the arrest of 318 and the forced detention in 'concentration camps' of an additional 4000 Resistance veterans, the majority of whom were said to be Hoa Hao.[16]

In February–March 1958 the RVN scored a notable triumph in Cai Be district, Dinh Tuong province.[17] Five underground Party cadres were arrested with documents listing the names of persons associated with the underground. Forty-two persons were arrested subsequently, including three senior Party officials and one district level cadre.[18] In addition three covert Party agents in the Dinh Tuong Civil Guard and a ring of 14 Party members operating under various legal covers were apprehended. Among the latter were Ma Thi Chu and her husband, Nguyen Van Hieu, two future members of the Central Committee of the National Front for the Liberation of South Viet-Nam.

Communist accounts of the ACDC are often contradictory and must be used with caution. The table below sets out the cumulative data provided by DRVN sources. Although they were issued with the disclaimer that they were based on 'incomplete figures' these estimates nevertheless serve as an upper limit in determining the effectiveness of the RVN's Anti-Communist Denunciation Campaign. Table 6.3 sets out the same figures arranged by time period. From this display one observes that the most intense period of the ACDC fell between November 1957 and February 1959. Thus there are grounds for the assertion by Party leaders that during several months of 1957 the Party apparatus experienced a brief respite.

The ACDC was directed indiscriminately at opponents of the Diem regime.[19] These included Communists and non-Communists alike. Among the latter were ex-Resistance veterans who were not Party members. These individuals were subject to the same abuses as Communist cadres and found themselves confined to 're-education centres.' Although estimates vary on the number of detainees, non-Communist observers put the total at about 50 000 over the 1954–60 period.[20]

Table 6.2 Cumulative results of the Anti-Communist Denunciation Campaign to 1959 based on PAVN complaints

Period (prior to)	Reprisals	Killed	Wounded	Arrested	Missing	Detained
February 1956[a]	–	1 563	4 636	40 768	732	–
October 1956[b]	5 529	1 775	4 725	53 350	761	10 024
April 1957[c]	5 777	2 124	5 159	57 353	778	10 000
November 1957[d]	6 172	2 148	4 182	65 211	880[e]	10 024
February 1959[f]	–	4 971	10 185	183 843	–	10 000

Sources:[a] Vietnam News Agency, May 4, 1956.
[b] Letter from Brig. Gen. Phan Trong Tue, head of the PAVN High Command, dated May 10, 1957, to Ambassador T.N. Kaul, chairman of the ICC; Vietnam News Agency, May 14,1957.
[c] *Nhan Dan*, December 3, 1957.
[d] Vietnam News Agency, November 1, 1958.
[e] Vietnam News Agency, August 7, 1958
[f] Quang Loi, *South of the 17th Parallel* (Hanoi: Foreign Languages Publishing House, 1959), p. 21; Loi cites documents prepared by PAVN. Wilfred G. Burchett, *The Furtive War* (New York: International Publishers, 1963), p. 38 states these figures, prepared by PAVN liaison officer to the ICC, cover the period April 11, 1955 to January 31, 1959.

From about mid-1957 onward, especially after October, the Communist underground struck back. By the following year they were inflicting casualties on the RVN's paramilitary forces at the rate of 40 men per week.[21] The Diem government responded by launching a new series of pacification operations. From March–October 1958, Operation Tho Lo was directed against dissidents in Binh Dinh and Phu Yen provinces. In April, Operation Nguyen Trai I swept through the eastern Nam Bo provinces of Binh Duong (Thu Dau Mot), Binh Long, Bien Hoa and Tay Ninh. During July–August 1958, Operation Hong Chau tackled the Chau Boi region along the Cambodian border. Finally, in September, Operation Nguyen Trai II shifted its operations to An Giang, An Xuyen, Ba Xuyen Kien Giang, Phong Dinh and Vinh Long provinces in western Nam Bo.

Table 6.3 Results of the Anti-Communist Denunciation Campaign by time period based on PAVN complaints

Period	Killed	Wounded	Arrested
July 1954–February 1956	1 563	4 636	40 768
February–October 1956	212	89	12 582
October 1956–November 1957	373	457	11 861
November 1957–February 1959	2 871	5 185	126 490

Sources: Same as table 6.2 above.

RURAL RESETTLEMENT

In order to cope with the influx of refugees from the north in 1954–55, to alleviate rural poverty in central Viet-Nam, and to banish politically suspect families, the RVN initiated a massive program of population resettlement. Security considerations were foremost as plans were drawn up to create a 'living wall' of new villages along the Viet-Nam–Cambodian frontier from Kontum province in the north to Ca Mau in the south.[22]

Two separate programs were implemented in the Highlands. The first, begun in April 1957, involved the resettlement of indigent and/or politically suspect families from the central coast into so-called land development centres. Within 18 months, a total of 31 000 persons had been moved into the Highlands.[23] The second program, the Highland Resettlement Scheme, was inaugurated in 1958. It aimed to resettle 88 000 person into eighty centres. In order to meet this target persuasion often gave way to coercion and in the view of one writer, 'as a result, the settlements, though reinforced by a sprinkling of demobilised soldiers, took on the wretched aspect of banishment camps . . .'[24] In the face of opposition by the victims, the scheme foundered and by 1960 virtually collapsed.

The influx of lowland Vietnamese into the Highlands immediately sparked off racial animosity between the new settlers and the Highland minority groups. This situation was only made worse by the heavy-handed efforts of the RVN to forcibly resettle Montagnard groups. These acts, coupled with Vietnamese ignorance of Highland customs and Diem's blatant disregard for traditional landholding practices, caused racial tension to rise.[25]

In early 1958 various Highland leaders came together and formed the Bajaraka Movement, an acronym formed from the names of the four tribes involved: Bahnar, Jarai, Rhade and Koho. In May, a provisional committee drew up a 'Special Charter' outlining Highland grievances and forwarded their demands for political autonomy to Saigon for action. In September the Bajaraka leaders called a general strike to draw attention to their claims. Diem responded by arresting all of the movement's leaders. Elsewhere in the Highlands, according to a party historian:[26] 'Saigon ran into the resistance of the ethnic minorities which culminated in the armed uprisings of the Raglay tribe in the Western part of Ninh Thuan province, the Bahnar tribe in Vinh Thanh in the western part of Binh Dinh province in early 1958, and the Kor and Hre ethnic minorities in Western Quang Ngai in 1959.'

In the lowlands, refugee resettlement had begun as early as 1955. In October 1957, five agricultural exploitation zones (AEZ) were created in the provinces surrounding Saigon and the Mekong Delta.[27] The most publicised of the AEZs was the Cai San resettlement area where between 40–43 000 persons were relocated on land which had been abandoned during the war. Press reports indicated that an additional 5500 persons were relocated in the Dong Thap Muoi AEZ and a further 19 839 resettled in the An Xuyen–Ba Xuyen AEZ by the end of February 1958.[28] Here too the government faced resistance on the part of some families who objected to being relocated after their regroupment to the south.

Families involved in the RVN's resettlement scheme were given the options of signing tenancy contracts or of buying the land on which they settled. They were not given free land. This aspect of the resettlement program caused confusion and resentment. As Robert Scigliano observed:[29]

> [the] peasants have not been able to understand why they have to sign tenancy contracts for unoccupied land which they assumed the Diem government was giving them. At the large Cai San development in southwestern Vietnam, for example, there was so much resistance to tenancy contracts by the 43 000 resettled refugees that the government cut off daily subsistence payments in order to bring the refugees around.

In order to grasp the crucial importance of the land tenure question it is necessary to turn to the larger issue of the RVN's land reform program .

LAND REFORM

Land ownership in the Mekong Delta was characterised by great inequality. In 1954 an estimated one quarter of one per cent of the rural population owned 40 per cent of the total rice land.[30] Most of these landowners held estates larger than 100 hectares in size. This contrasts with the average farm plot of 1.5 hectares.

Nearly 80 per cent of the population in the Mekong Delta was comprised of landless peasants with little or no security of land tenure. Prior to the Resistance War the lot of these tenant farmers was precarious indeed. They had little or no security of tenure and were often forced to pay exceeding high rental rates amounting to as much as 50–60 per cent of the crop. Quite often debt on the interest on loans borrowed to buy seed exceeded the original loan by as much as 70 per cent.

During the Resistance large numbers of estate owners, landlords, and contract labour retreated to the safety of the major towns and cities. During their absence, operating under the authority of decrees issued by the DRVN, resistance cadres implemented a rent reduction regime for the peasantry in areas under their control.[31] In addition, DRVN cadres also redistributed land taken from absentee landlords. The beneficiary was not required to pay rent on this land to the Resistance government but he was required to pay a tax, a financial obligation which was widely accepted as being quite separate from traditional rent. The impact of this land reform program was considerable as the Party controlled over half of the rural villages outside of the sect areas.[32]

After partition, and only as a result of prodding by American and French officials, Diem reluctantly agreed to act to alleviate the land tenure conditions, which adversely affected four-fifths of the rural population. Three major ordinances dealing with land reform were issued at this time. Ordinance No. 2 (January 8, 1955) addressed the problem of security of tenure. It provided for the registration of model contracts, and set a limit on the amount of rent and interest rates which could be charged by a landlord. On the face of it the application of Ordinance No. 2 appeared successful, for by mid-1959 80 per cent of all tenanted land (774 000 contracts) had been duly registered.[33]

Ordinance No. 7 (February 5, 1955) and its successor (Ordinance No. 28 of April 30, 1956) addressed itself to the problem of squatters who were farming on land abandoned during the war. Under the terms of this ordinance, village councils were empowered to lease abandoned land to suitable tenants. No rent was to be collected during the first year and reduced rates were set for the following two-year period. Ordinance 57 (October 22, 1956) dealt with the question of inequities in the ownership of rice lands and made provision for the redistribution of all holdings in excess of 100 ha.

The defects of ordinances Nos. 2 and 7 were well summarised by Robert Shaplen,[34] a close follower of the Vietnamese rural scene:

> While some peasants benefited from this part of the land reform program, it was hindered by bad administration and lack of proper enforcement. Peasants were frequently in arrears on their rents, and the system of agrarian courts established to settle landlord-tenant disputes soon came to be dominated by the landlords and by officials friendly to them, to the obvious disadvantage of the peasants. Furthermore, the peasants objected to paying rents for land that had been unoccupied because of the war—almost a third of the total rice land.

Shaplen's last point was a crucial factor influencing peasant discontent. During the war years, as we have already noted, most of the large landlords and tenant labour fled the countryside. Much of the fallow land was worked by new peasants, squatters in fact, under the Party's 'land-to-the-tiller' program. As a result of the RVN's land reform ordinances these people were subject to what were essentially regressive measures.[35] Absentee landlords who had remained for the most part in the towns, were now quite happy to collect some rent where no rent had been collected before. In many cases, the landlord hired local officials, or even local military units, to act on his behalf in collecting rent.[36]

Despite the stipulations of Ordinance No. 2, landlords regularly collected rent in excess of the upper limit of 25 per cent. Studies conducted in 1958 put the average rent at between 25 and 30 per cent.[37] In fact, even as these rents were charged, some landlords attempted to extort payment in full for rent unpaid during the war years.

The plight of the rural tenant assumes even greater proportions when set against the failure of the RVN to effect any meaningful land redistribution. First, individual landowners were allowed to retain an additional 30 hectares above the 100 ha. limit if they worked the land themselves. A further 15 ha. could be reserved for family graves and ancestral temples. Second, there was one significant catch to the redistribution program: all prospective new owners had to purchase the land from the government for the same purchase price the government had paid, but at a repayment rate spread over six years amounting to one-quarter of the annual gross yield. Third, rice land owned by French citizens, the Catholic Church, and land belonging to absentee landlords was not subject to expropriation.

Fourth, village communual land was not subject to Ordinance 57. This was especially important in central Viet-Nam where 99 per cent of the landowners were small holders. One hundred thousand farmers operated farms less than 1 ha. in size. These small holders depended on the allocation of communal land to supplement their inadequate personal holdings. Theoretically the institution of communal land served to benefit the poor but in practice, as land was let to the highest bidder, only the well-to-do benefited. As Denis Warner has recorded:[38]

> In practice, the system usually works as yet another means for squeeze and graft by appointed village chiefs and one of the worst forms of land exploitation. No security of tenure is given beyond the crop year, and there is no incentive for crop or land improvement when the poor peasants are allowed on the land. More often than not they do not get a chance at all, and the land goes to the richest and most prominent landlord.

Land devoted to crops other than rice, such as coffee, tea and rubber, was likewise not subject to expropriation. Thus, of the 2.45 million hectares of cultivable land in the delta, only 650 000 ha. owned by 2600 landlords was subject to expropriation and redistribution.[39] The surveying of this land and the transfer of titles were undertaken at a snail's pace. By December, 1960 for example, of 607 300 ha. acquired by the RVN only 376 600 ha. had been surveyed.[40] There were many other defects involved with the

Table 6.4   Land reform undertaken by the Republic of Viet-Nam 1957–61

Date	Amount of land (hectares)		
	Expropriated	Redistributed	New owners
July 1957[a]	–	35 700	18 800
January 1958[b]	–	104 370	49 968
May 1958[c]	–	148 445	64 877
September 1958[d]	–	258 969	97 229
July 1961[e]	415 843	–	109 438

Sources: [a] Viet-Nam Presse, July 15, 1957.

[b] Vietnam Press, *The Times of Vietnam*, February 27, 1958.

[c] *La Depeche du Cambodge*, July 9, 1958.

[d] Robert L. Sansom, *The Economics of Insurgency in the Mekong Delta of Vietnam*, p. 57, fn. 8

[e] Republic of Viet-Nam, State Secretariat for Information, *Bilan des realisations gouvernementales* (Saigon, 1961), p. 370

running of the RVN's land reform program. Private agreements were often struck between landlord and tenant which disregarded provisions of the various land reform ordinances. Wealthy landowners escaped expropriation by placing legal ownership of excess land in the hands of close family members. Table 6.4 sets out the results of Diem's land reform in the period up to July 1961.

The crucial point about land redistribution undertaken under Ordinance 57 was that it was too narrowly conceived. Only 30 per cent of the total cultivated rice land was liable to expropriation and of the number of tenants in 1955 only 10 per cent ever benefited.[41] As late as 1965, according to Sansom, some 817 000 tenants (87.5 per cent of the total) had yet to benefit from the provisions of Ordinance 57.[42] In brief the vast majority of tenants in the Mekong Delta laboured under abusive tenancy conditions.

The RVN's land reform of 1957–58 also struck at the heart of reforms implemented by the Party during the Resistance. According to Le Van Chan:[43]

This land-reform program had a great impact in the countryside, making the majority of the peasantry angry at the government. The peasants felt that they had spilled their blood to drive the French from the country, while the landlords sided with the French and fought against the peasants. Thus at the very least the peasants' rights to the land should have been confirmed. Instead, they were forced to buy the land, and thus they felt they were being victimised by the Government. At the same time the Party apparatus took advantage of this situation to propagandise on how bad the Government was, how it was the government of the landlords, stealing the land from the peasants.

AMERICAN MILITARY AND ECONOMIC INFLUENCE

In the 1955–61 period the United States lavished $US 1.7 billion in economic aid upon the Republic of Viet-Nam.[44] In May 1958 Saigon housed the largest US economic aid mission in the world and by 1961 was the third-ranking non-NATO recipient of American aid after Korea and Taiwan.[45] Table 6.5 sets out the figures on American economic and military aid to the RVN in the 1955–60 period.

Military influence

The major mechanism used in the disbursement of aid (except for direct military grants which comprised 25 per cent of the total program) was the Commercial Import Program, or CIP. Under the CIP the United States subsidised the running costs of the RVN in this way:[46]

> The two Governments agreed first on the size of the allocation of dollars [of U.S. aid for a given fiscal year]. Vietnamese importers—preferably industrial investors—applied for licenses to import from the U.S., or, in a variety of circumstances arising out of Washington's own balance-of-payments position, from a list of third countries that might change from year to year, the commodities they required, depositing at the National Bank in Saigon at thirty-five piastres for every dollar on the pro forma invoice. The US Treasury reimbursed the supplier in dollars, while the RVN government encashed the deposited piastres, crediting them to what was known as the Counterpart Fund, and incurred on the other side of the account such expenditures as had been agreed with the US—in the main, the pay and food of the armed forces.

Without the CIP or some other aid mechanism, the Diem regime would not have been able to survive as it had no other source of revenues sufficient to cover the expenses of running the country.[47] The solution to this problem, as we shall note below, was thought to

Table 6.5 US aid to the Republic of Viet-Nam, 1955–60 (in millions of US dollars by fiscal year [FY])

Obligations[a]	FY1955	FY1956	FY1957	FY1958	FY1959	FY1960
Economic[b]	322.4	210.0	282.2	189.1	207.4	182.0
Military	–	167.3	110.5	53.2	41.9	70.9
TOTAL	322.4	377.3	392.7	242.3	249.3	252.9

Source: John D. Montgomery, *The Politics of Foreign Aid: American Experience in Southeast Asia*, p. 284

Notes: [a] Not expenditures
        [b] Grants and loans

Table 6.6   US counterpart funding for the Republic of Viet-Nam, 1955–60 (in millions of piastres).

	1955	1956	1957	1958	1959	1960	Total
Local currency deposits:	167.1	239.4	256.0	203.4	170.2	181.8	1218.4
Withdrawals in support of RVN (defence budget)	97.1	202.5	204.5	152.9	176.0	166.6	999.6
Percentage of Total:	58%	85%	80%	75%	103%	92%	82%

Sources: 'U.S. Perceptions of the Insurgency, 1954–1960', *United States-Vietnam Relations 1945–1967*, Book 2, IV.A.5. Tab 4, p. 39.

Note: Under the Commercial Import Program, the US government issued credits in US dollars in American banks to licensed Vietnamese importers. The importers deposited piastres, the local currency, in Vietnamese banks. These deposits were known as counterpart funds which US officials in Viet-Nam drew upon to finance selected programs in the RVN's defence budget.

rest on encouraging Viet-Nam's economic self-sufficiency. Neither the CIP nor the RVN's efforts at economic development was successful.[48]

There were several problems associated with the running of the CIP. Initially the program encouraged the importation mainly of consumer goods (air conditioners, hi-fis, and automobiles). These made little contribution to economic development and tended to benefit mainly the urban middle and upper classes. Secondly, the piastre–dollar exchange rate was artificially low and licensed importers, after paying customs duties, would often sell goods at a lower price than their overseas value. One result was a massive stockpiling of goods in Saigon which could not be sold.[49] The RVN-imposed duties on the in-flow of goods under the CIP, in fact, soon became the government's prime source of revenue. According to one observer,[50] 'American aid has paid for most of Vietnam's imports since 1954. It has provided most of the revenues for the Vietnamese budget—about 60 per cent of all government revenues since 1954 have come directly or indirectly from American aid.'

The US used the CIP as the device through which it channelled over 80 per cent of its economic aid. In operation the money generated through the CIP did little to encourage RVN self-sufficiency. As table 6.6 sets out, 82 per cent of the counterpart funds were used by the RVN to meet defence needs.

Robert Scigliano has summarised this situation succinctly:[51]

Between 1956 and 1960, 43 per cent of all Vietnamese public expenditures were allocated directly to the military for the support of the army and Self-Defense Corps. The United States provided practically all of the money through the counterpart [fund] generated by the commercial import program. As a matter of fact, 78 per cent of all American aid given to Vietnam between these two years went into the military budget. In short, from 1956 to 1960 the Vietnamese government spent two-fifths of its total revenues, including over three-quarters of the money it obtained from the United States, in order to maintain its military establishment.

As for the disbursement of the remaining 20 per cent of US aid to Viet-Nam, a look at these expenditures reveals additional amounts spent on security and defence needs. The heading 'transportation', for example, includes funds spent on the repair or construction of roads. Although certain economic benefits accrued from this, military needs determined the priorities. The heading 'public administration' similarly contained expenditures related to the police and security services, mainly equipment.

The above figures do not reveal, however, the total picture. We have already mentioned that 25 per cent of the total American aid package comprised direct military grants (Table 6.6 above). These averaged $US85 million per year during 1955–61. Not included in RVN expenditure are accounts related to the technically 'civilian' Civil Guard, police and security services. And further, as Robert Scigliano has written, '[n]or do the figures on military and civilian expenditures indicate the extent to which provincial and other local authorities are likewise preoccupied with security matters.'[52]

Economic influence

The RVN's progress in economic development must be related to the security and defence priorities just outlined. In 1957, under American pressure, the RVN moved slowly to implement a program of economic development. A five-year development program was drawn up but it was, inexplicably, never published.[53]

In order to attain self-sufficiency the development plan placed emphasis on the export of rice and rubber, which then accounted for 70 per cent of export earnings. Rice production quickly reached pre-war levels (3.4 million tons in 1938) and a high point of 5 million tons was attained in 1959. Exports rose from 70 000 tons to 340 000 in the same period. In 1961, however, due to rural insecurity the Republic of Viet-Nam stopped exporting surplus rice. Rubber production similarly increased from a pre-war level of 60 000 tons in 1938 (51 000 tons in 1954) to 79 000 tons in 1960. Yet these developments were more than off-set by imports. While exports increased during the 1954–60 period, and while the total value of imports was reduced slightly at the same time (by $26.7 million), the ratio between exports to imports stood at 1:3 in the best year.[54]

Other problems beset economic planners. Because of the proclivities of Diem and Nhu, the massive amounts of foreign exchange

accumulated by the CIP were not reinvested in productive enterprises until after 1961. Second, because of the comfortable arrangement provided by the CIP the RVN took no steps to raise the
domestic revenues, preferring dependence on overseas aid. Taxa-
tion revenues fell drastically, perhaps by as much as 50 per cent.
Third, the RVN was extremely slow to encourage the development
of domestic industry whose growth would lessen dependence on
foreign imported goods. For example, an Industrial Development
Centre was established in 1957 to aid new enterprises; by 1959 it
had approved only 27 of 125 projects submitted to it.[55] Efforts to
attract foreign investment at this time were mainly unsuccessful.

The increase in American military and economic aid to the RVN
did not go unnoticed in Hanoi. Throughout this period Party
leaders kept a close watch on the growing American presence and
the comings and goings of high-level American delegations. Of
particular concern was the growth in the numbers of American
military advisers and the uncontrolled shipment into Viet-Nam of
military supplies and equipment. Although both developments
formed the subject of numerous complaints to the ICC, no
definitive action was undertaken due to the refusal of the RVN to
let ICC teams intrude where their presence might prove embarrass-
ing.

During 1956 various pressures built up on the United States to increase the numbers of its military advisers in Viet-Nam in excess of
the ceiling set in 1954. The ingenious solution was the creation of
TERM—Temporary Equipment Recovery Mission—a subterfuge[56] which enabled MAAG to surmount the Geneva limitations.
TERM was activated in June and reached maximum strength of
350 men three months later. It soon attracted the critical attention
of the ICC which petitioned the RVN for an explanation. After
months of procrastination and evasion the RVN agreed to provide
monthly reports to the International Commission. In its ninth
interim report (March 10, 1959) the Commission was moved to
state:[57]

> The Commission considered all relevant reports and docu-
> ments connected with TERM and informed the Government
> of the Republic that the Commission was of the view that
> TERM should be able to complete its remaining work by the
> end of June 1959, and that, the status of TERM being
> temporary, TERM should cease to exist thereafter and its
> personnel should leave the Republic of Vietnam.

Nearly a year later the issue had not been settled as the RVN informed the ICC that the discovery of further US equipment made it
impossible to determine when TERM would complete its activities.
Under ICC prodding the RVN eventually replied that TERM would

Table 6.7 US personnel in Viet-Nam, 1958–61*

United States Embassy[a]	90
United States Information Service (USIS)[a]	35
United States Operations Mission (USOM)[b]	555
Military Assistance Advisory Group (MAAG)[c]	1,000
Temporary Equipment Recovery Mission (TERM)[d]	350
Michigan State University Group (MSU)/CIA[e]	52
TOTAL	2,082

Sources: [a] Robert Scigliano, *South Vietnam: Nation Under Stress*, p. 192–3; he places USOM at less than 200, MAAG at less than 700 and American dependants at 800.

[b] John D. Montgomery, *The Politics of Foreign Aid*, p. 177; these include contract and career employees as of May 31, 1958.

[c] Bernard Fall, 'Will South Vietnam Be Next' *The Nation* (May 31, 1958); Fall writes, 'And a vast U.S. Military Assistance Advisory Group (MAAG)—its exact size is classified but including well over a thousand officers and men. . .' The official figures placed the number at 342; 'U.S. Denies Build-Up,' *The New York Times*, May 16, 1957.

[d] 'US Training of the Vietnamese National Army, 1954–1959', *United States–Vietnam Relations, 1945–1967*, Book 2, IV.A.4 Chronology, p. MM.

[e] Robert Scigliano and Guy H. Fox *Technical Assistance in Vietnam*, p. 8; prior to 1957 the figure stood at 34, in the 1957–62 period it never exceeded 52. Dennis Duncanson, *Government and Revolution in Vietnam*, p. 276 states that prior to 1961 the total number of employees assigned to USOM, USIS, MSU and the CIA was less than 300. This estimate obviously excludes the 372 USOM contract-employees.

Note: * These figures have been gathered from various sources and reflect different time periods. Figures for the U.S. Embassy and USIS may be maximum numbers for the period. USOM figures include contract-employees. Not included are various private US citizens engaged in business or missionary work, American dependants and temporary visitors.

be able to complete its work by the end of 1960. When the deadline was reached the RVN informed the Commission that it 'had ceased its activities and was disbanded on 31st December, 1960.'[58] PAVN protested that TERM had not disbanded but had remained in Viet-Nam under the cover of MAAG's Logistics Section. There may have been some truth in this as ex-TERM personnel transferred to MAAG's roster at that time.

PAVN High Command made further protests to the ICC concerning the nature of MAAG, the role of CATO (Combat Arms Training Organisation), TRIM (Training Relations and Instruction Mission), and the participation of RVN observers in various SEATO meetings. In May 1957, the DRVN Ministry of Foreign Affairs charged that the US had over 2000 military personnel in South Viet-Nam. American denials put the total at 692 and further stated that one-half of them were on 'temporary assignment.'

Hanoi may well have included civilian officials in their count (see Table 6.7). The PAVN High Command continued to note the arrival of American planes and ships bearing 'war material'. In 1957, the High Command addressed 69 letters to the ICC concerning alleged illegal arrivals of planes (70 cases) and shipment of 'illegal war material' (105 cases).[59] A review of Commission reports covering the period August 1956–February 1961 is shown in Table

Table 6.8   **PAVN complaints to the ICC concerning US military personnel and equipment**

Dates	ARTICLE 16[a]		ARTICLE 17[b]	
	PAVN complaints	Violations recorded	PAVN complaints	Violations recorded
1 Aug 1956–30 Apr 1957	96	5	114	3
1 May 1957–30 Apr 1958	31	13	45	6
1 May 1958–31 Jan 1959	16	27[c]	26	6
1 Feb 1959–31 Jan 1960	147	12	32	20
1 Feb 1960–28 Feb 1961	122	3	132	34

Sources: [a] Article 16 of the 1954 Geneva Agreements (parts a-g) bans the introduction of additional military personnel.
[b] Article 17 of the 1954 Geneva Agreements (parts a-f) bans the reinforcement of all types of arms, munitions, and other war material, such as combat aircraft, naval craft, pieces of ordnance, jet engines and jet weapons, and armoured vehicles.
[c] Complaints filed in one time period are usually determined in a later report. It is therefore possible for the number of violations recorded in one period to exceed the number of PAVN complaints at the same time.

6.8. The figures for violations are minimum figures as the ICC was prevented from controlling the arrival of numerous ships and aircraft at various RVN installations.

CONCLUSION

This chapter has attempted to provide an account of the major policies pursued by the Diem regime which had an impact on the underground Party apparatus during 1957–58. The next chapter will view this same period from the point of view of the Party. This overview of the 1957–58 period has been necessary for three reasons. First, it serves to indicate the continuing competition for rural legitimacy between the Diem regime and the various opponents of that regime. All too often this aspect has been overlooked by writers on this period. In other words, the RVN had to devote a large amount of its resources to establishing and maintaining its authority in rural areas. Both the large-scale military sweeps and the conduct of the anti-Communist denunciation campaign were part of this overwhelming concern to establish security in the countryside.

Second, a review of the 1957–59 period sheds light on the nature of the political problems confronting the Diem regime. Diem's failure to successfully cope with problems of rural indebtedness and tenancy, for example, left festering grievances which the Party attempted to exploit. The resettlement program, designed to secure Viet-Nam's borders against 'Communist infiltration' had the reverse impact in the Highlands. There the Party found a sympathetic audience for its anti-government propaganda. In the lowlands, meanwhile, the resettlement program was much more successful, as landless refugees were given a stake in the future. Nevertheless discontent arose between the newcomers and the locals as the latter felt Diem was giving the former special treatment.

Third, documentation of increasing American military and economic influence in the south provides an insight into genuine concerns and anxieties by Hanoi. The corruption and nepotism of the Diem regime, whether real or partly imagined, sparked domestic disaffection. Indeed, in September–October 1958 there appears to have been an attempt on the part of some civilians in alliance with disgruntled army officers to promote a coup, thus foreshadowing the more dramatic events of November 1960.

Growing American influence coupled with an increased acceptability of the RVN on the world stage (see chapter 8) only served to convince Party leaders that they must redouble their efforts to reunify Viet-Nam lest the southern Republic became too strong. There are two sides to the coin of rural discontent which emerged in Viet-Nam from 1957 onward. The actions and policies of the Diem regime which in themselves contributed to rural discontent represent one side. On the other side of the coin are the policies and actions of the Party's underground organisation, which was engaged in implementing the new strategy outlined in *Duong Loi Cach Mang Mien Nam.*

This situation has been aptly described by George Carver, a CIA official who served under civilian cover in Viet-Nam in 1959–60:[61]

The 1956–58 period was unusually complex, even for Viet-Nam. Diem, in effect, reached his political high-water mark sometime around mid-1957. After that, his methods of operation, traits of character and dependence on his family became set with ever increasing rigidity along lines which ultimately led to his downfall. Despite undeniable progress in its early years, his government was never successful in giving the bulk of the South Vietnamese peasantry positive reasons for identifying their personal fortunes with its political course. The administrators Diem posted to the countryside were often corrupt and seldom native to the areas to which they were assigned, a fact which caused them to be considered as 'foreigners' by the intensely clannish and provincial peasantry. Land policies, often admirable in phraseology, were notably weak in execution and frequently operated to the benefit of absentee landlords rather than those who actually tilled the soil. Such factors as these, coupled with the still manifest consequences of a decade of war, generated genuine grievances among the peasantry which the Communists were quick to exploit and exacerbate.

7

Maintaining and developing the struggle in the south

1957–58

THE 2ND CONFERENCE OF THE NAM BO REGIONAL COMMITTEE

In late 1956, the Nam Bo Regional Committee convened its 2nd Conference to discuss the implementation of the Central Committee's new policy line embodied in *Duong Loi Cach Mang Mien Nam*. This key document served to dispel disquiet among Party cadres in the south concerned at the receding chances for national unification in the face of the growing disparity of forces in favour of the Diem regime. According to a retrospective account:[1]

> the resolution of the [2nd] Regional conference considered the question of armed forces [*luc luong vo trang*]. According to this assessment, armed forces should be developed to cope with the renewal of fighting. The reason the conference mentioned this subject was because at that time the reality [of the situation] in Nam Bo was that all the armed forces opposing Diem belonged to the religious sects.

Among the long-range preparations set in train by the conference was the reorganisation of existing military units 'and unifying the command of these forces.'[2] In 1954, the Party embarked on a 'reduction of cadres' movement designed to streamline the Party apparatus. By 1957 Party membership had been reduced from 60 000 to 15 000.[3] It was upon this core of cadres that the Party relied in the new phase of consolidation and rebuilding. According to *Tinh Hinh Nam Bo*, a captured party document, 'from 1957 the people's struggle shifted to demanding social welfare and democracy. The political slogans used in 1955 and 1956 were seldom seen.' This reorientation of the struggle movement was reviewed by the Regional Committee's 1956 conference, which decided to inaugurate a 'second phase in the struggle movement in Nam Bo.'[4] Thus the change in emphasis, noticeable in late 1956, was re-affirmed. *Duong Loi Cach Mang Mien Nam* set forth three major themes that would be stressed by the renewed political struggle movement in Nam Bo: peace and unification, democracy, and social welfare.

POLITICAL STRUGGLE (1957–58)

The second phase of the struggle movement lasted until mid-1959 when, according to *Tinh Hinh Nam Bo*, it 'came to a deadlock.' By mid-1958 a loss of momentum was already noticeable. During this period 'the Party Regional Committee advocated that the main goals of the revolutionary movement were the struggle for democratic rights and the struggle for social welfare.' However the Regional Committee stressed that the struggle movement 'should not be conducted simultaneously and everywhere but should be concentrated in specific local areas and at an appropriate time.'[5]

Under the catchcry 'democracy' the Party focused its attention on abuses in the day-to-day operations of the Diem regime at all levels, especially in the hamlets and villages. Diemist officials provided many opportunities the Party could exploit. Abuses resulted from the conduct of military operations and the Anti-Communist Denunciation Campaign in the rural areas. Covert Party cadres noted the details and widely circulated embellished accounts of what occurred.[6]

Party cadres also encouraged protests against the renewal of conscription. In Quang Tri province, for example, scores of letters were sent to the provincial authorities demanding that youths eligible for the draft 'be allowed to stay home to look after their old parents.'[27] Face-to-face confrontations were arranged between the local people and government officials. Armed propaganda teams encouraged draft-eligible young men to flee to safe-havens.

Party cadres also directed their efforts at the sizeable Khmer Krom community in the Delta provinces.[8] One of the main grievances was the discriminatory policies of RVN officials who closed Khmer-language schools and restricted teaching in the Khmer language. Various delegations were organised to protest these activities. Tra Vinh province was the centre of these disturbances. At least one protest march clashed with the local Civil Guard.

After the commencement of Diem's land reform program, Party cadres put forward the argument that the present occupants of redistributed land should not cooperate with the RVN's schemes lest they provide absentee landlords with a basis for asserting legal ownership. In early 1957, the Party issued new guidelines on the land issue.[9] This policy sought to reap a dual harvest of landlord and peasant discontent over the implementation of RVN Ordinances Nos. 2 and 57. The Party's land policy took into account the transparent defects and shortcomings of the RVN's efforts. According to a later review,[10] 'one of the reactionary forces in the rural areas is the landlords. The enemy helps them collect taxes. His decrees, No. 57, 2 etc. . .are aimed at restoring to the landlords and Vietnamese traitors (*Viet gian*) the right of ownership of land previously confiscated during the Resistance.' However the Party also perceived differences between some landlords and the Diem regime:[11] 'Diem thought that his government was supported by all the landlords in Nam Bo but the fact is that his government received the support of only a small number, especially refugees from the North. A large number of landlords in Nam Bo were either neutral or disliked Diem.'

The Party's policy towards the landlords was conditioned in part on the basis of experience gained during the Resistance. At that time land was confiscated from landlords only if they were considered pro-French, 'traitors', cruel or corrupt. Landlords who remained in the liberated areas were permitted to collect rent, albeit on a reduced scale. In 1957 the Party attempted to play on discontent among landlords aroused by the RVN's land reform ordinances by suggesting that alternative arrangements be worked out with the tenants including, if necessary, the direct purchase of land.

Concerning the peasant farmers, the Party adopted the view that its main aim should be to keep them on the land they were presently tilling and to organise various forms of protests to delay the implementation of Ordinances Nos. 2 and 57. However the Party recognised that the peasants' strong desire to own their own land presented a complication. On the one hand, some peasants would resist all attempts to restore the *status quo ante* because they believed that land abandoned during the Resistance which the Party had redistributed, was theirs. On the other hand, other peasants could be stampeded by the provisions of Ordinances Nos. 2 and 57 into signing new model contracts or into purchasing a clear land title. Given these circumstances the Party formulated the following policy:[12]

> Temporarily set aside the slogan that the peasantry has achieved ownership of the land. Instead, pay attention to the principle of maintaining the current tiller on his land.

> This is the general policy for the entire South. Take care not to abandon the old policy [of the Resistance] all at once but rather rely on the local balance of forces to determine whether to continue emphasizing ownership or to abandon it temporarily.

In other words, the Party had assessed the 'balance of forces' between itself and the Diem regime and had decided 'to move one step back.' Diem would incur the opprobrium of the landlords, for restricting rents and expropriating land, and peasants, for upsetting the gains they had made during the Resistance. Due to the RVN's administrative weakness Party cadres in the villages could turn Diem's land reform to their own advantage. This important point has been aptly summarised by Samuel Popkin:[13]

> Viet Cong success has always been at least partially attributable to its ability to enforce and carry out GVN proclamations. Ironically, often only an 'illegal' group had this capability. The execution of Diem's land reform provides an example. The Viet Cong no doubt profited from the land problem, but not simply because Diem was a reactionary or an oppressive ruler. It was able to use land reform by transforming into a political issue a seemingly arbitrary set of decisions which peasants did not feel morally obligated to accept.
>   The Vietnamese system of land tenure could be exploited in many ways even without large-scale redistribution of land: rent levels, market prices, interest rates, and fertilizer prices. All could be manipulated to improve the welfare of the individual farmer, Diem's policies for dealing with these vagaries were often sound: set rent ceilings, provide for displaced persons, institute loan programs. But because he lacked effective organization for reaching into the village, Diem was unable to implement his programs. Only the Viet Cong had the necessary links with the peasantry. Thus, for many peasants the Viet Cong easily emerged as the champion of the just cause simply by carrying out the government's promises.

In addition to the land issue, the 'social welfare' component of the political struggle movement embraced a variety of other issues such as conditions in the refugee camps, American economic aid and cultural presence, and petty restrictions on trade imposed by the Diem government.[14] Two aspects of the American presence in particular came under attack. Firstly, 'depraved American culture' in the form of 'obscene films' and pornography was condemned. Secondly, the Commercial Import Program came under attack for threatening local industry. Party cadres launched a 'movement for support of locally made goods.'[15] Cadres also placed 'Yankee Go Home' leaflets in the mailboxes belonging to Americans serving in Saigon.[16]

Underground cadres in the cities encouraged various workers'
organisations to engage in protests and other public demonstrations
including strikes. These actions were classified as 'legal activities'
by the Party because they were specifically related to worker
grievances and they were conducted in a peaceful manner. In other
words they were designed to conform to the range of public activity
permitted by the Diem regime while at the same time acting as a test
of those limits.[17]

The extent of the Party's influence on urban protests is difficult to
measure, given its clandestine nature. Party-inspired accounts of
workers' and students' struggles are self-serving and highly exaggerated.[18] It is virtually impossible to determine how many strikes were
instigated by covert Party cadres and how many strikes occurred
independently. According to accounts published by Hanoi, 292
collective actions were undertaken in 1955, 504 in 1956 and 804 in
1957–58.[19] It does seem certain, however, that the Party encouraged and supported whatever actions workers decided to take
against their employers and that Party influence was strongest
among the workers on the rubber plantations. Although the main
emphasis was on economic grievances, the Party tried to link these
demands with those for 'democracy' and 'peace–independence–
reunification.' The Party was not always successful, however, as
Ton Vy observed: 'the South Vietnamese working class . . . clearly
realized that the economic struggle should be combined with
political and ideological struggle' in practice but 'at some times and
in some places, this triple aspect of the workers' struggle . . . [could
not be] maintained . . .'[20]

The Party muted the themes associated with reunification in
favour of more pragmatic concerns. Nevertheless a low-keyed effort
was conducted to keep these issues alive. On the occasion of the
RVN's National Day (October 26, 1958), for example, slogans
demanding 'peace and reunification' were daubed on walls in
Saigon, while posters printed by the RVN were defaced and torn
down. Elsewhere, in Quang Nam, Quang Ngai and Vinh Long
provinces, RVN soldiers and civil servants were subjected to
slogans shouted over loud hailers. During the year various leaflets
were circulated throughout Viet-Nam. One reproduced the
DRVN's March 8, 1958 call for the normalisation of north–south
relations.[21] Another, distributed in Ba Xuyen province, called upon
RVN government employees to:[22] 'Support the just struggle of the
people to overthrow the government of the Americans and Diem
[My-Diem], to establish a democratic regime in the South, and to
work for general elections which will reunify the country by
peaceful means.'

During the 18 month period from early 1957 to mid-1958 the
Party was relatively successful in its efforts to launch phase two of

the political struggle movement. But as time went on the capacity of the RVN to meet and overcome this challenge increased. According to one Party cadre,[23] 'the [Diem] government began to establish its village and hamlet apparatus in the remote rural areas where the French never dared to set foot. When the government local apparatus was established this naturally limited the Party's activities.' A Party history[24] of this period confirms these views concerning the timing and effectiveness of the RVN's pacification efforts, 'the enemy started this [pacification] program at the beginning of 1956, but the enemy did not succeed in oppressing the rural areas until the middle of 1958.' Yet the Party too was held to blame: 'as for the form of struggle the [Nam Bo Regional] Committee sometimes put too much emphasis on maintaining the struggle's legal position and for this reason in some areas the [political struggle] activities of the movement lost their revolutionary meaning.[25]

After mid-1958 the political movement 'gradually shifted from a strong to a weak position.' Cadres had great difficulty in initiating action and '[t]he movement demanding social welfare and democratic rights became sporadic and uncoordinated.'[26] According to Ton Vy, 'while the popular movement in the countryside, subjected to repeated attacks by the puppet regime, suffered setbacks in some places [during the first half of 1958], the workers and other labouring people in the cities availed themselves of the enemy's demagogy to extend and better organize their legal struggle.'[27] The 'legal' political struggle movement in the cities survived for another three months until 'a particularly harsh repression . . . caused some temporary setback to the worker movement.'

VIOLENCE IN THE COUNTRYSIDE

The sects and the Party

In 1955, when military forces loyal to Diem expelled the Binh Xuyen from Saigon, a group of Binh Xuyen men under the command of Vo Van Mon sought refuge in War Zone D and in the Plain of Reeds. That same year, two understrength breakaway Cao Dai battalions ensconced themselves in the Duong Minh Chau base area in neighouring Tay Ninh. In 1956 a Hoa Hao unit of 300 men, led by the son of Huynh Phu So, sought refuge near Can Tho. All three groups were contacted by Communist cadres. Past enmity was overcome when Party officials offered to assist these units in their fight for survival. In October 1956, for example, combined Binh Xuyen and Cao Dai units were successfully employed in attacks at Dau Tieng in Thu Dau Mot and Ben Cui in Bien Hoa. These actions led one historian[28] to observe:

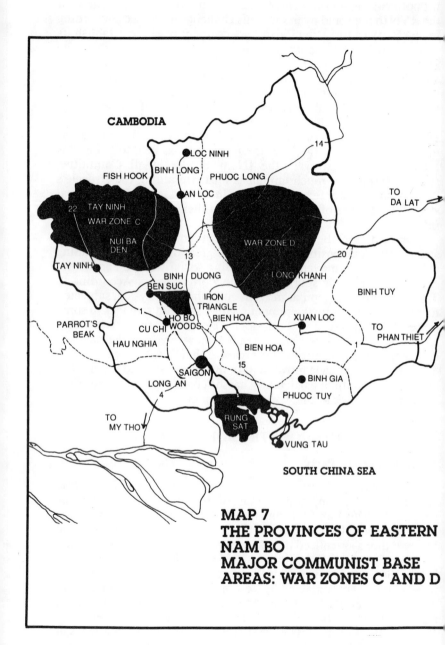

MAP 7
THE PROVINCES OF EASTERN
NAM BO
MAJOR COMMUNIST BASE
AREAS: WAR ZONES C AND D

[t]he anti-dictatorship armed forces in the years 1956–1957 actually became the prop of the people's struggle. In return, they enjoyed effective help from the people who provided them with food and manpower, enabling them to survive and develop. The armed forces of the religious sects, to enhance their reputation among the population and to break the encirclement by the Saigon army, launched a number of operations against military positions and political and economic centres of the Saigon regime around the resistance bases.

In December 1956 the Party instigated a mass escape of prisoners inside Bien Hoa jail. After seizing a quantity of arms, they fled to the safety of Zone D and the Plain of Reeds.[29] The Party then moved to unite the various armed sect units. Later that month various dissident leaders met in the Plain of Reeds to announce the unification of their armed forces under a joint general staff. This new alliance took the name Cao Thien Hoa Binh, an acronymn formed from its constituent members—Cao Dai, Thien Chua [Catholics], Hoa Hao and Binh Xuyen.[30] On operations, whether separately or in combination, each unit continued to bear its own sect designation as well as that of the new alliance.

Cao Thien Hoa Binh representatives soon made contact with Vietnamese exiles in Cambodia and France and tapped their financial resources. It is tempting to speculate that the renewal of opposition to Diem may have sparked other exile groups into action, such as the Dai Viet National Salvation Movement which formed six months later. In early 1957, approaches were made to individuals serving in sect units which had been integrated into the ARVN to enlist their support in a coup attempt against Diem. The plot failed and a purge of elements within ARVN suspected of disloyalty followed.[31]

A similar link-up between the Party and sect dissidents occurred in mid-1957 in Ca Mau province. There two sect leaders organised a military force to resist local RVN officials. According to Nguyen Tu Quang, a party cadre in Ca Mau at that time:[32] 'These men [Dinh Thien Hoang and Ngo Van So] had no particular political or ideological outlook . . . but since local leaders had sold out to Diem and they could not stand what was going on, Hoang and So organized some of the rank-and-file members of the sects and together with some other militants who had fled their villages because of repression, they formed two resistance battalions . . .'

In the various Party-controlled base areas, which dated back to the anti-French Resistance, Party cadres assisted the sect units by providing them with military and political training in the etiquette of people's war. US intelligence sources reported:[33]

The Communists are now believed to be actively cultivating the remnants of the Hoa Hao, Cao Dai, and Binh Xuyen dissident bands, dispersed by GVN [RVN] security forces in 1955. As many as 1500 armed non-Communist dissidents are believed still hiding in bands of various size in the delta region south of Saigon, the Plaine des Joncs, along the Cambodian border and northwest of Saigon. Through the years, the weapons of these outlaw bands have deteriorated, and ammunition has run low. The Communists are believed providing many of these bands with both assistance and guidance, in return for support or at least lip service to DRV aims.

The Party's attempts to win over various sect groups was a continuous affair. In September 1957, for example, the Long An province Party committee, located adjacent to the Cambodian frontier and the Plain of Reeds, instructed subordinates, 'to win over the progressive armed forces of the sects along the border to establish a situation which is favorable to ourselves'.[34] The process of 'winning over' the sects involved introducing Party members directly into the sect ranks as well as activating Party-controlled units to cooperate with the sect forces. According to *Tinh Hinh Nam Bo* (p. 22): 'Because of the conflict between religious sects and My-Diem, the Party planted a number of cadres among the dissident forces and activated armed units equipped with weapons we had hidden.'

The reactivated Party units styled themselves the Viet-Nam Liberation Army (Quan Doi Giai Phong Viet-Nam) or Viet-Nam People's Liberation Movement (Phong Trao Giai Phong Nhan Dan Viet Nam).[35] The newly formed sect alliance appears to have maintained a low profile until the final quarter of 1957 at which time a marked rise in rural violence was noticeable. Prior to then only sporadic clashes were reported. For example, in February 1957 the ARVN's ammunition dump and barracks at Go Vap was attacked twice by an unknown force.[36] In April, two French rubber plantations were subjected to brief hit-and-run raids by unidentified attackers.[37] This relative lull coincided with the withdrawal of ARVN units for American-styled re-training described in chapter 6.

Although the identity of the perpetrators of these earlier incidents remained unclear, such was not the case with subsequent armed attacks. Party historians of this period specifically mention the successes of 'resistance forces' (Party cadres, ex-Viet-Minh Front veterans and sect units) in attacking the towns of Minh Thanh in August and Trai Be in September 1957, the Self-Defense Corps post in Phu Long district of Binh Duong province in October, and Lo Than in December.[28] One of the most spectacular incidents of this period occurred on October 22, 1957 when two hotels serving as billets for US MAAG personnel and the USIS Library were bombed.[39]

A major escalation in the scope of fighting occurred in 1958. Two incidents in particular stand out.[40] The first occurred on January 4, when a battalion-sized unit seized the Minh Thanh rubber plantation in Thu Dau Mot after a mortar barrage. Members of the attacking force, described later as 'a cocktail of sect remnants and Communist officers', seized 1.5 million piastres from the manager's office, subjected the plantation work force to a political lecture, and set fire to the office buildings before making off. Among the topics stressed in the political lecture were American responsibility for Viet-Nam's continued partition, developments in the north, a condemnation of conditions in the south, and a request that taxes be redirected from the RVN to the guerrillas.

Seven months later 'resistance units' totalling perhaps as many as 500 attacked another rubber plantation in Thu Dau Mot, leading RVN and American observers to conclude that one purpose of the attacks was to disrupt the Republic of Viet-Nam's economy.[41] In a re-run of the earlier raid, the attackers seized a million piastres in cash and then set about systematically destroying the power plant, offices, storage sheds and processing facilities. On this occasion the attackers failed to make good their escape and 30 of their number were killed by ARVN forces. It was later established that the attacking unit was a Binh Xuyen force under the command of Vo Van Mon.[42]

These two attacks were unique when compared with other forms of rural violence then in progress, a development not unnoticed by US intelligence analysts. One US estimate stated for example: 'the guerrillas are able to marshall a force of several hundred men for major hit-and-run raids, as they demonstrated twice during 1958.'[43]

Starting in late 1957 and early the following year, as ARVN forces returned to the tasks of rural pacification, and as the ACDC intensified, the momentum built up by the Party-supported sect forces in 1957 began to slow down. Eventually the weight of Diem's political and military efforts achieved success and 'the resistance army of the religious sects dwindled into a mere token force'.[44]

The Party and its armed forces

Throughout the period 1954–60 US intelligence estimates placed the strength of Communist armed forces at between 5–8000 of whom no more than 2000 were ever considered active. Table 7.1 sets out in chronological order the various estimates produced at this time.

Although the Pentagon analysts argued that the phenomenal

Table 7.1   US Intelligence estimates of armed Communist strength in South Viet-Nam, 1955–59

Date	Source	Estimate
11 October 1955	National Intelligence Estimate	10 000
18 May 1956	Weekly Intelligence Digest	6–8 000
17 July 1956	Weekly Intelligence Digest	5 000
10 August 1956	Weekly Intelligence Digest	5–7 000
January 1957	MAAG Country Statement	1 370
15 July 1957	MAAG Country Statement	1 500
3 April 1958	Department of State	1 100–1 400
18 July 1958	Weekly Intelligence Digest	1–2 000
19 December 1958	Weekly Intelligence Digest	2 000
26 May 1959	National Intelligence Estimate	2 000

Source: United States-Vietnam Relations, 1945–1967, Book 2, 'U.S. Perceptions of the Insurgency, 1954–1960', pp. 9, 11, 13, 16 and 25. Estimates for this period, states a Pentagon analyst, are subject to great uncertainty. The numbers in the above table should be treated as order of magnitude. The American estimates provide no explanation for the large drop between August 1956 and January 1957. Paramilitary groups may have been included in the former estimates. Later estimates focused on active Communists. Otherwise the estimates reflect the success of the Diem government's anti-Communist suppression.

growth of the 'Viet Cong' in 1960 could be explained by previously low estimates,[45] this is only partly correct. Insofar as US intelligence specialists focused on regular troop strength they were probably accurate in the impression that force levels remained static. Their error lay in not focusing on the other levels and types of Communist military and paramilitary organisations.

With respect to force development during this period, the Party carried out two distinct programs, in addition to their cooperation with the sects. One program aimed at laying the foundations for a future expansion in armed strength. This involved the creation of village self-defence forces to fend off ARVN attacks. The other program aimed at maintaining and developing armed propaganda units at provincial level who were to carry out the 'killing tyrants' campaign (*tru gian*). All types of armed forces were developed to create an environment in which the political struggle movement could grow.

Captured documents made it clear that though the expansion in size of the armed forces began in 1957, it was not until two years later that the mission became one of national liberation.[46] Prior to 1959 the Party developed armed forces for self-defence purposes and for the conduct of the *tru gian* campaign (see below). During 1957 in what appears to have been a policy embracing all of South Viet-Nam, squads and platoons were created in Party-controlled base areas in Trung Bo (the Highlands, Binh Dinh and Quang Ngai), and in eastern (War Zone D) and central Nam Bo (Dinh Tuong and Long An) and western Nam Bo (Ca Mau). These basic

Table 7.2 Communist military units in South Viet-Nam; order of battle, 1957–58

Area	Description
Eastern Nam Bo[a]	Late 1956: two companies, located in Tay Ninh and Thu Dau Mot 1957: two companies, C40 and C45, formed including Binh Xuyen troops October 1957: Unit 250, the first battalion-sized concentrated unit, formed in War Zone D 1958: three companies Mid-1958: Eastern Nam Bo Command established consisting of three infantry companies and one sapper unit; plus C.1000, an enlarged company stationed in Tay Ninh End 1958: elements of two battalions
Central Nam Bo[b]	Late 1956: five companies August 1957: 4th Battalion located in Dinh Tuong province November 1957: 12th Company, 506th Battalion located in Long An. Party sources also report 16 squads in Long An
Western Nam Bo[c]	Late 1956: thirty companies 1957: two resistance battalions formed in Ca Mau 1958: 3 companies identified in U Minh area, other sources give 6 companies in U Minh
Interzone V[d]	2 battalions
Highlands[e]	3 companies

Sources: [a] *Cuoc Khang Chien Chong My Cuu Nuoc*, p. 24; Australian Army Training Information Letter, *Background Paper to the Vietcong in Military Region 7*, 14/1970 (November 1970), p. 414; Robert J. O'Neill, *Vietnam Task*, p. 8; *Tinh Hinh Nam Bo*, p. 22; Ta Xuan Linh, 'How Armed Struggle Began in South Viet-Nam,' pp. 22–23 reports 'about two battalions' of the Cao Thien Hoa Binh.

[b]*Cuoc Khang Chien Chong My Cuu Nuoc*, p. 24; *Tinh Hinh Nam Bo*, p. 22; 'Interrogation in 1958 of a prisoner who had been active in the "Resistance" since 1945 until his capture by GVN forces in 1956,' *Working Paper* Item 12, p. 14; Government of the Republic of Vietnam, 'Violations of the Geneva Agreements by the Viet-Minh Communists' (1959), p. 108; Republic of Viet-Nam, Ministry of National Defence, Joint General Staff, J2, *Study of the Activation and Activities of R*, p. 23; and Jeffrey Race, *War Comes to Long An*, p. 87.

[c]*Cuoc Khang Chien Chong My Cuu Nuoc*, p. 24; Wilfred Burchett, *Viet-Nam Will Win!*, p. 120; Republic of Vietnam, Ministry of National Defence, *Study of the Activation and Activities of R*, p. 23; Republic of Vietnam, 'Violations of the Geneva Agreements,' p. 20; and Ta Xuan Linh, 'How Armed Struggle Began in South Viet-Nam,' p. 22.

[d]Republic of Vietnam, 'Violations of the Geneva Agreements', p. 20.

[e]*Tinh Hinh Nam Bo*, p. 37.

Note: A company, *dai doi*, varied in size from 75 to 100 men; a battalion *tieu doi*, varied in size from 300 to 350 men. Both designations were rough classifications as the battle of order varied widely.

units were expanded in size to company and then battalion strength, the first of which was organised in October 1957 in War Zone D.[47] Other forms of rural violence sanctioned by the party included guerrilla raids on land development centres, (where dredges, tractors and other equipment were destroyed), rubber plantations, land reform and agricultural credit offices and local militia posts. Table 7.2 sets out a rough 'order of battle' for this period based mainly on Party sources.

There were various problems in maintaining these forces. Despite the fact that the Party controlled certain base areas which were kept out of RVN control, these were not capable of supporting battalion-sized units at this time.[48] The Party was therefore compelled to disperse its forces when not in operation. Although the Party left equipment, weapons and ammunition cached throughout South Viet-Nam at the time of regroupment, and indeed ARVN forces appear to have been successful in locating many of these,[49] the lack of weapons and ammunition at this time proved an inhibiting factor in the growth of the Party's armed forces. The Party relied on 'weapons we had hidden' to build up some of its forces; but it also had to attack ARVN posts to secure a sufficient supply. Ta Xuan Linh has written,[50] for example: 'After those resounding exploits [described above], the revolutionary armed units were supplied with more and better arms and equipment. With their assistance in cadres and armaments, Bien Hoa, Thu Dau Mot and Tay Ninh provinces founded their own armed units [after August 1958].'

In mid-1958 the Party had made enough progress in developing base areas to support armed units to form a Command of the People's Armed Forces in eastern Nam Bo to coordinate operations throughout southern Viet-Nam with the Cao Thien Hoa Binh General Staff.[51] Although the sects had 'dwindled into a mere token force' by that time, they still managed 'to muster their remaining force of about two battalions composed of the most determined persons . . . in a resistance base in Eastern Nam Bo.' There Zones C and D had been built up 'in all fields' and 'the Eastern part of Nam Bo became the centre of the armed struggle.'

Tru Gian: killing tyrants

According to a senior party cadre,[52] a secret directive accompanied *Duong Loi Cach Mang Mien Nam* authorising Party officials at the province level to organise armed propaganda groups to carry out a program of 'killing tyrants' or *tru gian*. This program, which began in mid-1957, was initially indistinguishable from other forms of rural violence, at least to RVN officials. By October of that year its broad outlines were apparent to outside observers[53] as underground Party cadres, organised in small selected armed groups were systematically kidnapping and/or executing local RVN officials. The prime targets included village officials (headmen, registrars, chairman of liaison committees, notables, and former notables), police and security personnel and village guards, RVN district, and in some instances provincial level, officials and civilians such as school teachers, social workers, members of malaria eradication teams, and cadres belonging to the Can Lao party and National Revolutionary Movement.[54]

According to a Party cadre:[55]

The principal purpose of the 'extermination of traitors' movement at that time [beginning in 1957, 1958 and 1959] was to protect the existence of the Party. Without exterminating the [government] hardcore elements, the Party apparatus could not have survived. A second purpose was to aid in the developing of the Party by creating fear in the enemy ranks and by creating faith among the masses in the skilled leadership of the revolution.

Tinh Hinh Nam Bo (p. 37) states that from 1957 'armed propaganda forces [*cac luc luong vo trang tuyen truyen*] were activated to carry out propaganda tasks and to kill tyrants.' It is extremely difficult to determine with precision the numbers killed as a result of the *tru gian* campaign, especially for 1957. In part this is due to the nature of RVN 'record keeping', in part also to the very real problem of determining who instigated a particular act and for what purpose. Various types of rural violence conducted by gangs and other sect remnants were occurring simultaneously. Nevertheless, even when these difficulties are taken into account, it is possible to discern a systematic program of violence directed against RVN government and administrative personnel. Both outside observers and Party sources are in agreement on this point.

In 1958 Bernard Fall was one of the first foreign observers to bring the *tru gian* campaign to public attention:[56]

Guerrilla activities in South Viet-Nam during 1957 and 1958 no longer represent a last-ditch fight of dispersed sect or Communist rebel remnants. On the contrary they have taken on a pattern of their own which is quite different from that followed by the Viet Minh during the struggle against the French. While the wartime Viet-Minh forces generally limited themselves to the intimidation of the local administrators (village chiefs, notables) into a state of 'positive neutrality,' the new terrorists seek out the local police chiefs, security guards, village treasurers, and youth leaders and kill them in as spectacular a manner as possible. It would be pointless to describe here the hundreds of cases reported in detail in the Saigon press but in general they document the fact that the objective of the rebels—gradual 'insulation' of the central authorities from direct contact with the grass roots—was achieved.

By way of corroboration, Ta Xuan Linh[57] has presented the following account:

Naturally, the more the people's self-defence organizations shrank, the more aggressive the cruel agents in the localities became and the bloodier the crimes they perpetrated. More and more cadres were arrested and many more revolutionary organizations in the villages and hamlets were broken up. The South Vietnamese people call this 'the darkest period'. Though this was a major setback of the revolution, the revolutionaries and the people had learnt the hard way that to survive and wage an efficacious political struggle they could no longer limit themselves to purely defensive methods. The most urgent thing was to punish the cruel agents and tyrants the most reactionary forces in the countryside. Step by step the self-defense organizations were restored in the form of 'armed youth organizations' or militia and guerrilla groups. By 1958, the punishment of local tyrants and the destruction of the grassroots administration of the Diem regime has become a widely-extending mass movement. Some of the tyrannical agents at the top of the administration at district and even provincial levels were executed one after another. This encouraged the population and had a sobering effect on the enemies of the revolution.

Estimates of the number of persons killed under this program vary. Figures for 1957, ranging from 75 to 700, are least reliable,[58] while estimates for 1958 (193 killed and 236 kidnapped) and 1959 (233 killed and 343 kidnapped) are probably closer to the mark despite the inaccuracies in gathering data of this kind.[59] The upper figure for 1957 apparently represents the total number of persons killed, whatever the cause, by groups labelled Communist by the RVN. The 1957 figures include both civilian (government officials and private citizens) and military (regular army, civil guard and self-defence corps) casualties. Some but not all the victims of the Party's *tru gian* campaign were found with a notice listing the reasons for execution attached to their corpses.[60]

During the following years RVN agencies improved their data collection and analysis techniques, thus enabling US officials to form a clearer picture of Party-directed rural violence. Table 7.3 sets out the figures for the numbers of RVN officials killed or kidnapped during 1958 and 1959. The trend appears to be a slow steady rise with monthly variations in both categories. Killings averaged 16 a month in 1958 and 19 a month in 1959; kidnappings rose from an average of 19 per month in 1958 to 28 per month in 1959. The final quarter of 1959 shows a marked increase for both killings and abductions. The fate of those who were kidnapped is unknown. In 1973, for example, the RVN released a list of 220 officials (civil servants, village officials, police, self-defence personnel and government cadres) who were abducted by the Communists during the period 1954–60 and on whom the RVN still sought information.[61]

Even more unreliable, except as gross indicators, have been US efforts to record and classify the number of 'armed terrorist incidents'. These included skirmishes between guerrilla bands and

Table 7.3 US estimates of Communist-directed assassinations and abductions, (1958–59)

Month	Assassinations 1958	Assassinations 1959	Abductions 1958	Abductions 1959
January	10	10	25	17
February	36	11	5	6
March	26	31	43	21
April	17	13	12	16
May	13	16	5	22
June	21	5	15	15
July	11	16	24	22
August	7	12	18	11
September	8	22	24	34
October	15	29	26	42
November	8	35	19	89
December	21	33	20	48
First six months	123	86	105	97
Last six months	70	147	131	246
TOTAL	193	233	236	343
Average/month	16.0	19.4	19.7	28.6

Source: 'Special Report on Current Internal Security Situation' prepared by the US Viet-Nam Country Team, dispatch No. 278 (March 7, 1960) from the American Embassy in Saigon to the US State Department in Washington, D.C. in *United States–Vietnam Relations, 1945–1967*, Book 10, V.B.3., pp. 1254–1275, especially p. 1273. The report relied on monthly figures gathered from three sources: MAAG intelligence summary based on ARVN figures; MAAG summary report of Self-Defense Corps activities based on figures supplied by the Self-Defense Corps; and 'Statistics of Communist and Rebel Activity in South Viet-Nam' gathered by the CIA Station (CAS) based on figures provided by the 'NPSS' an abbreviation not otherwise identified.

RVN forces, and guerrilla initiated attacks and ambushes. According to this methodology, less than 500 'Viet Cong incidents' occurred in 1957, around 500 took place in 1958, while the figure for 1959 jumped to 1500.[62] The tempo of conflict definitely picked up from 1958; one estimate places the number of military casualties suffered by both sides at 1000 in 1957 and 11 000 in 1959.[63] During 1958, according to another source, the RVN alone was suffering casualties at the rate of 40 government and 40 military personnel per month—or 960 for that year.[64]

Violence in the Central Highlands

In 1957, as we have noted in chapter 6, a resettlement program was begun which resulted in the migration of thousands of lowland ethnic Vietnamese into the Highlands. This was followed by another program designed to relocate highlanders into fixed camps which the RVN could more easily control. At the same time the Anti-Communist Denunciation Campaign attempted to identify

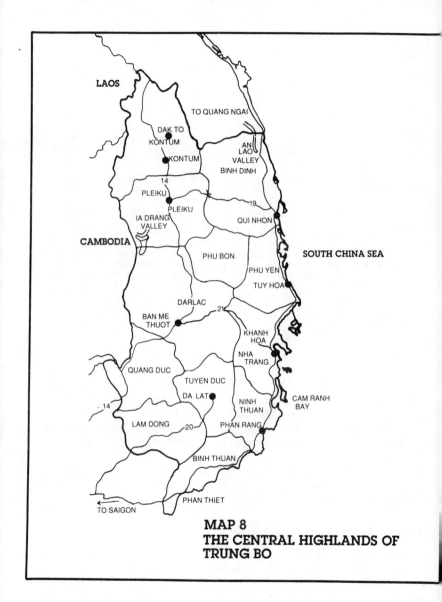

MAP 8
THE CENTRAL HIGHLANDS OF
TRUNG BO

and arrest Party cadres and their sympathisers. Thus anger at forced relocation, poor conditions in resettlement camps, as well as corvee labour, taxes, loss of land rights and the application of Vietnamese laws were all major issues which aroused discontent in the Highlands.

During 1955–56, as a result of the ACDC in the lowland provinces of central Viet-Nam, Party cadres began to seek refuge in the Highlands, particularly the western region of Quang Nam province.[65] The Party's underground absorbed these political refugees by dispersing them among secure villages. Later, these villages 'became revolutionary bases, inviolable bastions of the revolution'.

The balance of force began to shift in favour of the revolutionaries in 1957 and particularly during 1958. Several reasons account for this. First, the program of consolidation and expansion of base areas made rapid progress. In 1958 these resistance zones were 'extended to the mountains, the three border areas, and further north to areas bordering on the Central Highlands, parts untrodden by the resistance forces' previously.[66] Second, party cadres embarked on a program to make themselves economically self-sufficient, especially in food production. Third, the cadres conducted a program of cultural and political studies for themselves and for ethnic minority youths who had joined them. Finally, as the various RVN programs picked up pace, and more and more highlanders became alienated, a better operational environment was created for Party cadres. Thus, the foundation for an organised political movement was laid.

Some Party cadres were apparently quite successful in organising various tribal groupings (Kor, Hre, Katu, Bahnar, Raglay). By the end of 1957, according to one writer,[67] 'most leading bodies [i.e. Party-controlled organisations] at district level were staffed by cadres chosen from amongst the ethnic minorities. Most tribal chiefs and village patriarchs sided with the revolutionaries ...' In the face of this success, Party cadres faced the problem of how to respond to growing demands for armed violence which threatened to stimulate premature local uprisings. If cadres attempted to restrict the tempo of highland retaliation might they not lose their hard won positions of trust?

It would seem from the accounts available that the rise in highland violence preceded the Party's ability to control, let alone direct it. Many Highlanders chose to respond in the traditional way by withdrawing further upland away from Vietnamese control. When force or coercion was employed against them, they fought back, often with only primitive weapons.[68] Throughout 1957 and 1958 most of the targets were RVN officials involved in highland resettlement. In early 1957 members of the Katu were responsible for killing several RVN officials in western Quang Nam.[69] In

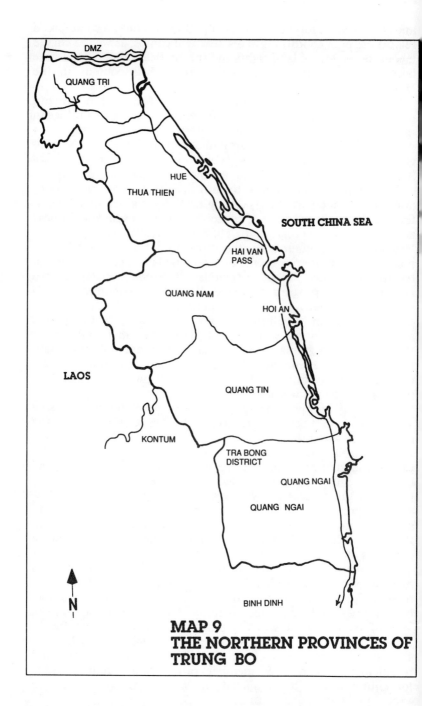

**MAP 9
THE NORTHERN PROVINCES OF
TRUNG BO**

another district in the same province tribal youths attacked the Thanh My resettlement camp 'with poisoned and incendiary arrows'. They later ambushed and killed three RVN officials. These and other highland attacks brought on increased RVN repression as both police and regular soldiers attempted to locate and punish those responsible. Party cadres quickly made contact with minority dissidents and attempted to channel their energies in Party-approved directions.

Throughout the remainder of the year developments picked up. In February, after a period of joint planning between Party cadres and Raglay tribesmen, Highlanders in the Camp Brawn resettlement centre were assisted in their escape from RVN control. Shortly thereafter, Raglay living at Tam Ngan were encouraged to do likewise. The following month members of the To Lo tribe evaded RVN efforts to resettle them along National Route One in Phu Yen. They too fled to the interior. Once out of the RVN's grip they set about preparing 'combat villages' (defended in the traditional manner with bamboo spikes and booby-traps) and organising self-defence groups. Minority leaders, some of whose ties to the Party dated back to the anti-French Resistance, approached the party for help.

As a result of these events and the pressures building up in the Highlands, Party leaders on the Trung Bo Regional Committee were forced to reconsider the question of armed struggle. Party officials took note of the sporadic yet ever-increasing independent attacks by tribal minorities against the RVN. These attacks coincided with progress in creating secure base areas and self-defence forces. The Party responded by providing training and equipment and various sorts of material. Nevertheless the question remained, what was the Party's policy on armed struggle? Part of this dilemma was summarised by Sao Nam,[70] a cadre who operated in Quang Nam and Quang Ngai provinces at that time:

> Before 1959, when we started to organize our real strength to try to find out where we stood, we asked people to wage a political struggle only—around economic questions, living standards, democratic rights; against unpaid labor, conscription and savage beatings . . . although we sometimes had arms hidden away, we remained disciplined. We had to put up with it [RVN repression] and do nothing. But when people saw that this passive attitude only encouraged the enemy, and when some of the tribes-people in the mountains decided to resist with armed struggle, using their rudimentary weapons, we agreed with them. This was not yet a real armed struggle but a legal struggle using rudimentary weapons in self-defense, such as spiked traps to limit the enemy's attempts to enter their villages.

Apparently the Party's line on armed violence—killing of tyrants but not armed struggle—was the subject of intense discussion among cadres in Trung Bo in late 1957. At that time, according to Ta Xuan Linh, they:[71]

> received materials sent from Nam Bo containing the view-points of the leaders of the struggle in South Viet-Nam as a whole. These documents indicated clearly that, because of the brutal fascist policies of the Saigon regime, there was no other way out than to use people's revolutionary violence. They also pointed out the necessity to prepare for an armed uprising to wrest back power for the people. They listed some experiences of the Nam Bo people and stated that timely armed activities in self-defense had been carried out and that the people's armed forces had been formed shortly after Ngo Dinh Diem's had started his atrocious campaign of terror.

As a result of the documents dispatched from Nam Bo, and in light of the discussions held between Party cadres and minority leaders, and 'pending the decision about a new line', Party officials in Trung Bo 'took the initiative of gradually changing the local movement into a combined political and military struggle'. According to Ta Xuan Linh, 'armed agitation groups were formed to eliminate cruel officials and traitors.'

These same officials decided to test this new strategy by limiting it to the western districts of Ninh Thuan and Quang Ngai provinces. Accordingly, Tran Nam Trung, the Party's most senior official in Trung Bo, gave the order to prepare for the first armed uprising in Tra Bong district of Quang Ngai. In July 1958 a meeting of Party cadres and representatives of the Kor, Hre and Ca Dong met in Tra Bong 'to discuss the waging of all possible forms of resistance to the Ngo Dinh Diem regime'.[72] It was from this time onwards that determined efforts were made to weaken the RVN by eliminating its officials, and building up the revolutionary forces. The tempo of the times has been aptly captured by Ta Xuan Linh:

> The building of revolutionary forces was speeded up. Leading bodies of villages and districts were strengthened and mass organizations were reorganized. Special attention was paid to the building of people's armed forces, the young people in secret camps were organized into militia units. Villages and hamlets were gradually organized into 'fighting' villages and hamlets were guarded by sharp bamboo spikes, booby traps, an alert system, and other measures.

The RVN responded by launching forays into the uplands as well as instigating an 'economic blockade' of dissident areas, aimed at denying the tribesmen essential goods such as salt.[73] While the RVN officials held North Viet-Nam responsible for inciting these disturbances, Party officials in the south were preoccupied with a different matter—were the other areas of the country similarly ripe for rebellion?

THE 3RD CONFERENCE OF THE NAM BO REGIONAL COMMITTEE (AUGUST 1958)

In the 18-month period between the second and third conferences of the Nam Bo Regional Committee, Party officials witnessed definite progress on all fronts.[74] The Party's organisation had been consolidated and maintained during the year. New recruits were attracted and old contacts reactivated. The existing resistance bases absorbed a variety of political refugees and served as ideal sites for indoctrination and training programs. New bases were established. The Party's clandestine apparatus extended its penetration into legal organisations, such as schools, professional associations, religious groups, and trucking companies, as well as various RVN civil and military groups.[75] Although the sect forces had been reduced, the Party itself had been successful in developing village self-defence groups. As the military base was strengthened, squads and platoons were gradually expanded into company and even battalion size. Similar progress was made in reorientating the form and content of the political struggle movement. The errors of the Diem regime offered fertile ground for exploitation. By the time the 3rd Conference convened in August 1958 the *tru gian* campaign had already begun to have an impact on raising the morale of the Party's supporters in addition to its intended effect on the RVN administration.

Despite these positive developments, the Party was far from able to take on the Diem regime in a full-blown campaign of armed struggle. The leaders in Nam Bo, despite whatever provocations they faced at the hands of the Diemists, remained cautious. Although they held that a resumption of armed struggle was necessary at some point in the future, they held back from encouraging premature action.

The Party and its various organisations did not operate in a vacuum. They faced intense competition and repression by the RVN authorities. By late 1957 and early 1958 the Diem regime took up the slack and renewed its efforts to extend control in the countryside. By the Party's own admission, RVN police and security officials, as well as hamlet and village officials, began to operate in areas where they had been absent for months. Thus the Party's newly rejuvenated political struggle began to wind downwards. In the words of a later Party review:[76] 'From the middle of 1958 to the end of 1959 the revolutionary movement in Nam Bo remained at a standstill. The political movement could not be initiated. The movement demanding social welfare and democratic rights was sporadic and uncoordinated.'

Wherever the RVN managed to re-install its administration, the Party encountered difficulties in conducting normal operations. According to a former Party cadre:[77] 'the Government began to establish its village and hamlet apparatus in the remote rural areas where the French never dared to set foot. When the [Diem] government local apparatus was established this naturally limited the Party's activities.'

The Party's nascent armed forces likewise encountered problems. Although the *tru gian* campaign was seen as successful, other operations were less so:[78]

> In some places where our armed forces appeared the enemy patrolled, controlled and terrorized the people. Sometimes our armed forces could neither counter enemy sweep operations nor could they protect the people because they were weak or had to act in accordance with the policy lines of the Party. They could not create favorable conditions for the political movement and they met many difficulties. The scattered killings of tyrants did not entirely affect the enemy's morale except to some small extent. As a consequence when the enemy terrorized the people, our armed forces were inadequate to protect the people. The people were afraid when our armed forces operated in their areas. The enemy always tried to locate the camp sites of our armed forces in order to attack them, separate them from the masses, and inflict casualties on them. At that time [from 1957 onwards] there were no military bases, our armed forces had to disperse and hide in thick jungles or in the middle of ricefields. They were thus driven into an isolated position. In places where the terrain features were disadvantageous to operate, our armed forces had to disperse widely among the people. They were quite weak. To maintain a lawful position for the people, we restricted armed activities and tried to prevent armed forces from interfering in the matters concerning the people's struggle movement.

This was one of the most intense periods of anti-Communist suppression. According to Communist figures presented in Table 6.3, 57 per cent of all persons killed during the July 1954–February 1959 period, were killed during the months November 1957–February 1959. The percentages of those missing and arrested during the same time period represent 50 per cent and 66 per cent respectively. In late 1957, the RVN also took steps to break the Party's influence in urban areas, targeting in particular the trade unions.[79] Early in the following year attempts to organise a student struggle movement around issues of educational reform foundered. Several of the self-defence organisations 'were broken up'. The sect forces had 'dwindled into a mere token force', while the armed forces had to be kept dispersed. Various Party cadres have since indicated that this was 'the darkest period'. These developments provided the background which the Nam Bo Regional Committee had to consider when it met in August for its third conference.

According to *Tinh Hinh Nam Bo* (p. 32):

> The resolutions of this conference were based on the content and spirit of the document *Duong Loi Cach Mang Mien Nam*. Although the entire Regional Committee realized that they no longer had the ability to peacefully change [the] political power [structure] in the South, they nevertheless affirmed that the Revolution in the South could only develop according to the line 'peaceful means must be employed flexibly with other means'. The subject of arms [i.e. violence] was stated more positively [i.e. affirmatively] than before but the approved line of struggle was not yet spelled out clearly.
>
> In fact the leadership of the Regional Committee more and more came to favor limiting the use of armed force. It criticized those who favored [an increase in armed violence] arguing that these persons' ideas were in opposition to the Party's line.

The point of the debate appeared to be, not whether to use armed force, but when, with what units (sects, companies, battalions) and for what purpose (self-defence, extermination of traitors, or a general uprising). As noted above, the Nam Bo leadership had already sent a review of its experiences with armed violence to the Trung Bo Regional Committee. The Nam Bo review asserted that 'there was no other way out than to use people's revolutionary violence', and that it was necessary 'to prepare for an armed uprising.'[80] By the time the third conference met in August, Tran Nam Trung had already taken the initiative in ordering preparations for an armed uprising in a carefully selected test area. It is likely the Nam Bo Committee was aware of these developments. Nevertheless they remained cautious. According to a CIA study[81] of this period: '[The] debate over strategy continued through 1958. Reports captured while being forwarded via Lao Dong [i.e. VWP] channels from South Vietnam to Hanoi indicate that some subordinates there clung to the belief that the Diem regime could be toppled without recourse to guerrilla warfare, and that others despaired of success without substantial military aid from the North.'

Although the Regional Committee continued to place restrictions on the widespread use of armed force they nevertheless permitted certain specific actions. In August, for example, Party-led units successfully attacked RVN posts in Dau Tieng and Bien Hoa, distributing the captured armouries to cadres in neighbouring Thu Dau Mot and Tay Ninh provinces so that they could develop their

own military forces.[82] The consolidation and development of
military units continued. Also, an estimated 300 selected cadres
joined the Party's Nam Bo organisation after completing the long
overland march from the north via Laos.[83] The RVN was quick to
react to these developments. In September Operation Nguyen Trai
swept through the western provinces of An Giang, An Xuyen (Ca
Mau), Ba Xuyen, Kien Giang (Ha Tien–Rach Gia) and Phong Dinh
(Can Tho) and continued until February 1959.[84]

By the start of 1959 the Party found itself, after a brief period of
respite, in another period of decline. In a later post mortem on the
policies pursued during this period, the Nam Bo committee was
criticised for not understanding the proper role of armed force in
carrying out a national democratic revolution. According to *Tinh
Hinh Nam Bo* (p. 22):

> In parts of 1957, '58 and '59 our armed forces did not obtain
> any good results for our movement. On the contrary, when our
> armed forces appeared the enemy tightly controlled the people
> and hunted down our forces. At that time [1957–58] our policy
> was to avoid fighting in order to protect [preserve] our armed
> forces. This situation made the people anxious. We did not
> launch any attacks because we operated under the name of the
> religious sects and therefore our influence [with the people] was
> not widespread ...
>
> Moreover, it was the policy of the Regional Committee to
> restrict armed activity. Because of this our armed forces were
> unable to support the [political struggle] movement. Nor could
> our armed forces develop as they had no operational guidelines
> [*phuong cham hoat dong*]. For that reason their very survival
> was threatened. The Regional Committee's operational guide-
> lines at that time were as follows: 'cause [the enemy's] lower
> echelon (administrators, spies) to shrink [from their assign-
> ments] so as to make [the enemy's] high echelons lack vigi-
> lance,' ... These operational guidelines greatly limited our
> armed forces. Therefore some of our people and cadres were of
> the opinion that 'not having armed forces was better than
> having armed forces' ...

Meanwhile developments in the DRVN had reached the point
where the Central Committee agreed to conduct a comprehensive
review of its policies throughout Viet-Nam. After two years of
implementation of the policies outlined in *Duong Loi Cach Mang
Mien Nam*, was the south now ready to enter a new stage? In order
to find out, Le Duan himself made an unpublicised inspection tour
of the south.[85] As the former secretary of the Nam Bo Regional
Committee Le Duan was the right man to conduct this assessment.
Le Duan returned to Hanoi sometime in December. His report was
considered by the VWP's 15th Plenum which met in January 1959.

In order to understand fully the background of this historic plenum it will be necessary to review the events of the 1957–58 period, focusing this time on the north. There the VWP had been charged with implementing the two other main missions set by the Party's 11th Plenum: consolidate the north and win the sympathy and support of the world's people.

8

Consolidating the north and winning the sympathy and support of the world's peoples

1957-58

The 11th Plenum of the Central Committee of the VWP debated the complex question of how to develop and implement an integrated national policy which took into account the differing circumstances in the north and south. The plenum reaffirmed that priority would be given to building and consolidating socialism in the north, which would then serve as the base for the national democratic revolution in the south.

On the eve of the Central Committee's 12th Plenum, the VWP celebrated its sixth anniversary (March 3, 1957). In a speech given in honour of that occasion, General Vo Nguyen Giap summed up the dilemmas facing the party throughout the country at that time:

> The revolutionary struggle of the people will still meet many difficulties, but by examining the prevailing situation in the world and in the country, and by making a comparison between the situation in the past and at present, we can say that we have favorable conditions — and this is a fundamental point — and although we still have many difficulties, these difficulties can certainly be overcome. One of the objectives is the strengthening of the North in its advance toward Socialism, and there is still another: The North will be transformed into a base for the struggle for the unification of the country.

Giap then highlighted what he termed the 'three main missions' for the future:

1. It is necessary to enlarge the anti-American-Diem front in the South, and rally and unite all people's forces which can be rallied and united, to patiently struggle against the fascist dictatorial policy, to demand democratic freedoms, to struggle against the policy of reducing [the people] to poverty, to demand the improvement of the living conditions of the people, and to demand rights of our people to a livelihood, basing ourselves on the ever-strengthened North.

2. We should hold fast and develop the people's movement and struggle in the South for the realization of the resumption of normal economic and cultural relations between the two zones ... We must struggle for the reestablishment of normal relations between the North and South to create favorable conditions so that the North and South may draw closer to each other and advance toward reunification of the country as provided by the Geneva Agreements.

3. Our practical missions [in the North] during 1957 are clearly very important and heavy. It is necessary to accomplish the mistakes-correction work in order to complete the agrarian reforms. It is necessary to concentrate all our forces to basically achieve economic recovery [to pre-war levels], and all other activities should be coordinated with these two fundamental tasks. On the other hand, we should study thoroughly the line of conduct and policy, the ideology and organization of our party in order to push forward the strengthening of the North through this transitory period. We must at the same time struggle for the reunification of the country.

In short, General Giap was foreshadowing the policy that would be pursued by Party leaders throughout the year. Earlier in his speech Giap drew parallels with the past to argue that the Party's line must be followed by all its members. Given the context it appears that Giap was directing his remarks at those cadres who had misgivings about the Party's priorities, and especially about policy toward the south. To quote Giap directly:

Through twenty-seven years of struggle [i.e. 1930–1957], our people's liberation work has scored brilliant success, but the revolutionary struggle has not always gone from one victory to another. During the time of secret activities [i.e. when the Party was illegal], our people met many difficulties and obstacles. Our movement had its ups and downs. In some places, it temporarily met with insuperable obstacles, and the revolutionary organizations were dissolved and the Party's leadership interrupted. However difficulties and dangers could never check the advance of the movement. Temporary failures could never affect the fighting spirit of the people and the Party. On the contrary, each difficulty and failure only encouraged our people to go bravely forward, and forged our Party's leadership, which became more experienced and clearsighted ... In each phase, the Party based itself on a comparison between the enemy forces and ourself to set up a strategy, to assemble all the forces which could be united, and to decide on the form of struggle which was sometimes secret and sometimes public, which sometimes appeared as a peaceful and sometimes as an armed struggle — thanks to all of which we succeeded in organizing and strengthening the revolutionary force and leading it to victory.

In other words, Giap was instructing Party cadres in the north and south who had become disillusioned, to put their faith in the VWP. No doubt the reduction of cadres movement then underway in the south was designed to weed out those individuals who were incapable of the discipline expected of them. Meanwhile in the north, the Party would take similar steps to improve political control over its members.

THE 12TH PLENUM (MARCH 1957)

The VWP's 12th Plenum focused on four major topics: the rectification of errors campaign, the maintenance of public order and security, the 1957 State Plan, and the modernisation and regularisation of the People's Army of Viet-Nam. All four topics were domestic issues, an indication that agreement on southern policy had been reached for the time being.

The rectification campaign, originally slated to conclude in March, was extended. It was not until November, when a series of provincial recapitulation conferences were held, that the campaign was concluded. The plenum's main concern in the public security field related to economic offences committed by speculators and hoarders. On May 19 it was announced that after an unsuccessful attempt to use ideological education, the DRVN government had issued a formal decree making speculation and hoarding a crime punishable by a range of penalties including confiscation, fines, or imprisonment.[2]

The 12th Plenum concentrated most of its attention on the economy and, to a lesser extent, military modernisation. The following objectives were written into the 1957 State Plan: the restoration of output to 1939 levels, and the strengthening, developing, and stabilisation of 'the people's democratic economy.'[3] The plenum set the main targets to be achieved by the State Plan in various sectors; it also designated seven 'important and urgent problems' for solution.[4] The aim of developing 'the people's democratic economy' was to broaden the socialist sector while 'readjusting and transforming' the private sector. It was hoped that progress in this area, coupled with the stabilisation of the market, would eventually permit planned construction along socialist lines.

The 12th Plenum also reviewed the changing role of the military in national defence in the period since 1954. The plenum concluded that the army would have to be modernised and regularised in order to carry out the tasks of static defence and routine training. Following the plenum, the PAVN underwent a major reorganisation at the central level. Major efforts were also undertaken to ensure party control through programs of political and ideological indoctrination. A political retraining program begun at this time continued until October. Thereafter, PAVN concentrated on 'modernisation and regularisation,' a process which accelerated the following year.

Once these plans were set in train, VWP leaders began to look ahead to the period when, after the period of restoration, the DRVN could embark on sustained economic development. In order to meet these plans, however, it would also be necessary to secure assistance from the socialist community.

PRESIDENTIAL TRAVELS (MAY 1957)

In 1957 the DRVN maintained diplomatic relations with only a small number of countries, mainly members of the socialist camp. The RVN, in contrast, had made rapid strides in gaining international acceptance. The previous year Diem had drawn up a constitution, elected a National Assembly and achieved domestic stability. Because Diem successfully refused to be bound by the terms of the 1954 Geneva Agreements, he had staked out a position from which he could argue that the Republic of Viet-Nam was a sovereign state, independent from North Viet-Nam. This was dramatically indicated on January 23, 1957 when the United States led 13 other members of the United Nations in sponsoring a resolution calling on the Security Council to recommend the republics of Viet-Nam and Korea for membership.

The Soviet Union, apparently without prior consultation with the DRVN, countered on the following day with a package proposal calling for the admission of North and South Korea as well as North and South Viet-Nam. While the Soviet proposal may have been a deliberate tactical ploy designed to provoke US rejection, it also implied the existence of two sovereign Vietnamese states. From Hanoi's point of view this was totally unacceptable. It is not surprising, therefore, that on January 25 Pham Van Dong addressed a letter of protest to members of the UN Security Council.[5] Undoubtedly Dong was in an awkward position as he was unable to criticise the USSR directly.

Five days later the General Assembly's Special Political Committee endorsed the US-backed resolution, while at the same time declining to consider the Soviet package deal. The UN General Assembly carried the matter further on February 28 when it voted 40 to 8 to recommend to the Security Council that the Republic of Viet-Nam be admitted into membership. Once again Dong protested.[6] This time he addressed a letter to the Soviet Union and Great Britain in their roles as co-chairmen of the Geneva Conference. This issue was still under consideration when on May 12 it was announced that 'at the invitation of President Ho Chi Minh, Marshal K.Y. Voroshilov, President of the Presidium of the USSR Supreme Soviet, will visit the DRVN in the near future.'[7]

On the eve of Voroshilov's trip to Hanoi, Ngo Dinh Diem embarked on a triumphal visit to the United States. The RVN President was accorded unusual honours for a visiting head of state. President Eisenhower despatched his personal plane, the *Columbine III* to fly Diem and his party from Hawaii to Washington. Eisenhower personally met Diem on arrival in the American capital, only the second time in four years that Eisenhower had greeted a visiting dignitary in such fashion. While in Washington, Diem met with the highest US officials and was accorded the honour of addressing a joint sitting of the Congress.

It was obvious that Diem's state visit was arranged to demonstrate the depth of American commitment to the RVN and to its president in particular. As one press account noted,[8] US economic aid during the current fiscal year amounted to $US250 000 000 — a sum only exceeded by US contributions (exclusive of military assistance) to South Korea. Both Diem and US officials were reportedly eager to increase this amount.

Voroshilov arrived in Hanoi on May 20 and departed four days later. His visit was billed by *Nhan Dan* (May 12, 1957) as 'an important historical event' and was accorded much publicity within the DRVN. At the time the announcement of Voroshilov's visit was made he had just completed a trip to China and was then touring Indonesia. There had been no prior indication that he would visit Viet-Nam. In other words, one explanation for Voroshilov's sojourn to Hanoi may well have been to counterbalance the effects of Diem's tour of the United States by shoring up the DRVN's international prestige.[9]

Voroshilov was accompanied on his tour by three Soviet officials: S. R. Rashikov, Vice President of the Presidium of the Supreme Soviet and President of the Uzbek Republic's Supreme Soviet; V. P. Yelyutin, Minister for Higher Education; and N. T. Fedorenko,

Deputy Foreign Minister. Rashikov accompanied Mikoyan on his visit to Hanoi in April 1956. The delegation's schedule and speeches made by the two presidents indicated that there were at least three main topics on the agenda: Soviet aid, prospects for Viet-Nam's reunification, and socialist bloc unity.

According to Donald Zagoria:[10]

> As prospects of early reunification faded, Hanoi had to come to grips with its acute economic problems. No longer able to count on incorporating the rice-rich South into its economy, it began to look for alternative sources of foodstuffs for the North and to lay the groundwork for a self-sustaining economy. It now came to believe that its best hope for eventual reunification lay in building up its own strength . . .
>
> In this situation, it was both necessary and logical for the DRV to turn to the Soviet Union. DRV requests were met with surprising alacrity by Moscow, despite the fact that the Soviet Union was already cutting down on its aid to China. Thus, then Soviet chief of state Klement Voroshilov went to Hanoi in May, 1957, and generously proffered offers of Soviet assistance to the Northern economy.

Throughout Voroshilov's visit, Ho Chi Minh repeatedly expressed Vietnamese gratitude for Soviet economic aid. In private discussions Ho appraised Voroshilov of Viet-Nam's developmental prospects, including the DRVN's forthcoming three-year plan which would lay the foundation for building socialism. Ho and other DRVN leaders also impressed upon their Soviet guests the need for trained Vietnamese specialists.[11]

In brief, in early 1957 the Soviet Union approved of Viet-Nam's three-year plan of socialist construction and decided to support it with much-needed development assistance. Significant amounts of Soviet aid began to reach Viet-Nam later that year, and in 1958 the USSR overtook China as Viet-Nam's number one provider of economic aid. In the second triennium (1958–60), while Viet-Nam was pursuing its first three-year plan, the Soviet Union increased its aid to $US133 million, up a modest 10 per cent (all in credits), while Chinese assistance fell by half to $US100 million (of which only $US25 million was an outright grant). Credits from Eastern Europe totalled $US26 million. Thus, in the post-1954 period, the DRVN received economic aid amounting to at least $US578.5 million; this compares to $US1 393.1 million, the amount of aid the US provided to the Diem regime during the same period (1955–60).

The issue of Viet-Nam's unification was also a continual theme in public remarks by Voroshilov and Ho Chi Minh. Although no public reference was made to Soviet diplomatic moves at the United Nations it would be remarkable if the issue was not touched upon in private. The speed of reunification was no longer as pressing a matter between the two parties as in the past, mainly because the Vietnamese had reconciled themselves to a prolonged resolution of this situation. It appears clear from Voroshilov's remarks that the USSR was anxious to keep the reunification of Viet-Nam a peaceful process. For example at a reception in his honour on May 20 he stated:[12]

> Acting on instructions of their foreign masters, the South Vietnamese authorities are inimical to the Geneva Agreements. But it is to be hoped that the popular masses in South Viet-Nam, all the progressive forces, including sober minded politicians, who are not blinded by hatred for Communism, will unite on the basis of the nationwide urge for a peaceful and democratic reunification of Vietnam. The Soviet Union has insisted and continued to insist on the unconditional implementation of the Geneva Agreements.

In an address before representatives of the Vietnamese people on May 21, following talks with Ho Chi Minh and senior party officials, Voroshilov appeared to acknowledge the potential dangers if the question of reunification was left unresolved. Nevertheless he failed to modify his government's position. In his words:[13]

> There is no doubt that the policy of trampling underfoot the Geneva Agreements and obeying foreign orders now pursued by the South Vietnamese authorities is a threat to peace not only in Vietnam but throughout Southeast Asia.
> We note with a feeling of profound satisfaction that the DRV Government, expressing the will of all the Vietnamese people, is unflinchingly conducting a policy of strict adherence to the Geneva Agreements, a policy directed toward the peaceful reunification of the country in a democratic way ...

Voroshilov's comments in this regard must be seen as part of a global policy on peaceful coexistence enunciated by Khrushchev at the 20th Congress of the CPSU in 1956. Events in Indonesia, India and Laos at this time no doubt reinforced the Soviets in this view. Prior to arriving in Viet-Nam, for example, Voroshilov visited Indonesia,[14] where the Indonesian Communist Party (PKI) had made a strong electoral showing in late 1956. Although excluded from the government, PKI officials were appointed to the 45-member advisory National Council in March following the resignation of the Ali Sastroamidjojo cabinet. In May, Voroshilov and Sukarno both toured Java and although the Soviet President refrained from endorsing the PKI publicly, his presence had a favourable effect on PKI support in the ensuing local elections held between June–August.

The Soviet 'parliamentary path to socialism' seemed vindicated by the electoral victory of the Communist Party in the Indian State of Kerala in April 1957. Meanwhile in Laos, progress was being made in negotiations between the Royal Lao Government and the Pathet Lao following the agreement of August 1956 which called for the inclusion of Pathet Lao representatives in a National Union Government. Voroshilov also strongly recommended the path of peaceful coexistence to Chinese leaders when he visited in April prior to coming to Viet-Nam.[15]

The problem from the Vietnamese point of view was not whether to accept or reject Soviet views on peaceful coexistence, but rather how to ensure that Vietnamese reunification under the terms of the 1954 Geneva Agreements was not forgotten altogether. This had been spelled out countless times by DRVN officials and was once again reiterated during Voroshilov's visit. The Vietnamese were evidently successful in obtaining Voroshilov's agreement to pub-licly endorse the 'strict adherence' of the Geneva Agreements as his remarks cited above attest. On the matter of the Soviet Union's UN tactics, after Voroshilov's visit the USSR dropped its four-nation package deal and vetoed the RVN's bid for membership in the General Assembly.[16]

The other area of discussion between Ho Chi Minh and Voro-shilov concerned socialist bloc unity[17] as a result of the events in Hungary and Poland in 1956, and differences voiced subsequently by China. Voroshilov's public references in Hanoi to China indicate that the two presidents may have discussed the PRC's new leadership role within the socialist camp. Chou En-Lai, it will be recalled, had undertaken a ten-day tour through the Soviet Union, Poland, and Hungary in January 1957. It also seems probable that Voroshilov and Ho Chi Minh discussed the latter's projected tour of Eastern Europe scheduled for July.

In summary, Voroshilov's visit to the Democratic Republic of Viet-Nam was significant because it marked a continuation of a trend which witnessed increased Soviet awareness of Viet-Nam's importance both in its own right and as a member of the socialist bloc.

THE DRVN'S FOREIGN RELATIONS (1957–58)

In 1957–58 both the RVN and DRVN initiated a wide-ranging series of international contacts.[18] Diem visited the US, Thailand, Australia, South Korea, India and the Philippines. Ho toured the socialist camp (including North Korea), Burma and India also. The sections below will review these developments under three head-ings, delegations received in Hanoi, Ho's overseas travels, and economic assistance received.

Major delegations received in Hanoi

Between March 1957 and December 1958, Hanoi hosted 15 important overseas delegations (excluding Voroshilov's).[19] Eight delegations came from the socialist camp: Czechoslovakia, Poland, Yugoslavia, Bulgaria, the Soviet Union, Rumania, Albania and North Korea. The remaining seven delegations included official representatives and non-governmental visitors from Algeria (provisional government), Indonesia, India, Burma and France (with two separate delegations from the latter two).

An analysis of the composition of the various socialist delegations and the public announcements, including joint declarations and final communiques, indicates the following reasons for their visits: an improvement in state-to-state relations, increased aid, trade and cultural ties, and liaison between officials of their respective ruling parties. The Czechoslovak, Polish, Soviet, Yugoslav, Bulgarian, Rumanian and North Korean delegations were led by either the chairman or vice-chairman of their respective governmental institutions (Council of Ministers or equivalent). Their trips to Hanoi were the first leg of a mutual exchange of visits and without exeception marked a first in state-to-state relations.

With the exception of a USSR parliamentary group, all other State delegations included the Minister of Foreign Affairs or a senior representative from that department.[20] These officials held discussions with their Vietnamese counterparts on the world situation as well as on specific items of bilateral interest. The Czech. Polish and Bulgarian delegations, by their size and composition, were obviously also concerned with trade and mutual assistance. All three delegations included their respective ministers for Foreign Trade. The Czech and Polish delegations, the largest to visit Viet-Nam, included a variety of senior ministers concerned with such areas as art and culture, finance, construction, public health, industry and economic planning.

As a result of joint negotiations between the visiting delegations and their Vietnamese counterparts, several major agreements were reached.[21] On March 20, 1957 Czechoslovakia and the DRVN signed a five-year contract on cultural cooperation. Poland agreed to step up its economic assistance to the DRVN, while Bulgaria and North Viet-Nam negotiated an agreement on the exchange of goods and payments for 1958. Under the terms of this agreement Bulgaria agreed to supply chemicals, textiles, electrical equipment, pharmaceutical products and consumer goods to Viet-Nam in exchange for mining, farm and handicraft products.

Another significant aspect of these visits, was the inclusion in the delegations from Czechoslovakia, Bulgaria, the Soviet Union and North Korea of the secretaries of the central committees of the

Communist Party. On the occasion of the visit by the USSR Parliamentary delegation it was reported that members of this group called on the VWP Politburo.[22] It is therefore probable that senior Party officials of the visiting delegations took the opportunity to hold discussions with their VWP counterparts. It also seems likely that VWP participation in the national Party congresses of the Soviet Union, Czechoslovakia and Bulgaria were touched upon at this time. The visit to Hanoi by a DPRK delegation led by Kim Il-Sung may have had a secondary purpose of balancing the visit to Saigon by South Korean President Syngman Rhee three weeks earlier.

Ho Chi Minh's overseas travels

During 1957–58 President Ho Chi Minh undertook three major trips overseas: to Korea, China, the Soviet Union and Eastern Europe (July–August 1957), to Moscow for the 40th anniversary of the October Revolution (discussed separately) and to India and Burma (February 1958). Ho's trip in mid-year was an unprecedented 55-day sojourn through eleven nations comprising the socialist camp: China, Korea, the Soviet Union, Czechoslovakia, Poland, East Germany, Hungary, Yugoslavia, Albania, Bulgaria and Rumania.

Ho Chi Minh's delegation included Hoang Minh Giam (the Minister of Culture), Hoang Van Hoan (a member of the VWP Politburo) and Pham Ngoc Thach (Vice-Minister of Public Health). All three of Ho's companions shared an expertise in foreign affairs. This suggests that the DRVN delegation's primary purposes were fourfold:[23] to enhance the prestige and international standing of the DRVN and to forge closer state-to-state ties with the other members of the socialist camp; to negotiate and coordinate various types of cultural, scientific and economic assistance to Viet-Nam, to obtain endorsement for the reunification of Viet-Nam under the terms of the 1954 Geneva Agreements, and to discuss relations among socialist countries, especially in light of the events of 1956.

The scope and intensity of these diplomatic initiatives illustrates the dramatic way in which VWP leaders set about ending Viet-Nam's relative isolation and 'winning the sympathy and support of the world's peoples' towards reunification. As a result of Ho Chi Minh's Eastern European tour four socialist governments sent high-level delegations to Hanoi—the Soviet Union, Yugoslavia, Bulgaria and Rumania. In 1959, a delegation representing the DRVN National Assembly toured five Eastern European countries — Czechoslovakia, East Germany, Hungary, Bulgaria and Poland.[24]

Ho Chi Minh also achieved a measure of success in developing contacts with the neutralist states of Asia. In February, 1958 Ho led a four-member delegation on a state tour of India and Burma.[25] Ho's visit to India counterbalanced New Delhi's earlier recognition of the Diem regime the previous November.[26] Ho Chi Minh sought and obtained Indian support for Viet-Nam's reunification (but failed in a bid to elicit India's condemnation of the RVN or the United States).[27]

After completing a 10-day tour of India, Ho Chi Minh flew to Burma where he was greeted by President U Win Maung and Premier U Nu. Once again Ho obtained general support for the reunification of Viet-Nam under the terms of the 1954 Geneva Agreements. On his return to Hanoi the DRVN President announced that presidents Prasad of India and U Win Maung, had accepted invitations to visit North Viet-Nam.

Economic assistance

The third major aspect of Viet-Nam's policy of 'winning the sympathy and support of the world's people' concerned obtaining much needed foreign assistance to help in economic rehabilitation and reconstruction. During 1957–58, the DRVN negotiated over 18 separate agreements and protocols governing various types of cultural and economic assistance.[28] Both China and the Soviet Union figured prominently in these agreements. The former agreed to supply raw cotton, textiles, medicines, rubber tyres, vehicles, rolled steel and machinery in exchange for Vietnamese timber, farm products and minerals.[29] The Soviet Union, for its part, agreed to provide petroleum products, fertilisers, laminated ferrous metals, cotton yarn, electrical appliances, machine tools, cars, lorries, tractors and farming machinery. In return, Viet-Nam exported rice, bananas, tea, coffee, plywood, clothing and footwear, jute and handcrafts.[30]

THE 7TH SESSION OF THE NATIONAL ASSEMBLY (SEPTEMBER 1957)

The preoccupation with 'consolidating the north' was clearly evident in the work of the National Assembly and Council of Ministers throughout 1957. In late June, the council met to consider reports by the Ministry of Finance and the Ministry of Water Conservation and Reconstruction. The budget for fiscal year 1956 was approved, as was the draft budget for FY1957. According to the communique issued by the council, the financial situation in 1957 was 'critical' and balancing the 1957 budget was declared to be 'fundamental' to the completion of the 1957 State Plan.[31] After hearing a report from the Ministry of Water Conservation and Reconstruction on the advanced preparations to meet typhoon flooding during the coming rainy season, the Council of Ministers also declared that the struggle against flooding 'is one of the most important works at the moment'.

The 7th Session of the DRVN's National Assembly was originally scheduled to convene in July 1957. However, due to severe flooding caused by typhoons this meeting had to be postponed until September.[32] In the interim, the Council of Ministers took charge of urgent government business. In August the Council met to consider three reports dealing with domestic matters. The first report, by the Ministry of Agriculture and Forestry, stated that in addition to flooding, drought had affected other areas of the countryside and that this would affect the autumn rice crop. Accordingly, the Council resolved:[33]

> The fight against drought must be considered a very urgent task, while flood-prevention work must not be neglected. According to the area and actual conditions, other tasks such as the correction of mistakes, collection of taxes must be coordinated with the work of struggling against drought and preventing floods. When floods and drought become serious, all other work may be stopped to permit consolidation of forces.

The second report considered by council was presented by the Central Land Reform Committee. It dealt with the rectification of errors campaign and efforts being made to compensate those who had been wrongly reclassified. According to this report 'the correction of mistakes has been completed in a number of regions and the majority of villages have entered the last phase of [mistakes] correction work.'[34] The Council of Ministers approved the report but recommended that various supplementary measures involving the restitution of property be carried out. The third report was presented by the Ministry of National Defence and concerned itself with various aspects of regularising the Army, that is drawing up rules and regulations concerning military obligations and terms of service. The council approved a draft law on national service and decided to implement it on an experimental basis in Vinh Phuc province. This then was the background to the 7th Session of the DRVN's National Assembly which met from September 10–19, 1957.

The rescheduled 7th Session, coming as it did more than five months after the previous plenary session of the VWP's Central Committee, was not convened especially to serve as a sounding board for newly ratified party policies which affected the state sphere of interest. Rather, the National Assembly was called into session to tidy up the outstanding problems that would face DRVN officials in the final quarter of the year. Of the eleven major reports delivered to the Assembly, nine dealt with domestic affairs. The other reports concerned Ho Chi Minh's overseas tour and the current situation in Nam Bo.

As the final resolution of the 7th Session made clear, the task of economic rehabilitation was almost, but not quite, complete:[35]

1. ... the 1957 State plan, ha[s] achieved many new gains and ha[s] brought the basic completion of the economic restoration in the North nearer and nearer to final success. At the same time, the National Assembly has realized that there were shortcomings in the realization of the state plan during the first six months of 1957—a number of monthly and quarterly plans have not been wholly completed either in quality or quantity.
2. The National Assembly agrees to charge the government with readjusting a number of points in the plan for the fourth quarter of 1957 ...
3. The National Assembly appeals to all people and cadres... to basically complete the restoration phase, make preparations for the development phase, bring the North nearer and nearer to socialism and turn it into a powerful base for the struggle for national unification.

In other words, priority was set in the last quarter of 1957 on overcoming shortcomings so that the VWP delegation to the Moscow Conference of Communist Parties (November 1957) could make a favourable report on progress in the DRVN. Once consolidation had been officially completed, the DRVN could then embark on a program of centralised planning.

Pham Hung's report 'On the Situation in Nam Bo' was a wide-ranging view of developments there.[36] His report gave no hint, however, that the party had made any alteration to the strategy outlined in *Duong Loi Cach Mang Mien Nam*.

The 7th Session of the DRVN's National Assembly ended its deliberations on September 19, in the shadow of the 12th anniversary of the South Viet-Nam Resistance Day (September 23, 1945). The party leadership chose to use this occasion to recall the lessons of the past. The most important commentary was made by Vo Nguyen Giap before a crowd of 10 000 in Hanoi. With obvious relevance for the present day, General Giap recounted the early years of resistance in the south and the contributions made by northern volunteers. He also stressed the role of the Party and resistance bases in maintaining the revolutionary movement in adverse conditions.

In speaking of the present Giap indirectly quoted from a VWP Central Committee resolution to indicate the strategy for the future:[37]

As pointed out by the resolutions of the Central Committee of the Lao Dong Party, our struggle for national liberation has not been terminated. While we are endeavouring to build the North into a socialist country, we have also the responsibility of uniting our entire people to carry on our struggle for the completion of the people's democratic national revolution throughout the country and to realize national unification on the basis of independence and democracy through peaceful means.

In the past, our compatriots from North to South united to acquire independence and unification for our country. Now under new historic conditions, we have shifted from an armed struggle to a political one. But the struggle for national unification remains the common responsibility of all our compatriots.

General Giap concluded by noting that Viet-Nam's struggle for national liberation was occurring in a 'new phase of a new historic era' in which the national liberation movement was in the ascendancy and colonialism on the decline. He pointed out that the paths of armed struggle and political struggle had enabled many countries (China, India, Indonesia, Burma, Cambodia, Laos, Egypt, Sudan, Morocco and Tunisia) to overthrow colonialism and advance toward 'socialism or to bourgeois democratic regimes'. As for Viet-Nam, Giap concluded, it would benefit from the previous phase of armed struggle, which successfully liberated the north. The north would now serve as the 'firm and powerful base for the revolution throughout the country'.

THE MOSCOW CONFERENCE (NOVEMBER–DECEMBER 1957)

Khrushchev's denunciation of Stalin and his endorsement of peaceful coexistence at the 20th Congress of the CPSU in February 1956 marked the start of the Sino-Soviet dispute. In the Chinese view.[38]

> From the very onset we held that a number of views advanced at the 20th Congress concerning the contemporary international struggle and the international Communist movement were wrong, were violations of Marxism-Leninism. In particular, the complete negation of Stalin on the pretext of 'combating the personality cult' and the thesis of peaceful transition to socialism by 'the parliamentary road' are gross errors of principle.

Khrushchev's remarks were apparently made *ex cathedra* and without the prior knowledge of the Chinese. The CCP responded by publishing two major editorial commentaries in the *People's Daily*: 'On the Historical Experience of the Dictatorship of the Proletariat' (April 5, 1956), and 'More on the Historical Experience of the

Dictatorship of the Proletariat' (December 29, 1956). In the period between the 20th Congress and the November 1957 Moscow Conference of Communist and Workers' Parties, CCP officials, in private discussion with their Soviet counterparts, brought up on no fewer than six occasions the question of how to interpret Stalin's contributions to Communism.[39] The CCP also challenged this Soviet presumption to speak for all socialist countries in other ways. In 1956, for example, the CCP defended the Gomulka regime in Poland against attacks by the Soviet press.

At the heart of the dispute over assessing Stalin's contibutions was the question of how the socialist bloc was to be organised in the post-Stalin era. The Chinese position has been summed up by Donald Zagoria in this way[40]:

> Peking sought what might be called a flexible, confederative approach to Bloc relations, as contrasted with the unitary approach insisted upon by Moscow. This confederative approach implied that there should be limits to Soviet prerogatives vis-a-vis other Bloc countries; that deviations from the Soviet model of socialist construction were not necessarily harmful; that honest differences of view, should be settled by genuine and frank discussion through intra-party channels and not in public; and, above all, that such honest differences, which inevitably arise, must be subordinated to the overriding common goals of all concerned—particularly to the struggle with the West.

The convening of a conference of Communist parties in Moscow following the celebrations of the 40th anniversary of the Soviet October Revolution set the stage for a renewal of Sino-Soviet debate. Clearly the CPSU intended to use the Moscow Conference to obtain international endorsement for the policies which Khrushchev had outlined at the 20th Congress. China was determined to thwart this. Mao Tse-tung himself led the CCP's delegation in an effort to bolster China's standing within the socialist bloc and to ensure that the new line for the Communist movement took cognisance of Chinese views. The VWP was probably aware of these differences as the CPSU had circulated a confidential draft of the conference's final declaration prior to the meeting.[41]

The Moscow Declaration was hammered out during November 12–14 at a special caucus of representatives of the 12 ruling Communist and Workers' parties. Sino-Soviet differences were clearly brought to the attention of other delegates. The CCP in fact circulated an 'Outline of Views on the Question of Peaceful Transition' on the eve of the 12-party gathering in an effort to alter the wording of the Soviet draft.[42] In the end the final declaration represented something of a compromise. According to a later Chinese account:[43]

> At this meeting the chief subject of controversy between us and the delegation of the CPSU was the transition from capitalism to socialism. In their original draft of the Declaration the leadership of the CPSU insisted on the inclusion of the erroneous views of the 20th Congress on peaceful transition. The original draft said not a word about non-peaceful transition, mentioning only a peaceful transition; moreover, it described peaceful transition as 'securing a majority in parliament and transforming parliament from an instrument of the bourgeois dictatorship into an instrument of a genuine people's state power'. In fact, it substituted the 'parliamentary road' advocated by the opportunists of the Second International for the road of the October Revolution and tampered with the basic Marxist-Leninist theory on the state and revolution.
>
> The Chinese Communist Party resolutely opposed the wrong views contained in the draft declaration submitted by the leadership of the CPSU. We expressed our views on the two successive drafts put forward by the Central Committee of the CPSU and made a considerable number of major changes of principle which we presented as our own revised draft. Repeated discussions were then held between the delegations of the Chinese and Soviet Parties on the basis of our revised draft before the Joint Draft Declaration by the CPSU and the CPC was submitted to the delegations of the other fraternal Parties for their opinions.
>
> As a result of the common efforts of the delegations of the CPC and the other fraternal Parties, the meeting finally adopted the present version of the Declaration, which contains two major changes on the question of the transition from capitalism to socialism compared with the first draft put forward by the leadership of the CPSU. First, while indicating the possibility of peaceful transition, the Declaration also points to the road of non-peaceful transition and stresses that 'Leninism teaches, and experience confirms, that the ruling classes never relinquish power voluntarily'.
>
> Secondly, while speaking of securing 'a firm majority in parliament', the Declaration emphasizes the need to 'launch an extra-parliamentary mass struggle, smash the resistance of the reactionary forces and create the necessary conditions for peaceful realization of the socialist revolution'.

Viet-Nam was represented at the Moscow Conference by a six-member joint party and state delegation led by Ho Chi Minh.[44] It consisted of Le Duan (newly appointed member of the VWP Politburo and Secretariat), Pham Hung (Minister attached to the Premier's Office and member of the VWP Politburo), Vo Dinh

Tung (Minister of War Invalids), Nguyen Xien (Minister of Social Welfare), and Nguyen Van Kinh (DRVN Ambassador to the USSR and member of the VWP Central Committee). Ho, Le Duan and Pham Hung represented the VWP at intra-party talks, including the 12-party gathering which approved the Moscow Declaration.

The inclusion of Le Duan on the joint DRVN–VWP delegation marked his ascendancy within the Politburo to a position second only to Ho Chi Minh. Le Duan served as Secretary of the Nam Bo Regional Committee until late 1956 when he was posted to the north. His reassignment coincided with Truong Chinh's dismissal as Party Secretary-General. Duan emerged into public view in the north in September as the third-ranking member of the VWP Politburo (after Ho Chi Minh and Truong Chinh). At the conclusion of the Moscow gathering Ho remained in the Soviet Union for discussions. Le Duan returned to Hanoi at the head of the DRVN–VWP delegation and addressed the Politburo on the significance of the Moscow Declaration. At this time he was now listed ahead of Truong Chinh.[45]

Virtually nothing is known about the role of the VWP delegation at the Moscow Conference, as the deliberations of the representatives of the 12 ruling Communist parties were kept secret. We can only speculate that the VWP leaders, while they may have favoured stronger references to the non-peaceful path to socialism, were not entirely dissatisfied by the wording of the final declaration. Le Duan's advocacy of increased violence in Nam Bo would have been common knowledge among members of the Politburo and Central Committee and may very well have been one of the reasons why he was included on the delegation.

The VWP, in approving the policies outlined in *Duong Loi Cach Mang Mien Nam* had committed itself to the use of force when conditions were ripe. In fact the wording of the 1957 Moscow Declaration clearly indicated that the use or non-use of violence would be determined by the behaviour of those holding state power. According to the Declaration:[46]

> The forms of the transition to socialism may vary for different countries. The working class and its vanguard — the Marxist-Leninist Party — seek to achieve the socialist revolution by peaceful means. This would accord with the interests of the working class and the people as a whole as well as with the national interests of the country...
>
> In the event of the ruling class resorting to violence against the people, the possibility of non-peaceful transition to socialism should be borne in mind. Leninism teaches, and experience confirms, that the ruling classes never relinquish power voluntarily. In this case the degree of bitterness and the forms of class struggle will depend not so much on the

proletariat as on the resistance put up by the reactionary circles to the will of the overwhelming majority of the people, on these circles using force at one or another stage of the struggle for socialism.

The possibility of one or another way to socialism depends on the concrete conditions in each country.

In short, Viet-Nam's preparations for armed struggle were not necessarily in conflict with the wording of the 1957 Moscow Declaration, especially as the document held open two possibilities in the transition to socialism. Presumably if the Diem regime continued to resort to violent repression of the Party's stepped-up political struggle movement, the VWP would be justified in resorting to armed force.

An editorial in *Nhan Dan* (November 24, 1957) endorsed the Moscow Declaration, calling it not only a 'political program for all the Communist and Workers' parties of socialist countries' but also 'a political program' guiding 'the building of socialism in North Vietnam as well as the struggle for Vietnam's reunification.' On November 30, after Le Duan and Pham Hung had arrived back in Hanoi, they immediately addressed a meeting of the VWP Politburo on the significance of the Moscow Conference. According to the Vietnam News Agency (December 1, 1957) the 'Politburo expressed elation and confidence in the growth and solidarity of the socialist countries and communist movement. Particular [attention] was paid to the Joint Declaration and Peace Manifesto.' The Politburo meeting then decided to convene an extraordinary session of the Party's Central Committee 'to hear reports on these two important international conferences'.

THE 13TH PLENUM (DECEMBER 1957)

Accordingly the 13th (enlarged) Plenum met on December 4 and heard a report by Le Duan on the Moscow Conference. According to an official account, a unanimous resolution was passed:

... reflecting agreement of the Party Central Committee with the observations and documents which these international congresses [of 12 Communist and Workers' Parties in socialist countries and 64 Communist and Workers' Parties in the world] had approved and appeal[ing] to the entire party to study the documents and widely disseminate them among the people...[47]

Interestingly, however, the communique of the 13th Plenum, which was published on March 23, 1958, made no reference to the 1957 Moscow Conference or its Declaration and Peace Manifesto.

The communique merely stated that the Plenum considered 'the living standards of workers, government officials and cadres; analysed the present wage system; and discussed ways of improving the wage system and increasing wages in 1958.'[48]

The lack of any reference to the Moscow Conference at this time, especially after the extensive inter-Party discussions, deserves explanation. Quite possibly the Central Committee was unable to reach a consensus on a statement dealing with the role and timing of revolutionary violence in the present stage of the Vietnamese revolution. The Central Committee may have been divided between those advocating the CPSU's peaceful approach and those who argued in favour of the CCP's position on non-violent forms of transition.

Ho recognised that the struggle for the unification of Viet-Nam could not be accomplished without support from the socialist camp as a whole, and this concern perhaps explains his prolonged absence from Hanoi at this time. Any attempt to step up the revolutionary movement in Nam Bo would need Soviet and Chinese support. It was obviously in Viet-Nam's interest to follow a policy which encouraged a unity of views between Moscow and Peking on the issue of Vietnamese reunification. Although information is lacking on the substance of Ho's talks in Moscow and Peking following the conference of Communist and Workers' parties, it seems likely that this is precisely the topic Ho raised with his hosts. In addition, Ho discussed issues affecting bloc unity and economic assistance to Viet-Nam.

According to a Pentagon analyst who reviewed the events of this period:[49]

> The new DRV–USSR understanding reached during 1957 definitely included the extension of material aid which North Vietnam needed for its economic advancement. It evidently also included Soviet concurrence in a more adventuresome policy toward reunification. Whether or not specific DRV advances upon South Vietnam were countenanced, it is evident that the DRV leaders had obtained Soviet recognition that North Vietnam's circumstances placed it outside the range of strategic and doctrinal considerations which had led Khrushchev et al. into 'peaceful competition' and 'peaceful coexistence'.

THE 8TH SESSION OF THE NATIONAL ASSEMBLY (APRIL 1958)

On New Year's Day 1958, Ho Chi Minh announced that 'the period of economic restoration has come to an end and the period of planned economic development has begun.'[50] In short, the national democratic revolution in the North was complete and the era of building socialism had begun.

The DRVN's economic development plans for 1958 and beyond were mapped out at the 8th Session of the National Assembly which met from April 16–29. In his report[51] to the meeting, Pham Van Dong set out two major tasks to be accomplished:

1. We must develop the state economy along socialist lines, turn Vietnam from a backward agricultural country into a prosperous agricultural and industrial country, and then into a rich, strong, advanced, and industrialized socialist country.
2. Simultaneously, and beginning now, we must pay particular attention to transforming the national economy, transforming the non-socialist economic sectors into socialist ones, and transforming agriculture, handicrafts, and private capitalist industry and commerce along socialist lines.

It was clear from this and other reports that the DRVN was preparing to initiate a three-year period of planned economic development in which every effort would be made to transform various sectors of the economy into State-owned enterprises. Although the socialised sector of the economy was 'the leading force', Dong pointed out that there still remained a large capitalist sector, especially in the areas of handicrafts, small business (retail trade) and agriculture. Each of these sectors was targeted for gradual transformation along socialist lines in the immediate future.

In rounding out his report Dong identified two areas of crucial importance. In Dong's view: 'socialist transformation of private capitalist commerce must be considered as one of the most important and urgent problems because in the private capitalist sector there are a number of bad elements who, by engaging in speculation and hoarding, have disrupted the markets, evaded taxes, etc.'

The other area of importance concerned agriculture where 'particular importance must be paid to the production of food, especially paddy'. Here, stated Dong, 'the most important problem at present' lies in solving the problem of irrigation, obtaining sufficient fertiliser and improving agricultural techniques. The answer lay in transforming the relations of production by encouraging individual farmers to join together in mutual aid teams and then in low-level agricultural producers' cooperatives which the State could assist.

The decision to step-up the process of agricultural collectivisation, coupled with a record grain harvest of 4.6 million metric tons in 1958, is clear evidence that the DRVN had overcome the disruptions caused by land reform. Pham Van Dong, in fact, declared at the 8th Session of the National Assembly that 'generally speaking, the mistakes committed during land reform have been corrected and the rectification of errors has brought good results. A number of remaining cases are still being redressed'.

The DRVN's economic development plans also called for the development of industry which, as Pham Van Dong indicated, depended 'on the cooperation and assistance of the socialist countries'. In this area the DRVN planned to concentrate on developing the means of production, producing consumer goods, and exploiting natural resources. Viet-Nam's friends were not found wanting, as their assistance to Viet-Nam continued to increase in 1958.

Throughout the remainder of the year the DRVN proceeded on the basis of economic plans approved by the 8th Session. In September the Council of Ministers summed up the prospects for continued economic development in this way:[52]

> There are advantages and difficulties in the present situa-
> tion. . . The rectification campaign has brought results in rural
> areas. Thanks to the patriotic emulation movement, the
> carrying out of the State plan has made notable progress in
> recent months, especially in the fourth quarter. In this 10th
> month crop, we have exerted new efforts to increase produc-
> tion and develop the manpower exchange and co-operative
> movement; the gradual reform of anti-socialist economic
> elements along socialist lines is being carried out, or prepara-
> tions are being made to carry it out in a steadfast and positive
> manner. We have begun to readjust our organisations and pay
> special attention to the problem of allotting managerial jobs.
> We have paid special attention to the political and ideological
> education of cadres and the people and achieved initial results.
> In State factories, we are embarking on a campaign aimed at
> teaching socialist thinking to workers, improving factory
> management, and extensively applying union laws.

In short, the DRVN was making progress in its efforts to develop the north, a fact recognised by the Soviet Union. In May 1958, for example, the DRVN's progress in building socialism was signalled when a representative of the VWP was invited for the first time to attend a meeting of the Council for Mutual Economic Assistance in Moscow.[53] Representatives of the CCP, Korean Labor Party, and the Mongolian People's Revolutionary Party were also invited to send observers. More importantly, on the occasion of the 1958 celebrations of the October Revolution the DRVN was for the first time listed in slogans marking that occasion as among the nations 'building socialism'.[54]

In addition to positive progress in the economic consolidation of the north, VWP leaders also achieved success in 1957–58 in consolidating their political position.[55] The Viet-Nam Workers'

Party, weakened by the land reform fiasco in 1956, was remoulded into an effective organisation following the rectification of errors campaign. PAVN was pared down and reorganised into a more modern fighting force, with various specialised branches.[56] During 1957–59 PAVN underwent a process of technological modernisation. At the same time Party political controls over the military were instituted at all levels. Also, as a result of decisions taken by the VWP's 12th Plenum, military units were assigned tasks in the civilian economy. The Army's involvement in this sector was increased in 1958 as designated units assumed responsibility for running State farms.[57]

Following the *Nhan Van–Giai Pham* Affair VWP authorities moved to crack down on intellectual dissent.[58] In 1957 a new writers' union was formed and a new journal *Van* (Literature) began publishing. In 1958, after a series of re-education courses and criticism sessions, musicians, fine artists, writers, and journalists' associations reorganised their executive committees. During June and July, numerous dissidents were expelled or suspended from membership. At the same time the government promulgated a variety of guidelines to control the activities of the intelligentsia.

In January 1957, the 6th Session of the National Assembly appointed a Committee to Amend the Constitution under the chairmanship of Ho Chi Minh. The purpose of this committee was to prepare a new document to replace the 1946 Constitution. In June 1958 it was announced that a referendum would be held to approve the committee's draft. The new constitution represented the legal cap stone in Viet-Nam's progress towards consolidating the north.

WINNING THE SYMPATHY AND SUPPORT OF THE WORLD'S PEOPLES

In 1957–58 the DRVN made great strides in expanding the level of its international contacts. Most progress was made within the socialist camp, where the DRVN negotiated a series of economic and cultural agreements. The DRVN and socialist countries also exchanged high-level delegations which served to draw the DRVN closer to its Eastern European allies. These efforts raised the DRVN's international prestige and served to match the efforts undertaken by the RVN in the diplomatic field. The DRVN also improved its relations with Burma and India as well as with neighbouring Laos and Cambodia.[59]

These international contacts became especially important in 1958 when the DRVN made another attempt to settle the issue of Vietnamese reunification by peaceful means. As we have noted above, the VWP was to reach a consensus on the issue of non-peaceful transition to socialism at its 13th Plenum. On the one hand there was disagreement over domestic factors. Some argued that a resort to force at that time would be premature. Others argued that priority should continue to be placed on developing the north. On the other hand, it would appear, there was also disagreement over external factors. Undoubtedly Sino-Soviet differences weighed heavily on these deliberations.

As we noted in chapter 4, when it became clear that the RVN would refuse to meet any of the deadlines on political issues set by the Geneva Agreements, the DRVN immediately launched a broad campaign proposing contacts on several levels. The DRVN also kept the issue alive by addressing letters to the ICC and the Geneva Conference co-chairmen. This same pattern continued during 1957 and 1958.

On June 8, 1957, Pham Van Dong forwarded a letter to the Geneva co-chairmen asking them to take all necessary measures to ensure that 'the Geneva Agreements are respected and correctly implemented.'[60] This was followed later in the year by repeated calls to expand postal, banking and trading relations.[61] On July 18, 1957 the DRVN once again proposed to the 'competent authorities' in South Viet-Nam that they hold a consultative conference to discuss reunification elections. In this note the DRVN reiterated its earlier proposals for the establishment of normal relations 'in all fields'.[62] The RVN responded with a communique dated July 26, 1957 scotching the proposals. These efforts to keep the issue of Vietnamese reunification alive also failed to evoke any response from the non-Communist Geneva powers.

While the DRVN initiatives of 1957 appear to be a continuation of its earlier attempts to put the onus on the RVN and to stimulate the political struggle movement in Nam Bo, a definite shift in intention was noticeable in 1958. On March 7, Pham Van Dong proposed not only the re-establishment of trading relations but also a bilateral reduction in armed forces.[63] This initiative immediately received endorsement from the the Soviet Union and China.[64] Dong's offer was rejected by the RVN as 'propaganda'.

Pham Van Dong's letter of March 7, and a follow-up statement issued by the Premier's Office on May 8,[65] were certainly more than mere propaganda. They went much further than the earlier initiatives designed to demonstrate the RVN's obstinacy and the DRVN's commitment to peaceful reunification. Coming as they did after the Moscow Conference, the 13th Plenum and Ho's lengthy discussions in Moscow and Peking, they appear designed as part of a campaign to demonstrate that the peaceful reunification of Viet-Nam was in fact impossible because of the attitudes of the RVN and the United States.

Throughout 1958 various ministries and organisations in the north flooded their counterparts in the south with requests for co-operation not only in the area of trade, banking and communications,[66] but also in the areas of literature, art, education, science, culture and health.[67] In September and in December, Pham Van Dong once again sent notes to the RVN proposing consultations, a reduction in military forces, freedom of movement and trading relations.[68]

Parallel with these initiatives, the DRVN also began to beat the drums of anti-Americanism. On March 19, 1958, the first of a series of anti-US demonstrations was held. Forty thousand people were reported to have gathered in Hai Phong and Nam Dinh, while another 35 000 attended a rally in Hanoi.[69] By April over 170 000 persons were estimated to have attended rallies throughout the country. In June, the DRVN inaugurated a 'film season against US imperialism' using material produced in the Soviet Union, China and other socialist countries.[70] The fourth anniversary of the Geneva Agreements (July 20, 1958) served as another occasion for displays of anti-American sentiment. According to media reports 30 000 rallied in Hai Phong while another 50 000 demonstrated in Hanoi.[71] Thereafter the pace of developments picked up, for by September, according to Xuan Thuy, over 2.25 million persons had been involved in these gatherings.[72]

Hand in hand with the anti-US rallies came revelations that foreign spy rings and saboteur groups were operating in the north.[73] On March 20, 1958 fourteen alleged espionage agents were tried in Hanoi. The group's leader was sentenced to death and publicly executed. A French diplomat allegedly implicated in the affair was expelled. Two months later both France and Britain were forced to close their consulates in Hai Phong.[74] The arrests of other spy rings were reported later in the year. By late 1958, the groundwork had been laid to step up the struggle to reunify Viet-Nam by non-peaceful means. In the eyes of party leaders, they had succeeded in 'consolidating the north and winning the sympathy and support of the world's peoples.' North Viet-Nam was now the reliable firm base to support the struggle of the people of South Viet-Nam for national liberation.

9

Founding the National Front for the Liberation of South Viet-Nam

1958–59

During 1958, despite the Soviet Union's policy of peaceful coexistence, the international situation grew more tense. In part this was due to the domestic politics of various countries, which affected the international system. In July, for example, as a result of a left-wing revolution in Iraq, that country withdrew from the Baghdad Pact. These events precipitated American military intervention in Lebanon. Sino-Soviet differences immediately came to the fore as China adopted a more militant attitude than the USSR towards the US.

In 1958 China was in the process of accelerating the Great Leap Forward, a radical domestic program, officially approved at the CCP's 8th Congress (second session) in May. Domestic radicalism spilled over into foreign policy. In late 1957, for example, as a result of the USSR's successful launching of an intercontinental ballistic rocket and the world's first satellite, the PRC was emboldened to adopt more militant policies.[1] This was reflected by Mao in the expression 'the East wind prevails over the West wind.' In mid-year Chinese leaders publicly announced plans to 'liberate Taiwan'. On August 23 the Formosan Straits crisis was precipitated when mainland gunners opened up on the Nationalist-held off-shore islands of Quemoy and Matsu.

Meanwhile the situation in Laos deteriorated. In May, 1958 the electoral success of the left-wing Neo Lao Haksat provoked a right-wing counter-reaction. In July, despite protests by the Communist powers, ICC operations in Laos were terminated. This caused neutralist Premier Souvanna Phouma to resign. In his absence, the right wing proceeded to dismiss all left-wing representatives from the Royal Lao Government on August 18. By the end of the year Laos was embroiled in a civil war.

During May–July relations between Cambodia and the Republic of Viet-Nam deteriorated as a result of incursions by ARVN units in pursuit of sect and Communist-led guerrillas.[2] Prince Sihanouk immediately sought to protect Cambodia's sovereignty by granting diplomatic recognition to China. In August the Prince journeyed to Peking where he met Mao Tse-tung.

These international developments set the backdrop for the deliberations of the VWP's 14th Plenum which met in early November and the 9th Session of the National Assembly which met the following month. The Central Committee discussed three reports: one by Le Duan on the international situation, another by Nguyen Duy Trinh on Viet-Nam's first three-year plan, and the third by Truong Chinh summarising the results of the land reform.

THE 14TH PLENUM (NOVEMBER 1958)

With respect to the international situation the plenum declared:[3]

> since the conference of twelve Communist and Workers' parties in socialist countries and the conference of sixty-four Communist and Workers' parties in the world held in Moscow last year, the forces of the socialist countries have shown themselves to be increasingly superior to those of the imperialist countries and that the East wind has continued to prevail over the West wind (*gio Dong tiep tuc thoi bat gio Tay*).

On the domestic scene, the plenum declared that:[4]

> the *immediate central task* is to step up the socialist transformation of the sector of individual economy of the peasants and handicraftsmen and that of the sector of privately-run capitalist economy, and at the same time to strive to develop the sector of state-run economy which is the leading force of the whole national economy. (emphasis in the original)

The policy priorities approved by the 14th Plenum were presented in public at the 9th Session of the National Assembly which met from December 9–12. The National Assembly approved the final draft of a 'Three-Year Plan for Economic Transformation and Cultural Development (1958–60)' which included three main objectives:[5]

1. To accelerate the development of agricultural and industrial production by considering agricultural production as the

      main point, to solve the food problem, while paying keen attention to industrial production, increasing means of production and satisfying the major part of the demand in consumer goods.
2. To endeavour to transform agriculture, handicrafts, private capitalist industry and trade along socialist lines, the main link in the chain being the acceleration of agricultural co-operation; simultaneously to develop and strengthen the State economic sector.
3. On the basis of developing production, to improve a step further the material and cultural life of the people, especially the toiling people and to consolidate the national defence.

The main task to be accomplished in the immediate future was agricultural co-operativisation. It was hoped, as a result, to raise agricultural production from the then level of 4.6 million tons to a minimum of 7.6 million tons of paddy per year. The three-year plan also highlighted increased investment in the light industrial sector as well as the construction of industrial zones at Viet Tri and Thai Nguyen.

Once again, the decision to accord priority to northern development provoked controversy. According to an official VWP history:[6]

    ... the Party also struggled to overcome inappropriate understanding of the close inter-relations of the task of the socialist revolution in the North and that of liberating the South, characterized by the fear that the advance of the North toward socialism would hinder the struggle for Viet Nam's reunification. The Party pointed out that i[t] was just in order to create favourable conditions for the struggle to liberate the South and achieve the reunification of the country that the North must advance rapidly, vigorously and steadily toward socialism.

    Under the specific conditions of our country ... while the country was still divided into two zones, what methods and forms should we use and what tempo should we adopt to advance toward socialism? Such were the very complex problems facing our Party [at the 14th Plenum in November 1958].

As a result, after approving the Three-Year Plan of socialist construction, the Central Committee also agreed to conduct a comprehensive review of policy toward the revolution in Nam Bo. In order to fully appreciate developments there Le Duan left Hanoi on a secret trip to the south to gather material for a report to the Central Committee at its next meeting. According to Pentagon analyst Paul Gorman:[7] 'US. intelligence came into possession of a directive from Hanoi to its subordinate headquarters in Inter-Sector (Zone) V during December, 1958, which stated that the Lao Dong Party Central Committee had decided to "open a new stage of the struggle ..." '

THE 15TH PLENUM (JANUARY 1959)

On December 1, 1958 during the course of a riot by detainees at the Phu Loi re-education centre in Thu Dau Mot province, inexperienced warders, members of the Civil Guard, panicked and machine-gunned to death a score or more of the demonstrators.[8] Among the dead and wounded were former members of the Resistance, peace activists and individuals associated with the sects. This incident was immediately seized upon by DRVN propagandists who alleged that an unsuccessful attempt had been made to poison the entire prison population of 6000 inmates. According to DRVN claims, 1000 persons were killed.[9] The Phu Loi incident became in effect the *casus belli* for the Second Indochina War.

Over the course of the following months the Phu Loi incident was given wide publicity in both halves of Viet-Nam by the VWP. It, and other alleged incidents of anti-Communist repression, were used as evidence of the 'fascist, warlike and dictatorial nature' of the Diem regime. It is undeniable that the Party's underground had suffered terribly at the hands of the RVN. As we have noted in chapter 6, after a period of recovery during early 1958 the Party's fortunes began to plummet later in the year. In the face of renewed repression the question of armed force was debated once again. One Party cadre has stated for example:[10]

> by 1959 the situation in the South had crossed to a stage which the Communists considered to be the darkest in their whole lives . . . Because of this situation Party members were angry at the Central Committee, and demanded armed action. Party members did not dare break discipline, but nevertheless there were instances of undisciplined behavior, kidnappings and assassinations, in order to resolve the problem of survival. At the same time the southern branch of the Party demanded of the Central Committee a reasonable policy in dealing with the southern regime, in order to preserve the existence of the southern organisation. If not, it would be completely destroyed.

According to an official Party history:[11]

> in January, 1959, in an important conference, South Viet-Nam's revolutionary leaders pointed out that South Vietnamese society was a neo-colonial and semi-feudal one. The Ngo Dinh Diem administration was a reactionary, cruel, war-like one which had betrayed the national interests. It was obviously a US tool for aggression and enslavement. The direction and task of (the) South Vietnamese revolution could not diverge from the general revolutionary law of using revolutionary violence to oppose counter revolutionary violence, rising up to

seize power for the people. It was time to resort to armed struggle, combined with political struggle to push the movement forward.

In the light of this conference, the people of South Viet-Nam passed from various forms of political struggle and armed struggle to insurrection, beginning with the simultaneous uprising of the people of Ben Tre province [on January 17, 1960].

The January conference was almost certainly the 15th Plenum of the VWP's Central Committee, which met at that time to hear Le Duan's report on his trip to the South. George Carver has written:[12]

he [Le Duan] presented a list of recommendations subsequently adopted by the Lao Dong (Party) Central Committee and referred to in Viet Cong cadre training sessions as 'Resolution 15'. These recommendations laid out the whole future course of the southern insurgency, including the establishment of a National Liberation Front to be controlled by the Central Committee of the South Vietnamese branch of the Lao Dong Party and supported by a South Vietnamese 'liberation army'. The Front was to be charged with conducting a political struggle, backed by armed force, designed to neutralize the South and pave the way for 'reunification'.

Other Communist sources confirm this account. According to *Cuoc Khang Chien Chong My Cuu Nuoc* (p. 30), Resolution 15 declared:

The basic path of development of the revolution in the South is to use violence, and that according to the specific situation and present requirements of the revolution the line of using violence is using the strength of the masses and relying principally on the political forces of the masses, in combination with armed forces to a greater or lesser degree, depending on the situation, in order to overthrow the rule of the imperialists and colonialists and set up a revolutionary regime of the people.

In order to attain those objectives it is necessary to have a long, arduous, and heroic struggle process and positively consolidate and meticulously develop forces, for only then could there be conditions for taking advantage of favourable opportunities and winning ultimate victory.

The development of forces referred to the creation of a new Front composed of a four-class alliance led by the Party. The operations of the Front were to be directly controlled by a special Central Committee directorate (*cuc truong uong*).

Resolution 15 not only approved the development of revolutionary armed forces, it also approved the use of armed violence to accompany the political struggle movement. In brief, the 15th

Plenum sanctioned an escalation of the conflict. Force was to be used to protect the Party and its bases, to disrupt and destroy RVN administration at the most basic level, and to create an environment in which it would be possible to launch a general uprising. At this stage, the VWP had no intention of employing PAVN regular units in an armed confrontation with ARVN; neither was the VWP sanctioning a policy of all-out attack on the Republic of Viet-Nam.

In other words, after two years of implementing the policies outlined in *Duong Loi Cach Mang Mien Nam* a majority of Central Committee members concluded that sufficient progress had been made in consolidating the north and winning the sympathy and support of the world's peoples to merit giving more attention to developments in the south. The decision to authorise the escalation of force appears to have been taken none too soon, for the VWP's underground had declined in strength from 15 000 members in 1957 to a mere 5000 by mid-1959.[13] The RVN inflamed the situation with the passage of Law 10/59, under which members of the Communist Party found guilty were executed by beheading.[14]

After Resolution 15 was approved, it was distributed to lower echelons for study and discussion, a process which took about four months. During this period Ho Chi Minh journeyed overseas to consult with Soviet and Chinese leaders. In May, after his return, the VWP Politburo met and decided that the time was now ripe to implement the Central Committee's resolution. A subsequent account noted:[15] 'the directive of the Politburo in May 1959 stated that the time had come to push the armed struggle against the enemy. Thanks to this, we followed the actual situation in order to formulate a program which we felt to be essential, and in October 1959, the armed struggle was launched.'

A similar process occurred on the highlands of Trung Bo where, as we have seen, preparations had long been underway to launch an armed uprising. According to Ta Xuan Linh:[16]

> [i]n the summer of this year [June–August 1959] a historic resolution reached them [Party cadres in the highlands], giving them the green light for switching from political struggle alone to political struggle combined with armed self-defense and support activities. A new page had been turned in the history of the South Vietnamese revolution.

In May, as a result of Politburo initiative, preparations were undertaken to infiltrate southern regroupees back to the south via Laos and down the central mountain range, the Truong Son, over what is now called the Ho Chi Minh Trail. Doan 559 (Group 559) was established at this time to set up and oversee some 20 way-

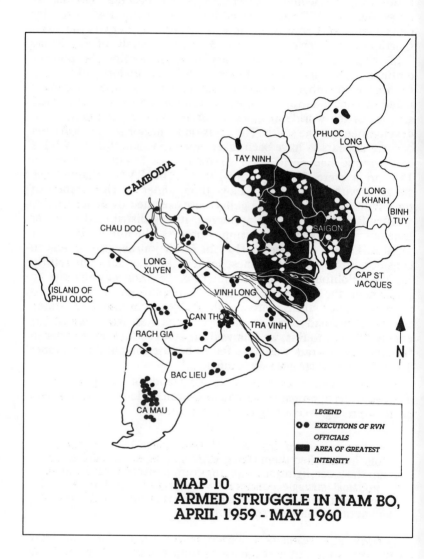

MAP 10
ARMED STRUGGLE IN NAM BO,
APRIL 1959 - MAY 1960

stations along this route.[17] Later in the year, Doan 759, a maritime unit, was set up to oversee movement by sea.[18] By the end of 1960 these groups successfully introduced some 4500 cadres into the south where they replenished a badly decimated Party underground.[19]

After the historic resolution of the 15th Plenum and the Politburo's May directive had been read and studied at all levels the Party's underground took to the offensive. In the final quarter of 1959 the number of RVN officials killed and kidnapped rose dramatically, reaching the 1400 mark by the end of 1960.[20] This tactic effectively cut off the RVN from rural areas where the Party developed larger-sized military units.

In March and April 1959, the first provincial armed units to be formed in the highlands since 1954 were created in Quang Ngai and Ninh Thuan provinces.[21] After receiving the 'resolution on the orientation of the movement' the Party implemented long-standing plans for an uprising in Tra Bong district of Quang Ngai. This took place in August.[22] The following month, party forces in Nam Bo successfully ambushed two companies of ARVN's 23rd Infantry Division.[23] The weapons captured in this attack were later used in a successful assault on the headquarters of ARVN's 32nd Regiment based at Trang Sup, Tay Ninh province during Tet 1960.[24] At the same time the Party conducted an uprising in Ben Tre province inaugurating the period of 'simultaneous' or 'concerted' uprising.[25]

The expansion of the Party's influence in the rural areas followed in the wake of armed violence. Party cadres concentrated on restoring underground cells and in creating the embryo of village revolutionary administrations and mass organisations. Ex-Resistance veterans were grouped together into an Association of Former Resistance Veterans which convened a much publicised meeting in March 1960 to call for the overthrow of the Diem government.[26]

Thus in the period from the 15th Plenum to September 1960, when the VWP held its 3rd National Congress, the Party's underground in the south witnessed a reversal of fortune. The new policy of armed violence permitted the VWP organisation to strike out at the RVN on the local level, severely crippling its administrative capacity. The Party's success in achieving these objectives led to the formal ratification of plans to create a new front. Le Duan, in his political report[27] to the Congress stated, for example:

> To ensure the complete success for the revolutionary struggle in south Viet Nam, our people there, under the leadership of the Marxist-Leninist Party of the working class, must strive to establish a united bloc of workers, peasants, and soldiers, and to bring into being a broad National United Front directed

against the US and Diem and based upon the worker-peasant alliance. This front must rally all the patriotic classes and sections of the people, the majority and the minority nationalities, all patriotic parties and religious groupings, together with all individuals inclined to oppose the US–Diem [regime]. The aims of the struggle of the National United Front against the US and Diem in the South are peace, national independence, democratic freedoms, improvement of the living conditions of the people and the peaceful reunification of the Fatherland.

By the time Le Duan made this statement, preparations to create such a front at the village level had been underway for nearly a year.[28] Apparently an unexpected (and unsuccessful) *coup d'etat* by ARVN military officers launched against the Diem government in November 1960 caused Party cadres to speed up their schedule. A month later, according to Bernard B. Fall:[29]

at 8 pm—exactly fourteen years to the hour from the beginning of the Viet-Minh's anti-French resistance—a small group of representatives of various South Vietnamese opposition groups met in the inaccessible forests north of Saigon . . . there may have been 'about fifty others attending as individuals'. The meeting lasted beyond midnight, and the resulting organization, the NFL, thus was proclaimed to exist as of December 20, 1960.

During the following year the VWP underground emerged under the guise of the People's Revolutionary Party (*Dang Nhan Dan Cach Mang*).[30] The various military forces were united under a single command, headed by a PAVN officer, and renamed the Liberation Armed Forces.[31] Various functional liberation associations (for peasants, women, youth, and students) were established and the embryo of the NFLSVN administrative structure, from province to village level, was created.

In February–March 1962 the NFLSVN held its First National Congress at which the provisional organising committee of 1960 turned over its duties to a newly chosen Central Committee.[32] The leadership of the NFLSVN consisted of long-time VWP cadres who had been active in the south, members of the sect forces, former non-Party members of the Resistance and non-Communist opponents of the Diem regime.[33] Rank-and-file membership consisted of rural folk long under the influence of the Party's underground or areas under the influence of dissident sect forces. The Liberation Armed Forces likewise included soldiers from the sects' armed units as well as newly recruited groups under the leadership of Party cadres. The National Front for the Liberation of South Viet-Nam quickly grew in size. According to Douglas Pike the NFLSVN had a membership of about 37 500 when it was founded in December 1960; by the time of its first Congress this figure had risen to 300 000.[34] It was the growth and influence of this organisation which so concerned President Kennedy when he took office in early 1961.

Conclusion

Previous accounts of the origins of the NFLSVN, as we have pointed out in the introduction, have often been greatly distorted by the nature of the debate over the merits of Western involvement in Viet-Nam. Official US and RVN interpretations correctly stressed the role of the Lao Dong Party but failed to indicate that the Party itself was a national organisation which had operated throughout Viet-Nam prior to partition. The official interpretations put forward in various White Papers overlooked the pre-existing areas of Party influence in the south. These same accounts also tended to overlook the widespread opposition to the Diem regime by the politico-religious sects and others, as well as the increasing alienation of various groups such as farmers, ethnic minorities, and urban intellectuals caused by Diem's repressive domestic policies.

Critics of the US and RVN, on the other hand, have correctly stressed the brutal treatment accorded ex-members of the Resistance as one of the major factors leading to a renewal of insurgency in the south. These writers, however, have overstressed the independence of cadres in the south in their relations with the Party Central Committee.[1] Although it is true that the demand to resort to armed force arose in the south it is also true that other cadres, particularly on the Nam Bo Regional Committee, felt that unification could be achieved by non-violent means.[2] In the course of internal disputes in the south, the Nam Bo Committee exercised strict discipline over lower-level cadres who violated the Party's guidelines. The Regional Committee only altered its policies after the Central Committee passed Resolution 15 which approved using revolutionary violence in support of the political struggle movement.[3]

These contending views concerning the origins of the NFLSVN fell into the semantic trap discussed in the introduction. In order to prove 'aggression from the north', official US and RVN interpretations stressed the crucial role of the Viet-Nam Workers' Party, which they held to be 'North Vietnamese'. In order to make their case, they pointed to important VWP meetings, such as the 15th

190

Plenum and 3rd Party Congress, which determined the scope and intensity of the conflict in the south.

Those who argued that the impetus for the creation of the NFLSVN came from the south downplayed the unity and cohesion of the VWP as a national organisation. These critics magnified the evidence which indicated that disgruntled cadres in Nam Bo forced the pace of developments. For example, Jean Lacouture has argued:[4]

> the actual birth of the National Liberation Front must be traced back to March 1960. At that time a group of the old resistance fighters assembled in Zone D (eastern Cochinchina), issued a proclamation calling the prevailing situation 'intolerable' for the people as a result of Diem's actions, and called upon patriots to regroup with a view toward ultimate collective action . . . the little Congress of March 1960 was in some ways the 'general call' for the creation of the Front, the signal that, coming from the South, was to force the government in the North to assume its responsibility.

This study has tried to present the case that the decision to create the National Front for the Liberation of South Viet-Nam in December 1960 was the outcome of a complex interplay of four sets of factors which operated over time: the international environment, domestic developments in the north, the state of the Party's underground in the south, and the policies of the Diem regime and its American ally. For purposes of drawing conclusions it will be convenient to view these factors as operating with varying degrees of influence on three levels: the international, national and decision-making levels.

THE INTERNATIONAL LEVEL

In 1954 the DRVN was born into an international system which was dominated by the power and Cold War rivalries of the Soviet Union and the United States. As a junior member of the socialist camp and as a small, divided and weak Southeast Asian state the DRVN had little leverage to alter the policies of either the USSR or China when these ran counter to the DRVN's declared objectives. In order to achieve its national objectives (territorial security, economic rehabilitation and development, reunification, and the end of foreign interference) the DRVN had little choice but to adhere loyally to the policies of the socialist bloc headed by the Soviet Union. Indeed Soviet and Chinese aid in the early years was indispensable in averting famine and in restoring the north's war-ravaged economy. Membership in the socialist camp also afforded the DRVN a measure of protection against attack by the United States, which was a constant fear of Hanoi's leaders.

The DRVN's attempts during 1954–56 to reunify Viet-Nam under the terms of the 1954 Geneva Agreements foundered on the central fact that neither superpower found it in its interests to support such a settlement. The United States was hostile to the Geneva Conference from the beginning. Immediately a political settlement was achieved the US adopted a policy of shoring up the Diem government and abetting it in its refusal to hold negotiations with the north. The Soviet Union, although willing to grant limited support for DRVN initiatives, was in fact more concerned with obtaining concessions from the West in Europe than in pushing the issue of Vietnamese unification.

China too gave limited support to DRVN initiatives. And France, which had some economic interests in the north, quickly divested itself of all responsibilities by withdrawing the French Expeditionary Corps prior to the July 1956 electoral deadline. In the face of these developments the attitudes of India and other Asian states, however sympathetic, were immaterial.

The DRVN adjusted to these setbacks by adopting a long-range policy of building up international contacts and awaiting more favourable circumstances. These arose in 1957 as a result of the deepening Sino-Soviet dispute. The solidarity of the socialist bloc was shaken as a result of Khrushchev's denunciation of Stalin and as a result of the Polish troubles and Hungarian uprising of 1956. In November 1957, the CCP and the CPSU aired their differences on several matters, including the issue of peaceful or non-peaceful transition to socialism before a meeting of 12 Communist and Workers' parties in Moscow. China's adoption of a militant line in foreign affairs in 1958 created an environment which enabled the VWP leadership to move without the previous constraints. According to a Party review of this period:[5]

> If one took the world situation as the model for the policy line for our country, which had its own special characteristics, it would be inappropriate to do so even if the revolution in a particular country depended greatly on the international situation. Concerning the possibility of advancing revolution by peaceful means even the resolution of the 20th Congress of the CPSU stated that it could be achieved only in certain countries which already had democratic institutions. South Viet Nam is an American colony dominated by the My-Diem system; it therefore has its own laws governing revolution. It cannot take the general guidelines concerning the world for its own ... according to declaration 12 [i.e., the Moscow Declaration], the Party stated: 'Whether the Revolution is violent or not will not depend on us, but on the attitude of our enemy'.

In January 1959, after two years of economic progress and after strengthening contacts with socialist bloc countries, the leaders of the VWP were in a position to approve a more militant policy in the south. In short, the international constraints which applied in an earlier period were partially removed. The new low-risk policy which the VWP adopted was designed to take advantage of this.

As the situation in neighbouring Laos deteriorated, bringing first American then Soviet involvement, the VWP undertook bolder steps. Military coups in Laos and South Viet-Nam in late 1960 may have prompted this. In December 1960 the NFLSVN was formed, with the twin purpose of overthrowing the Diem government and liberating the south from the influence of the American imperialists. In short, Viet-Nam became an example of a 'just war of national liberation' to which the Chinese and Soviets would be expected to give some measurement of support.

THE NATION-STATE LEVEL

The second level of analysis, the nation level, focuses primarily on internal developments within a country in order to explain policy outcomes. In the case of Viet-Nam two features in particular appear significant, the role of the Marxist-Leninist Viet-Nam Workers' Party (its ideology and previous experiences), and the fact of national partition. The VWP, as a Marxist-Leninist Party, subscribed to the two stage theory of revolution, that of a national democratic phase followed by a phase of socialist revolution. In this respect one of the most important components of VWP ideology was the idea of a Front (*mat tran*), a broad union of various social classes, suited to 'the objective circumstances' of each historical period. Thus in the Resistance War the Viet Minh–Lien Viet Fronts served as the main instruments of national mobilisation. Because the historic period was one of armed struggle, the role of the People's Army was also important.

During the 1954–56 period, when the VWP shifted to political struggle, the Fatherland Front served as the prime organisation for mobilisation in the north. It never became a mass organisation in the south, mainly because of the hostile environment in which the party organisation had to operate. Nevertheless it existed in embryo, ready to expand should the Diem government collapse and a coalition favourably disposed towards reunification take its place.

The partitioning of Viet-Nam must be seen as a fundamental factor influencing Party policy because for the first time it became impracticable for the Party to pursue the same objectives throughout the country. In short, Party leaders asserted that there were two major interrelated objectives in the post-1954 period: socialist construction in the north and the carrying out of national democratic revolution in the south. The decision to accept the partitioning of Viet-Nam and the decision to pursue two objectives simultaneously almost proved impossible to implement. In the period 1954–55, when it appeared that reunification could be achieved by peaceful means under the terms of the Geneva Agreements, the contradictions in this dual approach were less evident. Afterwards, however, the difficulty of carrying out these two objectives became apparent as US support for the Republic of Viet-Nam upset the power ratio within Viet-Nam.

In the north the VWP was faced with the immense task of restoring a war-damaged economy and avoiding famine. The pace of recovery depended not only on the success of Party policies and programs but also on the nature and extent of foreign assistance. In 1956 the Party faced a serious crisis in the aftermath of its land reform campaign, a campaign impelled by the ideology of the VWP. The ramifications of this crisis, which sparked peasant disturbances in Quynh Luu district and which encouraged disaffection by sections of the intelligentsia, drained the party's energies and resources.

Simultaneously, the VWP had to face the impact of US and RVN policies in the south. As the Diem regime grew stronger, and as US assistance increased, the ability of the VWP underground to respond diminished accordingly. The problem for the VWP, of course, was to cope with both sets of problems at the same time. In late 1956, a new policy was devised which continued to place priority on the consolidation of the north (economic stability and development, public order and security, and regularisation and modernisation of PAVN). Its other components consisted of maintaining and developing the movement in the south and winning international sympathy and support (which contributed to both objectives). After two years of implementing this policy, progress in the north had reached a level where it became possible to contemplate a step-up in the movement in the south.

There, meanwhile, Party leaders faced a dilemma. On the one hand the repressive policies of the Diem regime (military operations, security laws, anti-Communist denunciation campaigns) severely weakened the Party. On the other hand, various policies of the RVN (land reform, resettlement, regroupment in the highlands, press censorship) raised the level of discontent and also the potential for rebellion, as group after group became alienated from the incumbent government.

Restrictions on the use of armed force severely hampered the Party's underground in its attempts to defend itself. The Party therefore relied on the armed sect forces and, in 1957, on a 'killing tyrants' program carried out by armed propaganda teams.

Both policies achieved mixed success. In 1959, Party cadres in both the north and south argued that sufficient progress had been made in building up the DRVN and in obtaining international support to permit a change in strategy in the south. The use of armed violence was then sanctioned as a counter to the actions of the Diem regime. In order to avoid US retaliation on the DRVN, the movement in the south had to rely as much as possible on its own resources. The creation of the NFLSVN was designed to demonstrate that the people in the south supported the overthrow of Diem and the end of American influence.

THE DECISION-MAKING LEVEL

This level of analysis attempts to explain policy outcomes by focusing on the decision-making structure of the country being studied and on the role of various organisations and individuals within that structure. In the case of Viet-Nam it is immediately apparent that the key decision-making structure rested within the Viet-Nam Workers' Party. This study has focused on the importance of the regular plenary sessions of the VWP's Central Committee during the 1954–60 period. It is evident that, since the Central Committee met on average only twice a year, the implementation of policy on a regular basis was the responsibility of the Politburo. However because of the nature of the data, it has not been possible to analyse thoroughly the role of this body (only three crucial meetings have been discussed in the text, September 1954, October 1956 and May 1959).

During the period under consideration, VWP policy towards the south was set at the plenary session of the Central Committee at which the views of the subordinate Nam Bo Regional Committee were considered. Decision-making was an interactive process by which party officials on the Central Committee had to consider the input demands of various sectors in the light of existing priorities, limited resources and poor communications. The evidence presented here indicates that the VWP's organisation in the south, while it did agitate for policy change on some occasions, was extremely reluctant to take the initiative and sanction the use of force. In fact in early 1959 after the VWP Central Committee had approved the use of armed violence, the Nam Bo Regional Committee was still restricting its use in the south; indeed, it was misleading the Central Committee about the pressures building there in favour of armed struggle.[6]

It is also evident that Le Duan played a key role within the VWP Central Committee. During 1954–56 as Secretary of the Nam Bo Regional Committee he consistently advocated the employment of armed force. His proposals were not accepted in their entirety because of the pressing nature of problems in the DRVN. It was only with the demise of Truong Chinh following the land reform campaign that Le Duan was brought into the inner-circle of decision-makers, where he tipped the balance in favour of greater commitment to the revolutionary movement in the south. Not only did Le Duan draft the important policy guidelines embodied in *Duong Loi Cach Mang Mien Nam* but he also submitted the crucial report to the VWP's 15th Plenum. By the time of the VWP's 3rd National Congress in September 1960 the influence of those advocating a more militant line in the south was clear in appointments made to the secretariat and Central Committee. Le Duan himself was appointed First Secretary of the Party. Thereafter the VWP further increased the tempo of revolutionary activity in the south.

Finally, the evidence presented in this book has indicated that the disputes within the Central Committee were, in all probability, based more on the relative priorities to be assigned to the consolidation of the north and the national democratic revolution in the south than on the question of a pro-Soviet or pro-Chinese orientation. In conclusion, it would appear that the birth of the National Front for the Liberation of South Viet-Nam was a far more complex process than has usually been suggested. The decision to create the NFLSVN in December 1960, and not earlier, has been explained in this study by examining four major factors which influenced the decision-making process of the Viet-Nam Workers' Party: the constraints imposed by the international environment; the process of economic, social and political development in the north; the success of the VWP's underground in the south; and the policies of the RVN and its American allies.

Notes

Introduction

1   Truong Nhu Tang, *Vietcong Memoir: An Inside Account of the Vietnam War and Its Aftermath* (New York: Harcourt Brace Jovanovich Publishers, 1985), pp. 66–80.

2   Arthur M. Schlesinger, Jr., *A Thousand Days* (Boston: Houghton Mifflin Co., 1965), pp. 302–303.

3   United States Department of State, Bureau of Public Affairs (Washington, DC: US Government Printing Office, Dec. 1961), pp. 1–2.

4   George McT. Kahin and John W. Lewis, *The United States in Vietnam* (New York: Dell Publishing Company, Revised Edition 1969), p. 119.

5   Point 6 of the Final Declaration in Great Britain, *Further Documents Relating to the Discussion of Indochina at the Geneva Conference*, Miscellaneous No. 20 (1954), Command Papers, Cmd. 9239 (London: Great Britain Parliamentary Sessional Papers, XXXI, 1953–1954), pp. 9–11.

6   United States Department of State, *The Communist Subversive Threat in Vietnam, Cambodia and Laos* (Washington, DC: Office of Intelligence Research, Dec. 29, 1955), pp. 8–10. *The New York Herald Tribune*, March 1, 1955 states, 'Estimates of the dimensions of the problem vary rather widely, to be sure. If you ask the Americans here [in Saigon] they will tell you that outside the feudal domains of the military religious sects, anywhere from 50 to 70 per cent of the southern Indochinese are subject to Viet Minh influence or control. French experts give still higher percentages, between 60 and 90.' According to census figures the population south of the 17th parallel was about 10 million; this would have placed the population in the liberated areas at between 2.1 and 3.6 million; Viet Nam Cong Hoa, *Viet Nam Nien Giam Tong Ke* (Saigon: Bo Kinh Te Quoc Gia, 1956), Vol. 4 (1952–53) and 6(1956). Pham Van Dong stated that the population figure was 3 million of whom 2 million had been under DRVN government since the 1945 August Revolution, Wilfred Burchett dispatch from Geneva in *The Daily Worker*, July 26, 1954.

7   The discussion which follows relies on Ivo D. Duchacek, *Nations and Men: An Introduction to International Politics* (Hinsdale, Illinois: The Dryden Press, 3rd edition, 1965), pp. 14–30.

8   For example the Saigon press referred to a DRVN delegation headed by Ton Duc Thang as a 'Viet Cong Parliamentary Group'. See Vietnam Press, *The Times of Viet Nam Weekly*, Oct. 13, 1956.

197

9   Jean Lacouture, *Vietnam: Between Two Truces* (New York: Vintage
    Books, 1966), p. 52.
10 In the sense used by Samuel P. Huntington, *Political Order in
    Changing Societies* (New Haven: Yale University Press, 1968).
11 John T. McAlister and Paul Mus, *The Vietnamese and Their Revol-
    ution,* (New York: Harper and Row, 1970), pp. 31–35.
12 I am referring to a process described in great detail for China, Japan
    and Korea by John K. Fairbank, Edwin O. Reischauer and Albert M.
    Craig in *A History of East Asian Civilization* (Boston: Houghton
    Mifflin Co., 1965), Vol. II, *East Asia: The Modern Transformation,*
    pp. 4–10.
13 These developments are dealt with by David G. Marr, *Vietnamese
    Anticolonialism 1885–1925* (Berkeley: University of California Press,
    1971), pp. 44–76.
14 John T. McAlister, *Viet Nam: The Origins of Revolution,* (New York:
    Alfred A. Knopf, 1969), pp. 256–272 and 319–364; George Modelski,
    'The Viet Minh Complex', in Cyril E. Black and Thomas P. Thornton,
    Communism and Revolution: The Strategic Uses of Political Violence
    (Princeton: Princeton University Press, 1964), pp. 185–214; and
    Bernard B. Fall, *The Viet-Minh Regime: Government and Adminis-
    tration in the Democratic Republic of Viet-Nam* (New York: Institute
    of Pacific Relations, 1956).
15 McAlister, *Viet Nam: The Origins of Revolution,* p. 4.
16 David Easton, *A Framework for Political Analysis* (Englewood Cliffs,
    New Jersey: Prentice-Hall Inc., 1965), pp. 35–135 for a discussion of
    political systems and the interaction between the environment and
    political system.

Chapter 1 Regroupment and reorientation

1   Dispatch by Tillman Durdin from Geneva, *The New York Times,* July
    25, 1954.
2   'Replies to a Swedish Correspondent (November 1953)', in Ho Chi
    Minh, *Selected Writings (1920–1969)* (Hanoi: Foreign Languages
    Publishing House, 1973), pp. 153–154.
3   Philippe Devillers and Jean Lacouture, *End of a War: Indochina, 1954*
    (London: Pall Mall Press, 1969), pp. 249–253.
4   According to French estimates (no official Vietnamese figures have
    been released), PAVN losses may have exceeded French casualties
    (15 000) by 30 to 100 per cent; Pierre Rocolle, *Pourquoi Dien Bien
    Phu?* (Paris: Flammarion, 1968), pp. 553–557.
5   Janos Radvanyi, *Delusion and Reality* (South Bend, Indiana: Gateway
    Editions, Limited, 1978), p. 6.
6   Strobe Talbot, editor and translator, *Khrushchev Remembers* (Lon-
    don: Sphere Books Ltd., 1971), pp. 442–443.
7   'How the Dien Bien Phu Battle Was Won', *Vietnamese Studies* (March
    1965), No. 8, pp. 68–69.
8   'The Outcome for the Communists', in *United States–Vietnam Rela-
    tions* (Washington, DC: US Government Printing Office, 1971), Book
    2, III.D.1., pp. D8–D9.

9 Ta Xuan Linh, 'South Viet Nam at the Time of Dien Bien Phu', *Vietnamese Studies* (1976), No. 43; *Dien Bien Phu: Before, During, After,* pp. 56–57.

10 Point Seven of the Final Declaration in Great Britain, *Further Documents Relating to the Discussions of Indochina at the Geneva Conference*, p. 9–11.

11 P. J. Honey, 'North Vietnam's Party Congress', *The China Quarterly* (Oct.–Dec. 1960), No. 4, p. 70.

12 P. J. Honey, *Communism in North Vietnam: Its Role in the Sino-Soviet Dispute* (Cambridge: The MIT Press, 1966), p. 6.

13 Jeffrey Race, *War Comes to Long An: Revolutionary Conflict in a Vietnamese Province* (Berkeley: The University of California Press, 1972), p. 34.

14 Seymour Topping, *Journey Between Two Chinas* (New York: Harper and Row, 1972), p. 151.

15 'Viet Minh policy document on post-Geneva strategy (November 1954)', in United States Department of State, *Working Paper on the North Vietnamese Role in the War in South Viet-Nam* (Washington, D.C:, 1968), Appendices, Item 200, p. 7. Cited hereafter as *Working Paper.*

16 King C. Chen, *Vietnam and China, 1938–1954* (Princeton: Princeton University Press, 1969), pp. 294–295.

17 Charles B. McLane, 'The Russians and Vietnam: Strategies of Indirection', *International Journal* (Winter 1968/69), Vol. XXIV, No. 1, p. 49, footnote 3.

18 Ho Chi Minh, *Nhung Chang Duong Lich Su Ve Vang* (Hanoi: Nha Xuat Ban Quan Doi Nhan Dan, 1973), pp. 77–90. Quotations in the text from this speech are taken from this source. See also: War Experiences Recapitulation Committee of the High-Level Military Institute, *Cuoc Khang Chien Chong My Cuu Nuoc, 1954–1975: Nhung Su Kien Quan Su* (The Anti-U.S. Resistance War for National Salvation, 1954–1975: Military Events) Hanoi: Nha Xuat Ban Quan Doi Nhan Dan, 1980, p. 3. Cited hereafter as *Cuoc Khang Chien Chong My Cuu Nuoc.*

19 Devillers and Lacouture, *End of a War*, p. 255.

20 D. R. SarDesai, *Indian Foreign Policy in Cambodia, Laos, and Vietnam, 1947–1964* (Berkeley: The University of California Press, 1968), p. 48.

21 'Sino-Soviet Objectives and Strategy' in *United States–Vietnam Relaions*, Book I, III.C.2., p. C–23.

22 Ban Nghien Cuu Lich Su Dang Trung Uong, *Bon Muoi Lam Nam Hoat Dong Cua Dang Lao Dong Viet-Nam* (Hanoi: Nha Xuat Ban Su That, 1976), p. 74.

23 See note 6, Introduction.

24 Xu Uy Nam Bo [Nam Bo Regional Committee], *Tinh Hinh Nam Bo Tu Sau Hoa Binh Lap Lai Den Hien Nay* [The Situation in Nam Bo from the Restoration of Peace to the Present] (typescript, circa 1960). Cited hereafter as *Tinh Hinh Nam Bo.*

25 Vu Can, 'The People's Struggles Against the US–Diem Regime from 1954 to 1960', *Vietnamese Studies* (1968), Nos. 18/19, p. 103.

26   Radio France-Asie, August 9, 1954; and 'Vietnam Sets Up 2 Sedition Courts', *The New York Times*, August 4, 1954, p. 2.
27   Xu Uy Nam Bo, *Tinh Hinh Phong Trao Dau Tranh Chinh Tri o Nam Bo Tu Hoa Binh Lap Lai Den Hien Nay* (The Situation of the Political Struggle Movement in Nam Bo From the Restoration of Peace to the Present), typescript, circa 1960/61. Cited hereafter as *Tinh Hinh Phong Trao*.
28   *Working Paper* Item 200. References in the following paragraphs are taken from this source. See also *Cuoc Khang Chien Chong My Cuu Nuoc*, p. 5.
29   *Working Paper* Item 200, p. 10.
30   *An Outline History of the Viet Nam Workers' Party* (Hanoi: Foreign Languages Publishing House, 1970), p. 81. See also *Cuoc Khang Chien Chong My Cuu Nuoc*, p. 6.
31   *Tinh Hinh Nam Bo*, pp. 24–25.
32   ibid.; Race, *War Comes to Long An*, pp. 32–33; and *Working Paper*, Item 200, pp. 15–16.
33   The legal position is defined here by the Party as reflecting the point of view of the incumbent government.
34   *Tinh Hinh Nam Bo*, pp. 15–16; *Tinh Hinh Phong Trao*, pp. 16–17; and 'Translation of a Lao Dong Party document acquired on November 29, 1954, in the Saigon-Cholon area', *Working Paper* Item 29, pp. 1–6.
35   ibid.
36   ibid., p. 6.
37   Dispatch by Tillman Durdin from Saigon in *The New York Times*, September 29, 1954 and Anita L. Nutt, *Troika on Trial: Control or Compromise?* (Washington, DC: US Department of Commerce, Sept. 1967), Vol. I, pp. 175–178.
38   'Rebellion Against My-Diem', in *United States–Vietnam Relations*, Book 2, IV.A.5, Tab 2, p. 49; B. N. S. Murti, *Vietnam Divided: The Unfinished Struggle* (New Delhi: Asia Publishing House, 1964), p. 224; J. J. Zasloff, *Origins of the Insurgency in South Vietnam, 1954–1960: The Role of the Southern Vietminh Cadres* (Santa Monica: The RAND Corporation, May 1968), p. 1; and 'Commentary: Bernard B. Fall on Bui Van Luong', in Richard W. Lindholm, editor, *Viet-Nam The First Five Years: An International Symposium* (East Lansing: Michigan State University Press, 1959) p. 57.
39   'US Perceptions of the Insurgency, 1954–1960', in *United States–Vietnam Relations*, Book 2, IV.A.5, Tab 4, p. 25.
40   *Tinh Hinh Nam Bo*, p. 25; and Voice of the Dai Viet National Liberation Troops, December 6 and December 20, 1955.
41   *Working Paper* Item 29, pp. 1 and 4.
42   Voice of Nam Bo, November 27, 1954.
43   Radio Hanoi, November 27, 1954.
44   Vietnam News Agency, November 27, 1954.
45   It was not until January 1955, for example, that France terminated the Pau Agreement of 1950 and transferred control of finances and economic matters to the State of Viet-Nam; 'General Monetary and Commercial Convention Between France and State of Viet-Nam'

Notes et Etudes Documentaires (Jan. 25, 1955), No. 1973, pp. 41–43 translated and reprinted in Allan B. Cole, editor, *Conflict in Indo-China and International Repercussions: A Documentary History, 1945–1955* (Ithaca: Cornell University Press, 1956), pp. 199–202.

46 Edward G. Lansdale, *In the Midst of Wars: An American's Mission to Southeast Asia* (New York: Harper and Row, 1972), p. 175.

47 United Press dispatch from Saigon in *The New York Times*, March 9 and March 13, 1955.

48 'Indochina Aid Now Direct', *The New York Times*, January 1, 1955.

49 Bernard B. Fall, *The Two Viet-Nams: A Political and Military Analysis* (New York: Frederick A. Praeger, 1967), pp. 245–246; Joseph Buttinger, *Vietnam: A Dragon Embattled* (New York: Frederick A. Praeger, 1967), Vol. 2, pp. 1101–1107 and 1115; and William Henderson, 'South Viet Nam Finds Itself', *Foreign Affairs* (January 1957), Vol. XXXV, No. 1, pp. 287–288.

50 Radio France-Asie, December 1, 1954; and 'Vietnam Soldiers Fight with Police', *The New York Times,* December 2, 1954.

51 Donald Lancaster, *The Emancipation of French Indochina* (New York: Octagon Books, 1974), p. 384.

52 There were a variety of Vietnamese politicians in exile in Paris, most notably Buu Hoi, who might have replaced Diem in 1954–55. Hoi was already on record as favouring a rapprochement with the DRVN; United Press dispatch from Saigon in *Le Monde*, August 18, 1954.

53 Dispatch from Saigon in *The New York Times*, November 18, 1954.

Chapter 2 Political struggle under the Geneva Agreements

1 Communique of the Conference of the Lien Viet National Committee, Voice of Vietnam, Jan. 20, 1955.

2 Message Sent by the National Conference of the Delegates of the Lien Viet to the Compatriots of the South, Voice of Vietnam, Jan. 17, 1955.

3 'Socialist Construction and Anti-US Resistance: Chronology of Events (1954 1970)', *Vietnam Courier* [Hanoi] (August 10, 1970), No. 281, p. 4. See also *Cuoc Khang Chien Chong My Cuu Nuoc*, p. 10.

4 President Ho Chi Minh's Speech at Opening Meeting of the Seventh Session of the General Executive Committee of the Labor Party of Viet Nam, Voice of Vietnam, April 29, 1955.

5 Pham Van Dong's speech was broadcast in instalments by the Voice of Vietnam on March 22, 1955 and released by the Vietnam News Agency on March 23, 1955. All references to this speech in the text are from these sources. See also *Cuoc Khang Chien Chong My Cuu Nuoc*, p. 10.

6 ibid.

7 Vo Nguyen Giap's speech was broadcast by Voice of Vietnam on March 23, 1955. All references to this speech in the text are from this source.

8 'The Text of the Joint Communique by the Prime Minister of India and Shri Pham Van Dong Deputy Prime Minister and Foreign Minister of the Democratic Republic of Viet Nam in New Delhi on April

       10, 1955', in *Foreign Policy of India: Texts of Documents, 1947–1959*
       (New Delhi: Lok Sabha Secretariat, 1959), p. 169.
9   SarDesai, *Indian Foreign Policy*, p. 89.
10   Vietnam News Agency, March 6 and May 21, 1955.
11   Vietnam News Agency, June 6, 1955.
12   'The Text of the Joint Declaration by Marshal Bulganin and Shri
       Nehru Issued in Moscow on June 23, 1955', in *Foreign Policy of
       India*, pp. 185–187.
13   'The Text of the Joint Statement By the Prime Ministers of India and
       Poland Issued in Warsaw on June 27, 1955', ibid., pp. 191–92.
14   'Premier Diem States Policies Regarding Country-Wide Elections
       (July 16, 1955)', Embassy of Vietnam (Washington, DC), Press and
       Information Service, Press Release, July 22, 1955), Vol. 1, No. 18
       reprinted in Cole, *Conflict in Indochina*, pp. 226–227.
15   Vietnam News Agency, July 20, 1955.
16   The information on Ho's visits to Peking and Moscow has been
       culled from a variety of sources: Allan W. Cameron, 'The Soviet
       Union and Vietnam: The Origins of Involvement', in W. Raymond
       Duncan, editor, *Soviet Policy in Developing Countries* (Waltham,
       Massachusetts: Ginn Blaisdell, 1970), p. 200; Harold C. Hinton,
       Communist China in World Politics (Boston: Houghton Mifflin
       Company, 1966), p. 256; Roy Jumper and Marjorie Weiner Nor-
       mand, 'Vietnam', in George McT. Kahin, editor, *Governments and
       Politics of Southeast Asia*, 2nd Edition (Ithaca: Cornell University
       Press, 1964), p. 506; William Kaye, 'A Bowl of Rice Divided: The
       Economy of North Vietnam', in Honey, *North Vietnam Today* (New
       York: Frederick A. Praeger, 1962), p. 112; and McLane, 'The Rus-
       sians and Vietnam', op. cit., p. 60. For the texts of the two joint
       communiques see: New China News Agency, July 8, 1955 and Soviet
       Home Service (Moscow), July 18, 1955.
17   'Ho Gets Burmese Rice', *The Economist*, September 24, 1955, pp.
       1022–1023.
18   Welles Hangen dispatch from Moscow in *The New York Times*, July
       16, 1955. For remarks reportedly made by the Chinese to Viet-Nam
       at this time consult *Cuoc Khang Chien Chong My Cuu Nuoc*, p. 21.
19   Cameron, in *Soviet Policy in Developing Countries*, p. 200.
20   'Taking Indo-China Gently', *The Economist*, July 30, 1955, p. 373.
21   Reuters dispatch from Geneva in *The New York Times*, July 24,
       1955.
22   'Bao Cao Cua Ho Chu Tich Ve Viec Doan Dai Bieu Cua Chinh Phu
       Ta Di Tham Lien Xo va Trung Quoc', [Report by Chairman Ho
       Concerning the Work of the Delegation of Representatives of Our
       Government on Their Visit to the Soviet Union and China] *Nhan
       Dan*, July 24, 1955.
23   For an overview consult: Robert Shaplen, *The Lost Revolution: The
       U.S. in Vietnam, 1946–1966* (New York: Harper and Row, 1966), pp.
       120–26; Lansdale, *In the Midst of Wars*, pp. 260–281; and Lancaster,
       The Emancipation of French Indochina, pp. 381–397.
24   Murti, *Vietnam Divided*, p. 136; Buttinger, *A Dragon Embattled*, Vol.
       2, pp. 870 and 1105; Ta Xuan Linh, 'How Armed Struggle Began in

South Viet Nam', *Vietnam Courier* (March 1974), New Series No. 22, p. 21; United Press dispatch from Saigon in *The New York Times*, March 9, 1955; Associated Press dispatch from Saigon in ibid., March 11, 1955; and Voice of the Dai Viet National Liberation Forces, April 20; August 5 and 8, and Oct. 3, 1955.

25 Nguyet Dam and Than Phong, *Chin Nam Mau Lua Duoi Che Do Gia Dinh Tri Ngo Dinh Diem* [Nine Years of Blood and Fire Under the Nepotism of Ngo Dinh Diem] (Saigon: Tac Gia Xuat Ban [published by the authors], 1964), pp. 48–50.

26 Francis J. Corley, 'Viet Nam Since Geneva', *Thought* [Fordham University Quarterly] (Winter 1958/59), Vol. XXXIII, No. 131, pp. 546–547.

27 Denis Warner, *The Last Confucian* (Baltimore: Penguin Books, 1964), pp. 103–104.

28 Paul Ely, *L'Indochine dans la Tourmente* (Paris: Librairie Plon, 1964), p. 171.

29 *Tinh Hinh Nam Bo*, p. 15; Radio Hanoi, August 31, 1955 reports the arrest of several committee members.

30 The text of the communique of the 8th Plenum was broadcast by Vietnam News Agency, Aug. 22, 1955. All references in the text are from this source. See also *Cuoc Khang Chien Chong My Cuu Nuoc*, pp. 13–14.

31 ibid., and 'Lam Cho Nghi Quyet Cua Hoi Nghi Trung Uong Lan Thu 8 Tham Nhuan Den Moi Dang Vien', [Every Party Member Should Thoroughly Implement the Resolution of the Central Committee's 8th Plenum] *Nhan Dan*, September 26, 1955.

32 Vietnam News Agency, May 2, 1955.

33 At least three members of the committee were former members of the Viet Minh and this gave rise for concern in some quarters; Warner, *The Last Confucian*, pp. 103–104.

34 'Interrogation in 1958 of a prisoner who had been active in the "Resistance" since 1945 until his capture by GVN [i.e. RVN] forces in 1956', *Working Paper*, Appendices, Item 12, p. 14.

35 Vu Can, 'The People's Struggles Against the US–Diem Regime', op. cit., pp. 75 and 109.

36 US Central Intelligence Agency, *Current Intelligence Weekly Review*, October 27, 1955 cited in 'The Role of Hanoi', in *United States–Vietnam Relations*, Book 2, IV.A.5. Tab 3, p. 45.

37 Jean Sainteny, *Ho Chi Minh and His Vietnam: A Personal Memoir* (Chicago: Cowles Book Co., Inc., 1972), pp. 105–159.

38 Dispatch by Max Clos from Hai Phong in *Le Monde*, Jan. 23, 1955.

39 Bui Cong Trung, 'The Food Problem', *Nghien Cuu Kinh Te* [Economic Research] (February 1961) translated by United States Joint Publications Research Service, No. 10, 1974, p. 13.

40 Bui Cong Trung, 'Aid by Countries in the Socialist Camp in Restoring and Developing the National Economy of the Democratic Republic of Vietnam', in *Demokratichevskaya Respublika V'yetam* (Moscow: Institute of the Peoples of Asia of the Academy of Sciences USSR, 1960), translated by U.S. JPRS No. 4925 (1961), p. 24.

Chapter 3 The Fatherland Front

1 'Tuyen Ngon cua Mat Tran To Quoc Viet Nam', [Manifesto of the Viet-Nam Fatherland Front] *Nhan Dan*, Sept. 14, 1955. References in the text to the manifesto are taken from this source.
2 'Cuong Linh cua Mat Tran To Quoc Viet Nam' [Platform of the Viet-Nam Fatherland Front] *Nhan Dan*, Sept. 14, 1955.
3 'Bao Cao cua Chinh Phu Truoc Khoa Hop Thu Nam cua Quoc Hoi', [Report of the Government Before the 5th Session of the National Assembly] *Nhan Dan*, Sept. 17, 1955. References in the text to this report are taken from this source.
4 The Cao Dai sect is not, as is commonly assumed, a unified movement. The *Minh Chon Dau* (Bright and True) Cao Dai is a component of one of three major groupings within the Cao Dai sect which emerged in the 1930s. Various 'Holy Sees' were created throughout the Mekong Delta in rivalry to the better known Holy See in Tay Ninh province. The centre of the *Minh Chon Dau* is in Bac Lieu province, adjacent to Ca Mau. During the Resistance War a grouping of Twelve Unified Sects, including the Minh Chon Dau, was active with the Viet Minh and Lien Viet Fronts. Its leader, Cao Trieu Phat, regrouped to the north and played an active role in the Viet-Nam Fatherland Front.
5 These were Operation Liberty, conducted in the Ca Mau regrouping zone, and Operation Giai Phong, conducted in the Quang Ngai-Binh Dinh regrouping zone; Lansdale, *In the Midst of Wars*, pp. 228–243.
6 Race, 'The Origins of the Second Indochina War', *Asian Survey* (May 1970), X, 5, p. 362.
7 Burchett, *North of the 17th Parallel* (Delhi: People's Publishing House Ltd., 1956), p. 247.
8 *Tinh Hinh Nam Bo*, p. 15.
9 Voice of the Dai Viet National Liberation Troops, August 8, 1955.
10 'Ho Gets Burmese Rice', *The Economist*, Sept. 24, 1955, pp. 1022–1023.
11 US Central Intelligence Agency, *Current Intelligence Weekly Review* (October 27, 1955) in *United States–Vietnam Relations*, Book 2, IV.A.5 Tab 3, p. 45.
12 'Mr Diem's Visitor', *The Economist*, August 27, 1955, p. 684.
13 Radio France-Asie, Sept. 8, 1955.
14 *Cuoc Khang Chien Chong My Cuu Nuoc*, p. 11.
15 'From a conversation between an agent of the government of Vietnam [i.e. RVN] and a North Vietnamese [i.e. Communist Party cadre] who had good contacts among political groups in North and South Vietnam', and '[Intelligence report of] Viet Minh collaboration with the Hoa Hao and penetration of the Cao Dai and agricultural organizations in the Plaine des Joncs, October 1955', *Working Paper*, Appendices, Items 21, p. 1 and 205, pp. 1–2, respectively.
16 *Working Paper*, Appendices, Item 21, pp. 1–2.
17 *Working Paper*, Appendices, Item 205, pp. 1–2.
18 Voice of the Dai Viet National Liberation Troops, Oct. 9, 1955.
19 Voice of the Dai Viet National Liberation Troops, Oct. 18, 1955.

20 *Working Paper*, Appendices, Item 205, pp. 1–2.
21 *Working Paper*, Appendices, Item 22; Voice of the Dai Viet National Liberation Troops, November 2, 1955; for background information on Muoi Tri, see: Hilaire du Berrier, *Background to Betrayal: The Tragedy of Vietnam* (Boston: Western Islands Press, 1965), pp. 56–58. For an official biography consult: *Who's Who of the Republic of South Viet-Nam* (South Vietnam: Giai Phong Editions, 1969), p. 47.
22 Lucien Bodard dispatch from Saigon in *France-Soir*, Oct. 26, 1955.
23 Colonel Melvin Hall, 'The Dragons Lash Their Tails in Indo-China', *Journal of the Royal Central Asian Society* (April 1956), XLIII, II, pp. 113–120; John Osborne, 'The Tough Miracle Man of Vietnam', *Life* (May 13, 1957), 42, 19, p. 164; Lancaster, *The Emancipation of French Indochina*, p. 399; and Fall, *The Two Viet-Nams*, p. 257.
24 Fall, *The Two Viet-nams*, p. 319.
25 'Taken together, available evidence indicates that infiltration of re-groupees from North to South Vietnam began as early as 1955 ... However, from all indications, the early infiltration was quite small scale, involving no more than a few hundred persons in all'. 'Hanoi and the Insurgency in South Vietnam', in *United States–Vietnam Relations*, Book 2, IV.A.5 Tab 3, p. 34.
26 'Interrogation to two Vietnamese Communist captives picked up in 1956 by GVN [i.e. RVN] forces', *Working Paper*, Appendices, Item 17, p. 1; United States Central Intelligence Agency, *Memorandum: The Organization, Activities, and Objectives of the Communist Front in South Vietnam* (September 22 1965—Secret), Appendices, p. A–18, which comments on Huynh Tan Phat.
27 *Working Paper*, Appendices, Item 12.
28 'Interrogation of a Viet Minh cadre who deserted in 1956 and turned himself in to South Vietnamese [i.e. RVN] authorities' and 'Report of an informant who was employed by the South Vietnamese [i.e. RVN] Security Service and in contact with a Viet Minh cadre from the Rach Gia area', *Working Paper*, Appendices, Items 16 and 25–A, respectively.
29 Ta Xuan Linh, *Vietnam Courier*, March 1974, p. 21.
30 *Working Paper*, Appendices, Item 30.
31 Interview with Phan The Ngoc, a party cadre who served in Cambodia at the time, RVN Ministry of Open Arms, Saigon, June 8, 1972; Voice of the Dai Viet National Liberation Troops, October 2, November 16, and 28, December 20, 1955; and Voice of the National Army (Saigon), Jan. 19, 1956.
32 Voice of the Dai Viet National Liberation Troops, November 2 and 12, 1955.
33 Vietnam Press (Saigon), 'Seizure of a Junk of Rice' and 'North Bound Junk Seized' in *The Times of Viet Nam*, April 21 and May 19, 1956, respectively.
34 US Department of State, Office of Intelligence Research, *Intelligence Brief* (February 7, 1956) in *United States–Vietnam Relations*, Book 10, p. 1049; and Voice of the Dai Viet National Liberation Troops, Nov. 16, and Dec. 6 and 20, 1955.

35   US Central Intelligence Agency, *Current Intelligence Weekly Review* (November 10, 1955) in *United States–Vietnam Relations*, Book 2, IV.A.5 Tab 3, p. 45.

36   Robert MacAlister, The Great Gamble: United States Policy Towards South Viet-Nam from July 1954 to July 1956, MA thesis, The University of Chicago, 1958, p. 122; and *Working Paper*, Appendices, Item 17.

37   US Central Intelligence Agency, *Probable Developments in North and South Vietnam Through Mid-1957*, National Intelligence Estimate (July 17, 1956), NIE No. 63–56 in *United States–Vietnam Relations*, Book 10, p. 1067.

38   US Central Intelligence Agency report from Singapore, CS-82270 (January 16, 1956) cited in *United States–Vietnam Relations*, Book 2, IV.A.5., Tab 3, pp. 48–49.

39   'Hanoi and the Insurgency in South Vietnam', *United States–Vietnam Relations*, Book 2, p. 49.

40   'Document purportedly issued by Lao Dong Party Central Committee for Guidance of Cadres in GVN [i.e. RVN] Zone', *Working Paper*, Appendices, Item 204.

41   'Translation of a document found on the person of a political officer with Communist forces in Zone 9 of the Western Interzone on Nov. 27, 1956', *Working Paper*, Appendices, Item 19 and Item 204.

42   The following paragraphs are based on *Working Paper*, Appendices, Item 31.

43   *Working Paper*, Appendices, Items 12 and 31; *Tinh Hinh Nam Bo*, p. 22.

44   'Communique of the Political Bureau of the Central Committee of the Viet-Nam Labor Party', Voice of Vietnam, March 31, 1956.

45   'Mot Su Kien Co Y Nghia Lon' [An Event of Great Significance], *Nhan Dan*, March 23, 1956.

46   'DRV propaganda suggested some expectation that new aid or economic agreements might result', US Central Intelligence Agency, *Probable Developments in North and South Vietnam Through Mid-1957*, p. 1071.

47   'Text of the Statement by Molotov at Meeting of United Nations General Assembly', *The New York Times*, Sept. 24, 1955.

48   ' "Happy Talk" in Indo-China,' *The Economist*, Oct. 15, 1955, p. 199.

49   Paul Kattenburg, 'Viet Nam and U.S. Diplomacy 1940–1970', *Orbis* (Fall 1971), XV, 3, pp. 822–823.

50   'Bao Cao cua Ho Chu Tich Truoc Quoc Hoi', [Speech by Chairman Ho before the National Assembly] *Nhan Dan*, Sept. 21, 1955.

51   US Central Intelligence Agency, *Probable Developments in North and South Vietnam Through Mid-1957*, p. 1069.

52   'Khrushchev's Twentieth Congress Speech', in G. F. Hudson, Richard Lowenthal and Roderick MacFarquhar, *The Sino-Soviet Dispute* (New York: Frederick A. Praeger, 1961), p. 43. The following quotations are taken from this source.

53   TASS, April 4, 1956 and 'Bai Noi cua Ho Chu Tich Trong Cuoc Mit Tinh cua Nhan Dan Hanoi Mung Doan Dai Bieu Chinh Phu Lien-Xo', [Text of Speech by Chairman Ho at a Meeting of the People of

Hanoi to Greet a Delegation of Soviet Government Representatives]
Nhan Dan, April 4, 1956.

54   'Bao Cao cua Dong Chi Truong Chinh o Hoi Nghi Trung Uong Lan
     Thu 9 mo rong (19–24.4.1956)', [Report by Comrade Truong Chinh
     at the 9th Enlarged Session of the Central Committee (19–24 April
     1956)] *Nhan Dan*, April 28, 1956. The following quotations are taken
     from this source. See also *Cuoc Khang Chien Chong My Cuu Nuoc*,
     pp. 15–18.

55   See the statement by a spokesman of the People's Army High Com-
     mand, Vietnam News Agency, Dec. 3, 1955.

56   These broadcasts were transcribed by the US Foreign Broadcast In-
     formation Service.

57   'Bao Cao cua Dong Chi Truong Chinh o Hoi Nghi Trung Uong Lan
     Thu 9 mo rong', op. cit.; unattributed quotations in the text are taken
     from this source.

58   People's Radio, Revolutionary Committee (Saigon), Sept. 27, 1955.

59   US Central Intelligence Agency, *Probable Developments in North and
     South Vietnam Through Mid-1957*, p. 1069.

60   'Lansdale Team's Report on Covert Saigon Mission '54 and '55', in
     Neil Sheehan, compiler, *The Pentagon Papers* (New York: Bantam
     Books, 1971), Document No. 15, pp. 53–66.

61   The list included the former commander of TRIM, the Commanding
     General of US Armed Forces in the Pacific, the Commander in Chief
     of the US Navy in the Pacific, the Secretary of the Army, the Chair-
     man of the Joint Chiefs of Staff, the Secretary of the Air Force, the
     Chief of Naval Operations and the Secretary of State.

62   Vietnam News Agency, Aug. 7, 1958. Various complaints were
     lodged by the PAVN High Command to the Central Joint Armistice
     Commission; see: Vietnam News Agency, Sept. 14, 1955. Vietnam
     News Agency, December 5, 1955 carries a PAVN protest to the Inter-
     national Commission.

63   'Nghi Quyet cua Hoi Nghi Ban Chap Hanh Trung Uong Dang Lao
     Dong Viet-Nam Lan Thu 9 (mo rong) (19–24.4.1956)', [Resolution of
     the 9th Enlarged Session of the Central Executive Committee of the
     Viet-Nam Workers' Party (19–24 April 1956)] *Nhan Dan* , April 27,
     1956. See also *Cuoc Khang Chien Chong My Cuu Nuoc*, p. 16.

64   According to US intelligence the portion of the speech in brackets
     was dropped from the 1956 text on publication in 1961/62 and the
     portion in italics added; see: US Central Intelligence Agency, *Central
     Intelligence Weekly Review* (May 10, 1956) in *United States–Vietnam
     Relations*, Book 2, IV.A.5 Tab 3, p. 47. For a copy of the speech as it
     was published in 1962 consult: Ho Chi Minh, *Selected Works* (Hanoi:
     Foreign Languages Publishing House, 1962), Vol. IV, pp. 153–156.

Chapter 4 Political struggle reaffirmed

1   'Saigon, Bastion of the Anti-US Struggle', *Vietnam Courier* (June
    1975), New Series, No. 37, p. 25.

2   US Department of State, *A Threat to Peace*, pp. 3–4.

3   *Tinh Hinh Phong Trao*, p. 15.

4   *Tinh Hinh Phong Trao*, p. 4. A retrospective account reveals that in
    June 1956 the Politburo issued a resolution entitled 'The Situation
    and Missions of the Revolution in the South' in response to requests
    for guidance. The resolution stressed the importance of consolidating
    the southern party organisation as 'a key, decisive task', building a
    strong mass base and forming a broad united front. See *Cuoc Khang
    Chien Chong My Cuu Nuoc*, pp. 16–17.
5   Data was gathered from *Journal d'Extreme-Orient* and Vietnam
    News Agency for the May–September 1956 period. See also *The
    Times* [London], June 25, 1956.
6   Great Britain, *Documents Relating to British Involvement in the Indo-
    China Conflict 1945–1965*, Cmnd. 2834, pp. 93–94.
7   Nutt, *Troika on Trial*, p. 356; and SarDesai, *Indian Foreign Policy*, p.
    98.
8   Nutt, *Troika on Trial*, p. 359.
9   Great Britain, *Vietnam and the Geneva Agreements: Documents Con-
    cerning The Discussion Between the Representatives of Her Majesty's
    Government and the Government of the Union of Soviet Socialist Re-
    publics Held in London in April and May 1956*, Vietnam No. 2 (1956)
    Command Paper, Cmd. 9763 (London: HMSO, May 1956), p. 4. See
    also dispatches from Singapore, Hong Kong, Moscow and London in
    The New York Times, July 21, 1955; Jan. 31; March 4; and May 11,
    1956.
10 Vietnam News Agency, April 27, 1956.
11 Vietnam News Agency, May 1, 1956.
12 US Central Intelligence Agency, *Probable Developments in North and
    South Vietnam Through Mid-1957*, pp. 1068 and 1071; Murti, *Viet-
    nam Divided*, pp. 176–177; and dispatch from London in *The New
    York Times*, May 11, 1956.
13 Great Britain, *Documents Relating to British Involvement in the Indo-
    China Conflict 1945–1965*, Cmnd. 2834, p. 96
14 US Central Intelligence Agency, *Probable Developments in North and
    South Vietnam Through Mid-1957*, p. 1068.
15 Vietnam News Agency, May 12, 1956.
16 Democratic Republic of Viet-Nam, *Documents Related to the Imple-
    mentation of the Geneva Agreements Concerning Viet-Nam* (Hanoi:
    Press and Information Department, Ministry of Foreign Affairs,
    1956), pp. 146–149.
17 Reuters dispatch from Peking in *The New York Times*, June 2, 1956.
18 Vietnam News Agency, July 16, 1956.
19 Vietnam News Agency, Aug. 14, 1956.
20 Vietnam News Agency, July 6, 1956.
21 Ho Chi Minh, 'Letter to the Cadres from South Vietnam Regrouped
    in the North,' *Selected Works*, Vol. IV, pp. 157–161; it was this letter,
    among other indications, which led US analysts to conclude that the
    DRVN had resigned itself to partition, see: *United States–Vietnam
    Relations*, Book 2, IV.A.5., Tab 3, pp. 24 and 47.
22 Vietnam News Agency, July 22, 1956; unattributed quotations in the
    text are taken from this source.
23 Lacouture, *Vietnam: Between Two Truces* (New York: Vintage Books,
    1966), p. 68.

24 Dispatch from Saigon in *The Observer*, January 15, 1956.
25 Voice of the Dai Viet National Liberation Troops, February 26, 1956.
26 Ambassadorial level talks between the United States and the People's Republic of China began in Geneva in August 1955.
27 This account is drawn from the following: Associated Press dispatches from Can Tho in *The New York Times*, June 12; Paris in ibid., July 5; and Saigon in ibid., July 10, 1956; Reuters dispatch from Saigon in ibid., July 13, 1956; and United Press dispatches from Saigon in ibid., May 26, and June 28, 1956.
28 This account is drawn from: *Journal d'Extreme-Orient*, August 14 and 27, 1956; Radio Hanoi, Aug. 24, 1956; and Voice of Vietnam, June 3, and September 11, 1956.
29 Cited by Robert Scigliano, *South Vietnam: Nation Under Stress* (Boston: Houghton Mifflin Company, 1964), p. 168.
30 The Committee listed 15 473 Communists as having been denounced, 5906 surrendered and 87 456 'who broke with the Party'; Committee for the Denunciation of Communist Subversive Activities, *Achievements of the Campaign of Denunciation of Communist Subversive Activities, First Phase* (Saigon: The People's Directive Committee for the National Congress of Denunciation of Communist Subversive Activities, May 1956), p. 116.
31 Vietnam News Agency, May 8, 1956. The figures are for the period July 1954–February 1956 and include, in addition to the ones cited in the text, 1563 persons killed and 4636 persons wounded by the RVN authorities in the course of the ACDC.
32 *The Fight Against the Subversive Communist Activities in Vietnam* (Saigon: Review Horizons Special Edition, 1956), p. 4.
33 John Osborne, *Life*, May 13, 1957, p. 166.
34 Cited in Kahin and Lewis, *The United States in Vietnam* , p. 100 and 121.
35 ibid., pp. 100–101 and Osborne, *Life*, May 13, 1957, p. 164–165.
36 This account is drawn from the following: Voice of the Armed Forces, May 10, 1956; *Tinh Hinh Nam Bo*, pp. 7 and 25; Vietnam Press, 'Cleanup Operation on the Plain of Camau', *The Times of Viet-Nam Weekly*, May 5 and 'Operation "Nguyen Hue" Ends', ibid., June 2, 1956; United Press dispatch from Saigon in *The New York Times*, Aug. 10, 1956; and *Journal d'Extreme-Orient*, Aug. 13, 23, and 29, 1956.
37 *Tinh Hinh Phong Trao*, p. 6.
38 US Central Intelligence Agency and National Security Council briefs of July 2nd and 19th, 1956 cited in *United States–Vietnam Relations*, Book 2, IV.A.5., Tab 3, p. 47, footnote 157.
39 Interview with Bui Cong Tuong, former chief of the training and propaganda section of the Long-Chau-Ha tri-province committee; Ministry of Open Arms, Saigon, June 9, 1972.
40 *Tinh Hinh Nam Bo*, p. 16. For the Politburo's view on the use of armed force at this time consult *Cuoc Khang Chien Chong My Cuu Nuoc*, pp. 16–17.
41 *Working Paper*, Appendices, Item 301, pp. 2–3.
42 United States Department of State, *A Threat to Peace*, p. 4.

43 'From the end of 1954 until 1956 most of the Party regional committee's plans, under a resolution of this period, did not change', *Tinh
Hinh Nam Bo*, p. 30.

44 'Nang Cao Chi Khi Phan Dau, Tich Cuc Cung Co Mien Bac Vung
Manh, Tiep Tuc Dau Tranh De Gianh Thong Nhat Nuoc Nha', [En-
hance the Will to Struggle, Actively Consolidate and Strengthen the
North, Continue the Struggle for the Realization of National Unity]
Nhan Dan, July 22, 1956. Unattributed quotations in the text are
from this source.

45 *Tinh Hinh Nam Bo*, p. 30.

46 Race, *War Comes to Long An*, p. 74.

47 'The July 1956 Situation Report submitted by the U.S. Army Attache
(Colonel L. B. Woodbury) in Saigon', *Working Paper*, Item 25–B.

48 US Central Intelligence Agency, *Probable Developments in North and
South Vietnam Through 1957*, p. 1077.

49 'U.S. Perceptions of the Insurgency, 1954–1960', in *United States–
Vietnam Relations*, Book 2, IV.A.S.Tab 4, p. 26.

50 *Tinh Hinh Nam Bo*, p. 30.

51 Republic of Vietnam, Ministry of National Defence, Joint General
Staff, J2, *Study of the Activation and Activities of R* (Saigon: Combined Documentation Exploitation Centre, 1969), No. 075/69, p. 18.

52 *Tinh Hinh Nam Bo*, p. 25.

53 Linh, op. cit., *Vietnam Courier* (March 1974), p. 22.

54 Le Duan's draft was prepared in August; *Cuoc Khang Chien Chong
My Cuu Nuoc*, p. 18. *Duong Loi Cach Mang Mien Nam* refers to the
recent US presidential elections.

55 See the discussion in the following chapter.

56 'Thu cua Ho Chu Tich Goi Dong Bao Nong Thon va Can Bo Nhan
Dip Cai Cach Ruong Dat o Mien Bac Can Ban Thanh Cong' [Letter
to Rural Compatriots and Cadres from President Ho on the Occasion
of the Basic Success of Land Reform in North Vietnam], *Nhan Dan*,
Aug. 18, 1956.

57 Ho addressed a National Day rally in Hanoi on September 2nd, while
Vo Nguyen Giap delivered an important speech on October 29th
1956.

58 'Thong Cao cua Hoi Nghi Lan Thu 10 (mo rong) cua Ban Chap Hanh
Trung Uong Dang Lao Dong Viet-Nam' [Communique of the 10th
enlarged Session of the Central Executive Committee of the Viet-
Nam Workers' Party], *Nhan Dan*, Oct. 30, 1956. Unattributed quotations in the text are taken from this source.

59 'Thong Cao cua Hoi Nghi Lan Thu 10 cua Ban Chap Hanh Trung
Uong Dang Lao Dong Viet-Nam Ve Viec Cu Lai Tong Bi Thu Ban
Chap Hanh Trung Uong' [Communique of the 10th Plenary Session
of the Central Executive Committee of the Vietnam Workers' Party
Concerning the Appointment of the Secretary General of the Central
Executive Committee], *Nhan Dan*, Oct. 30, 1956 and 'Thong Cao
Cua Hoi Nghi Lan Thu 10 cua Ban Chap Hanh Trung Uong Dang
Lao Dong Viet-Nam ve Viec Thi Hanh Ky Luat Doi Voi Nhung
Dong Chi Uy Vien Trung Uong Pham Sai Lam Trong Viec Chi Dao
Cong Tac Cai Cach Ruong Dat va Chinh Don To Chuc' [Communi-
que of the 10th Plenary Session of the Central Executive Committee

of the Vietnam Workers' Party Concerning Carrying Out Discipline Towards Comrade Members of the Central Committee for Mistakes in the Work of Carrying Out the Tasks of Agrarian Reform and Reorganization of Organizations] *Nhan Dan*, Oct. 30, 1956.

60 'Thong Cao cua Hoi Nghi Lan Thu 10 (mo rong) cua Ban Chap Hanh Trung Uong Dang Lao Dong Viet-Nam', loc. cit.

61 'Doan Ket Nhat Tri, Kien Quyet Chap Hanh Nghi Quyet Cua Hoi Nghi Trung Uong Lan Thu 10' [Unite Unanimously and Resolutely Implement the Resolutions of the 10th Session of the Central Committee], *Nhan Dan*, Oct. 30, 1956.

62 Mentioned in radio reports but not in the press; Voice of Vietnam, Nov. 2, 1956.

63 'Thong Cao Cua Hoi Nghi Uy Ban Trung Uong Mat Tran To Quoc Viet-Nam', [Communique of the Conference of the Central Committee of the Viet-Nam Fatherland Front], *Nhan Dan*, Nov. 3, 1956.

Chapter 5 Policy revision

1 *An Outline History of the Viet Nam Workers' Party*, p. 82.

2 See: Edwin E. Moise, *Land Reform in China and North Vietnam* (Chapel Hill: The University of North Carolina Press, 1983) and Christine P. White, Agrarian Reform and National Liberation in the Vietnamese Revolution: 1920–1957, unpublished Ph.D. thesis, Cornell University, 1981.

3 *An Outline History of the Viet Nam Workers' Party*, p. 83.

4 Edwin E. Moise, 'Land Reform and Land Reform Errors in North Vietnam', *Pacific Affairs* (Spring 1976), 49, 1, p. 78. Moise nevertheless acknowledges that the figure could range as high as 15 000. A former DRVN state employee who worked on economic affairs in the north at this time reports that the figure of 15 000 was mentioned in internal documents which he read. Conversation with Vo Nhan Tri, Singapore, Jan. 31, 1988.

5 'Nghi Quyet cua Hoi Dong Chinh Phu Ve May Chinh Sach Cu The De Sua Chua Sai Lam Ve Cai Cach Ruong Dat va Chinh Don To Chuc', [Resolution of the Council of Ministers Concerning Several Concrete Policies on the Rectification of Land Reform Errors and Readjustment of Organizations] *Nhan Dan*, Nov. 7, 1956.

6 Moise, *Pacific Affairs* (Spring 1976), 49, 1, pp. 85–87.

7 Bernard B. Fall, 'Crisis in North Vietnam', *Far Eastern Survey* (January 1957), XXVI, 1, pp. 12–15.

8 This account is based on: Vietnam Press dispatch from Quang Tri in *Journal d'Extreme-Orient*, Nov. 19, 1956; 'Tin Them Ve Vu Bon Phan Dong Gay Lon Xon O May Xa Thuoc Huyen Quynh-Luu (Nghe-An)', [Further Information About Reactionary Groups Causing Disturbances in the Villages of Quynh Luu district (Nghe An province)] *Nhan Dan*, Nov. 18, 1956; Voice of Vietnam in Vietnamese, Nov. 20, 1956; and dispatch from Ben Hai in *Journal d'Extreme Orient*, Nov. 20, 1956.

9 *The Quynh Luu Uprisings* (Saigon: Viet-Nam Chapter of the Asian People's Anti-Communist League, 1957), p. 16; and *Seventh Interim*

Report of the International Commission for Supervision and Control in Vietnam, August 1, 1956 to April 30, 1957 (London: HMSO, Dec. 1957), Cmnd. 335, p. 11.

10   Voice of Vietnam, November 20, 1956. Eyewitness accounts to these events stated that as many as 12 000 persons were involved in the confrontation with PAVN troops but that only a few were killed due to the crowd control technique of the army regulars, see: United Press dispatch from Saigon in *The Bangkok Post*, November 29, 1956. This report is based on refugee accounts and a briefing by the United States Information Service in Tourane (Da Nang); it tallies closely with the official version.

11   Voice of Vietnam, Nov. 21, 1956.

12   J. Price Gittinger, 'Communist Land Policy in North Vietnam', *Far Eastern Survey*, (Aug. 1959), XXVIII, 8, p. 120.

13   *Tram Hoa Dua No Tren Dat Bac* [The Blooming of the Hundred Flowers in North Vietnam] (Saigon: Mat Tran Bao Ve Tu Do Van Hoa, 1959); and Hoa Mai, editor, *The 'Nhan Van' Affair* (Saigon: Asian People's Anti-Communist League, 1958).

14   Hoa Mai, ed., *The 'Nhan Van' Affair*, pp. 38–41 and Nhu Phong, 'Intellectuals, Writers and Artists', in Honey, ed., *North Vietnam Today*, pp. 70–92. The titles translate Literary Works and Humanity, respectively. *Nhan Van* was a pun on the party's paper, *Nhan Dan* (People).

15   P. J. Honey, 'The Revolt of the Intellectuals in North Vietnam', *The World Today*, XIII, 6 (June 1957), pp. 250–260.

16   Hoang Van Chi, *From Colonialism to Communism* (New York: Popular Library, 1964), pp. 233–243.

17   Nhu Phong, in Honey, ed. *North Vietnam Today*, p. 82.

18   Vietnam News Agency, Dec. 14, 1956.

19   Nam Moc, 'A Few Observations on Our Literary Theory and Criticism during the Past Fifteen Years', *Nghien Cuu Van Hoc* [Literary Research] (October 1960) translated by US Joint Publications Research Service, Selected Translations on North Vietnam (May 18, 1961), No. 3, JPRS 8304.

20   Vietnam News Agency, Nov. 16, 1956.

21   There are other interpretations. Brian Shaw, 'China and North Vietnam: Two Revolutionary Paths', *Current Scene* [Hong Kong] (November 7, 1971), IX, 11, p. 4, suggests that instability in the north may have prompted China to consider intervention. Another view suggests Chou came to shore up the flagging fortunes of Truong Chinh's pro-China faction in Hanoi; see: Elizabeth Godfrey, The Emergence of a Communist State in Vietnam, MA thesis, Cornell University, 1962, pp. 69–72 and 85–86.

22   Vietnam News Agency, Nov. 19, 1956.

23   Vietnam News Agency, Nov. 21, 1956.

24   Mao Tse-tung, 'Opening Address at the 8th National Congress of the Communist Party of China', in *Eighth National Congress of the Communist Party of China* (Peking: Foreign Languages Press, 1956), Vol, I Documents, p. 10.

25   Mao Tse-tung, 'On the Ten Great Relationships', in Stuart Schram,

editor, *Mao Tse-tung Unrehearsed: Talks and Letters: 1956–1971* (Harmondsworth: Penguin Books, 1974), pp. 81–83.

26 Klaus Mehnert, *Peking and Moscow* (New York: Mentor, 1964), p. 372.

27 Vietnam News Agency, Nov. 22, 1956.

28 Fall, *The Two Viet-nams*, p. 189. According to Huynh Kim Khanh, Chou En-lai's visit was occasioned in part by difficulties in the relations between Chinese specialists serving the DRVN and their Vietnamese hosts. Professor Khanh bases his remarks on confidential conversations he has had with high-level DRVN officials passing through Singapore. Conversation with Huynh Kim Khanh, Singapore, Jan. 15, 1976.

29 Voice of Vietnam, Nov. 19, 1956.

30 ibid. In 1956, in a telegram sent to the VWP's Central Committee, the Central Committee of the CCP reportedly recommended 'setting a protracted ambush, building up forces, forming ties with the masses, and awaiting the opportune moment'; see: *Cuoc Khang Chien Chong My Cuu Nuoc*, p. 20.

31 Vietnam News Agency, Nov. 22, 1956.

32 Voice of Vietnam, Nov. 19, 1956.

33 The inclusion of PLA Marshal Ho Lung in Chou's delegation raises the possibility that military assistance may have been discussed.

34 'Tang Cuong Doan Ket, Nang Cao Tinh To Chuc Va Boi Duong Chi Khi Chien Dau Trong Toan Dang', [Reinforce Unity, Raise the Quality of Organization and Foster the Will to Struggle in the Party] *Hoc Tap* (November–December, 1956), No. 11, reprinted in *Nhan Dan*, Dec. 30, 1956. Henceforth referred to as 'Tang Cuong Doan Ket'.

35 The issue of reunification received extensive coverage; in addition to the reports by Pham Van Dong and Pham Hung, reports which touched upon the issue were also given by Ton Quang Phiet, Huynh Van Tieng, and Xuan Thuy. The National Assembly passed a resolution on reunification and also addressed an open letter to the people of the South.

36 Pham Hung, 'Dau Tranh Cho Thong Nhat Nuoc Nha', [The Struggle for National Unification], *Nhan Dan*, Jan. 6, 1957.

37 'Tang Cuong Doan Ket', *Nhan Dan*, Dec. 30, 1956. References in the text are taken from this source.

38 According to one account 'the situation was increasingly difficult. Most Party members had no confidence in political struggle and in the Party's policies. They wanted to activate armed forces and these forces had to be expanded. In some areas Party members automatically killed enemy spies and furnished the people with weapons to counter the enemy's terrorism. However there were only a few incidents due to the close control of the higher echelons', *Tinh Hinh Nam Bo*, p. 25.

39 'Tang Cuong Doan Ket', *Nhan Dan*, Dec.30, 1956.

40 'Dau Tranh Cho Thong Nhat Nuoc Nha,' *Nhan Dan*, Jan. 6, 1957.

41 Ho Chi Minh, 'Appeal Made After the Successful Conclusion of the Geneva Agreements (July 22, 1954)', in Bernard B. Fall, editor, *Ho Chi Minh On Revolution* (New York: Frederick A. Praeger, 1967), p.

271; these remarks were also cited by Pham Hung and Pham Van Dong in their reports to the National Assembly.

42 'Tang Cuong Doan Ket', *Nhan Dan*, Dec. 30, 1956.

43 'Dau Tranh Cho Thong Nhat Nuoc Nha', *Nhan Dan*, Jan. 6, 1957.

44 'Thong Cao Cua Hoi Nghi Lan Thu 11 (mo rong) Cua Ban Chap Hanh Trung Uong Dang Lao Dong Viet Nam', [Communique of the Eleventh Enlarged Plenary Session of the Central Executive Committee of the Viet-Nam Workers' Party], *Nhan Dan* Jan. 12, 1957.

45 'Tang Cuong Doan Ket', *Nhan Dan*, Dec. 30, 1956.

46 *Cuoc Khang Chien Chong My Cuu Nuoc*, p. 20.

47 *Working Paper*, Appendices, Item 301, p. 3.

48 Race, 'Origins', *Asian Survey* (May 1970). p. 355; Race, *War Comes to Long An*, pp. 81–84; and Ronald H. Spector, *Advice and Support: The Early Years of the US Army in Vietnam 1941–1960* (New York: The Free Press, 1985), p. 312.

49 Party historians in Hanoi have yet to release the official text of this document. The version used here was captured by RVN security officials in Long An province in March 1957. *Duong Loi Cach Mang Mien Nam* [The Line of the Revolution in the South], may be located in Jeffrey Race, compiler, *Vietnamese Materials* (Chicago: Center for Research Libraries, 1968), Microfilm Reel No. 1, Document No. 1002.

50 Notwithstanding the recently acquired atomic capacity of the Soviet Union, which is viewed here as contributing towards world peace.

51 The following points have been summarised by the author and represent a close paraphrase of the points made in *Duong Loi Cach Mang Mien Nam*.

52 Quotations in this and the following paragraphs are taken from Vietnam News Agency, January 2, 1957.

53 *Ban So Ket Hoc Tap ve Duong Loi Cach Mang Mien Nam*, [Preliminary Report on the Study of 'The Path of Revolution in the South'], p. 1. Race, compiler, *Vietnamese Materials*, Document 1002b.

54 'Dau Tranh Cho Thong Nhat Nuoc Nha,' op. cit.

55 US Central Intelligence Agency, The North Vietnamese Party Leadership (Langley, Virginia: typescript, 1972), p. 10 states that he probably remained in the south until mid-1957. Thomas Latimer, a former CIA analyst, states that no public reference to Le Duan was made until September 1957; Latimer, Hanoi's Leaders and their South Vietnam Policies, 1954–1968, Ph.D. thesis, Georgetown University, 1972, pp. 50–51.

Chapter 6 Domestic policies of the Diem regime

1 *Journal d'Extreme-Orient*, October 19, 1956.

2 *Journal d'Extreme-Orient*, October 3 and November 30, 1956.

3 *Journal d'Extreme-Orient*, January 4, 1957.

4 *Journal d'Extreme-Orient*, October 15, 1956.

5 *Journal d'Extreme-Orient*, April 17, 1957.

6 Race, *War Comes to Long An*, p. 97.

7 *The Fight Against the Subversive Communist Activities in Vietnam*, p. 4.

8   Linh, *Vietnam Courier* (March 1974), p. 22.
9   Vietnam News Agency, March 31 and May 25, 1958.
10   Vietnam News Agency, Feb. 27, 1957.
11   Voice of Vietnam, May 8, 1957 and Vietnam News Agency, June 10, 1957.
12   Voice of Vietnam, Aug. 22, 1957 and Vietnam News Agency, Nov. 26, 1957 and June 12, 1958.
13   Vietnam News Agency, March 20, 1958.
14   Vietnam News Agency, April 5, 1957.
15   Vietnam News Agency, April 7, 1958.
16   Vietnam News Agency, April 7, 1958.
17   William R. Andrews, *The Village War: Vietnamese Communist Revolutionary Activities in Dinh Tuong Province, 1960–1964* (Columbia: University of Missouri, 1973), p. 44 which reports that all 20 members of a village Party committee had been arrested by mid-1958; the fate of a financial cadre in Dinh Tuong is mentioned in Zasloff, *Origins of the Insurgency*, p. 13.
18   'Communist Cell for Subversion of Free Viet-Nam Press Discovered', *The Times of Viet-Nam*, March 21, 1958; 'Communist Ring Uncovered in Cai Be District', ibid., March 22, 1958; and Voice of Vietnam, June 26, 1958.
19   Zasloff, *Origins of the Insurgency*, p. 9 and P. J. Honey, 'The Problem of Democracy in Vietnam', *The World Today* (February 1960), 6,2, p. 73.
20   Georges Chaffard, *Indochine: dix ans d'independance* (Paris: Calmann-Levy, 1964), p. 168–169, cites RVN Ministry of Information figures of 48 200 arrested between 1954–60. Fox Butterfield, 'Origins of the Insurgency in South Vietnam', in Sheehan, compiler, *The Pentagon Papers*, p. 17, places the figure of detainees at over 50 000. The number held varied from year to year from a low of 15 000 to a high of 30 000.
21   'US Training of the Vietnamese National Army', *United States–Vietnam Relations*, Book 2, IV.A.4., p. 24.
22   John D. Montgomery, *The Politics of Foreign Aid: American Experience in Southeast Asia* (New York: Frederick A. Praeger, 1962), p. 73.
23   Bruce Russell, 'New Life Surges in the Highlands', *The Times of Viet-Nam*, July 14, 1959.
24   Dennis J. Duncanson, *Government and Revolution in Vietnam* (London: Oxford University Press, 1968), p. 247.
25   Bernard Fall has written, 'The mountain tribesmen of the vast plateau area which covers almost 65 percent of South Viet Nam were the subject of political and economic oppression which American experts as early as 1957 considered tantamount to genocide', Fall, 'Viet Nam in the Balance', *Foreign Affairs* (Oct. 1966), 5,1, p. 6.
26   Linh 'How Armed Struggle Began', *Vietnam Courier* (March 1974), p. 22.
27   Vietnam Press dispatch in *The Times of Viet Nam*, Oct. 1, 1957.
28   Vietnam Press, 'Dong Thap Muoi Land Development Zone Towards Full Prosperity', *The Times of Viet Nam*, April 9, 1958 and 'An

Xuyen–Ba Xuyen Land Development Area Develops Steadily', ibid., April 10, 1958.

29 Scigliano, *South Vietnam: Nation Under Stress,* p. 12.
30 R. Michael Pearce, Land Tenure and Political Authority: Changes in Land Attitudes and Land Relations in Vietnamese Villages of the Mekong Delta Since 1954, unpublished PhD thesis, the University of Washington, 1968, p. 108, fn. 6.
31 ibid., pp. 99–101 and Fall, *The Viet-Minh Regime,* pp. 119–138.
32 See footnote 6, Introduction.
33 Duncanson, *Government and Revolution,* p. 96.
34 Shaplen, *The Lost Revolution,* p. 144.
35 'This reversal of traditional roles was caused in part by the peasants' continued recognition of earlier "expropriation" by the Viet Minh of the land of absentees and "traitors". Entering into lease agreements would have validated the claim of ownership by landlords who had been thus "expropriated". Farmers would then have been forced to pay rent on land they felt was largely their own. Tenant reluctance was also a tribute to the continuing influence of Communist organization and propaganda. Viet Minh agents repeated incessantly in the villages that after the projected July 1956 elections, the South would come under the jurisdiction of the Democratic Republic of Viet Nam which would confirm earlier Communist expropriation of land.' David Wurfel, 'Agrarian Reform in the Republic of Vietnam', *Far Eastern Survey* (June 1957), XXVI,6, p.85.
36 John Mecklin, *Mission in Torment* (New York: Doubleday & Co., 1965), p. 86.
37 Warner, *The Last Confucian,* p. 140; James B. Hendry, *The Small World of Khanh Hau* (Chicago: Aldine Publishing Company, 1964), pp. 36–41; and Price Gittinger, 'Rent Reduction and Tenure Security in Free Vietnam', *Journal of Farm Economics* (May 1957), XXXIX, 2, p. 438. Robert L. Sansom, *The Economics of Insurgency in the Mekong Delta of Vietnam* (Cambridge: The MIT Press, 1970), p. 56 places the rent as high as 40 per cent.
38 Warner, *The Last Confucian,* p. 139.
39 Pearce, op. cit., PhD thesis, Uni. of Washington, 1968, p. 114.
40 ibid., p. 118.
41 Committee on Government Operations, House of Representatives, United States Congress, *Land Reform in Vietnam* (Washington: US Government Printing Office, 1968), 20th Report, 90th Congress, 2nd Session, p. 5 and Pearce, op. cit. PhD thesis, Uni. of Washington, p. 118.
42 Sansom, *The Economics of Insurgency,* p. 57.
43 Race, *War Comes to Long An,* p. 97–98.
44 Scigliano, *South Vietnam: Nation Under Stress,* pp. 111–112.
45 'U.S. Perceptions of the Insurgency', *United States–Vietnam Relations,* Book 2, IV.A.5. Tab 4, p. 37.
46 Duncanson, *Government and Revolution,* p. 284.
47 Scigliano, *South Vietnam: Nation Under Stress,* p. 111.
48 Duncanson, *Government and Revolution,* p. 277–282 and Edward R. Wright, *Barriers to Progress in South Vietnam: The United States Experience* (Seoul: Pomso Publishers, 1973).

49 Bernard B. Fall, 'Will South Viet Nam Be Next?' *The Nation* (May 31, 1958), p. 490 and Milton C. Taylor, 'South Viet-Nam: Lavish Aid, Limited Progress', *Pacific Affairs* (1961), XXXIV, 3, pp. 242–256.

50 Scigliano, *South Vietnam: Nation Under Stress*, p. 111.

51 ibid., p. 113.

52 ibid., p. 114.

53 Vu Quoc Thuc, 'National Planning in Vietnam', *Asian Survey* (September 1961), I, 7, p. 4.

54 Scigliano, *South Vietnam: Nation Under Stress*, p. 116 and 125 and Fall, *The Two Viet-Nams*, pp. 294–296.

55 Frank C. Child, *Essays on Economic Growth, Capital Formation, and Public Policy in Vietnam* (Saigon: Michigan State University Vietnam Advisory Group, May 1961), p. 133–134.

56 In responding to a request by Senator Mike Mansfield for information on MAAG, Lt. Gen. Williams, chief of MAAG in Viet-Nam, cabled a copy of his reply to the Office of the Secretary of Defense/International Security Affairs on May 20, 1960. Within the text of the cable the following appears: 'Following sentence classified CONFIDENTIAL: Change over of TERM excess to MAAG ends subterfuge as actually TERM has had undercover mission as logistical advisors since activation.' *United States–Vietnam Relations*, Book 10, V.B.3., pp. 1279–1280.

57 *Ninth Interim Report of the International Commission for Supervision and Control in Vietnam, May 1, 1958 to January 31 1959*, Vietnam No. 1, (1959) Cmnd. 726, (London: HMSO, May 1959), paragraph 31, p. 13.

58 *Eleventh Interim Report of the International Commission for Supervision and Control, February 1, 1960 to February 28, 1961*, Vietnam No. 1, (1961) Command Paper Cmnd. 1551, (London: HMSO, Nov. 1961), paragraph 49, p. 17.

59 Vietnam News Agency, April 7, 1958.

60 US Department of State, *Intelligence Report: The Outlook for North and South Vietnam*, No. 8008, (May 5, 1959), p. 9. In February 1957 an assassin unsuccessfully tried to kill Diem: 'Last News: President Diem Undisturbed By Fanatic's Shooting', *The Times of Viet Nam*, Feb. 23, 1957; Jacques Lefebvre, 'After the Ban Me Thuot Attempt', ibid. Feb. 25, 1957; and dispatch from Ban Me Thuot by Foster Hailey in *The New York Times*, February 23, 1957. There may have been a second attempt on President Diem's life by soldiers stationed at the Saigon airport, see Voice of Vietnam, Jan. 30, 1958.

61 Carver, 'The Faceless Viet Cong', *Foreign Affairs* (April 1966), 44, 3, p. 358–359.

Chapter 7 Maintaining and developing the struggle

1 *Tinh Hinh Nam Bo*, p. 32. See also *Cuoc Khang Chien Chong My Cuu Nuoc*, p. 11.

2 Republic of Viet-Nam, Ministry of National Defence, *Study of the Activation and Activities of R*, p. 17.

3   *Tinh Hinh Nam Bo*, p. 25 and Pearce, PhD thesis, Uni. of Washington, 1968, op. cit., pp. 138–139 reports on the classification of cadres into two groups.
4   ibid., p. 23.
5   ibid., p. 33.
6   See the publication by the Long An province committee, *Hoa Binh Thong Nhut* [Peace and Unification] (December 22, 1958), Nos. 39/40 in Race, compiler, *Vietnamese Materials*, Microfilm Reel No. I, document 1014.
7   Vietnam News Agency, September 10, 1957.
8   Vietnam News Agency, November 22, 1957; see also Wilfred G. Burchett, *Vietnam: Inside Story of the Guerilla War* (New York: International Publishers, 1968), pp. 178–179.
9   Xu Uy Nam Bo, *Chanh Sach Dien Dia* [Policy on Land] (October 1957), pp. 1–4 in Race, compiler, *Vietnamese Materials*, Microfilm Reel No. I, document 1005.
10 *Tinh Hinh Nam Bo*, p. 9.
11 ibid., p. 13.
12 Xu Uy Nam Bo, op. cit., in Race, *Vietnamese Materials* document 1005.
13 Samuel Popkin, 'South Vietnam: Villages Under Diem', in Steven Spiegel and Kenneth Waltz, eds., *Conflict in World Politics* (Cambridge, Massachusetts: Winthrop Pub. Inc., 1971), pp. 267–268.
14 Ton Vy, 'The Workers' Struggle', *Vietnamese Studies* (1966), No. 8, p. 80.
15 Voice of Vietnam, July 21, 1957.
16 Fall, *The Two Viet-Nams*, p. 331.
17 Jeffrey Race, 'How They Won', *Asian Survey* (Aug. 1970), X, 8, pp. 640–641.
18 Vu Can, *Vietnamese Studies* 1968, pp. 55–129 and To Minh Trung, 'The Students' and Pupils' Struggle', ibid. (1966), No. 8, p. 112–180.
19 Ton Vy, 'The Workers' Struggle', op. cit., p. 94 and 'Saigon: Bastion of the Anti-US Struggle', *Vietnam Courier* (June 1975), New Series No. 37, p. 25. The Vietnam News Agency, Jan. 16, 1958, reported that over 200 struggles took place between January and November in 1957.
20 Ton Vy, 'The Workers' Struggle', op. cit., p. 96.
21 'Cong Ham Cua Thu Tuong Chanh Phu Nuoc Viet Nam Dan Chu Cong Hoa Goi Tong Thong Cong Hoa Viet Nam' [A Diplomatic Note from the Premier of the Democratic Republic of Viet-Nam to the President of the Republic of Viet-Nam] (December 22, 1958) reprinted by the Long An province committee; in Race, compiler, *Vietnamese Materials*, Microfilm Reel I, document 1013.
22 Cited by Robert Scigliano, *South Vietnam: Nation Under Stress*, p. 138.
23 Race, 'Origins', *Asian Survey* (May 1970), p. 371.
24 *Tinh Hinh Nam Bo*, p. 9.
25 ibid., p. 33.
26 ibid., pp. 19 and 23.
27 Ton Vy, op. cit., *Vietnamese Studies* (1966), p. 95.

28 Ta Xuan Linh, 'How Armed Struggle Began', *Vietnam Courier*, (March 1974), p. 21.

29 Vietnam News Agency, Dec. 15, 1956.

30 Viet Hong, 'Vai Net Ve Dau Tranh Vo Trang Va Luc Luong Vo Trang o Nam Bo Truoc Cuoc Dong Khoi 1959–1960', [The Armed Struggle and the Armed Forces in Nam Bo Before the 1959–60 General Uprising] *Nghien Cuu Lich Su* (March–April 1974), No. 155, p. 43 and Hiliare du Berrier, 'Report from Saigon', *American Mercury* (Sept. 1958), 87, 416, pp. 43–51.

31 du Berrier, op. cit., *American Mercury* (Sept. 1958), p. 47.

32 Wilfred G. Burchett, *Vietnam Will Win!* (New York: Monthly Review Press, 1970), p. 120.

33 US Department of State, *Nature and Extent of the Communist Subversive Threat to the Protocol States of Vietnam, Cambodia and Laos* (April 3, 1958) in *United States–Vietnam Relations*, Book 2, IV.A.5. Tab 4, p. 18.

34 du Berrier, op. cit., *American Mercury* (Sept. 1958), p. 50.

35 These designations are mentioned in: Bo Tu Lenh Giai Phong Quan Viet Nam [High Command of the Vietnam Liberation Army], Tai Lieu Quan Nhu Tai Chanh Nam 1957 [Document on Military Supplies and Finance for the Year 1957] (May 19, 1957), pp. 1–4 and 'Hanh Chanh Giai Phong Khu Vuc' [Administration—Special Liberated Zone] Chi Thi So 17/CTKV [Directive No. 17/CTKV] in Race, *Vietnamese Materials*, Microfilm Reel I, documents 1006 and 1007. Republic of Vietnam, *Violations of the Geneva Agreements by the Viet-Minh Communists* (Saigon, July 1959), p. 20 refers to Army of National Liberation.

36 Vietnam News Agency, March 9, 1957.

37 Vietnam News Agency, April 13, 1957.

38 Ta Xuan Linh, 'How Armed Struggle Began', *Vietnam Courier* (March 1974), p. 23; Viet Hong, op. cit., *Nghien Cuu Lich Su* (March–April, 1974), pp. 47–48. These were later referred to as 'appropriately scaled attacks'; *Cuoc Khang Chien Chong My Cuu Nuoc*, p. 23.

39 Dispatch by Greg MacGregor from Saigon in *The New York Times*, October 23, 1957.

40 'A Large Group of Pirates Attack and Destroy French Rubber Plantation North of Saigon', *The Times of Viet Nam*, Jan. 7, 1958 and 'While Viet Nam Battalions Track Down Minh Thuan [sic] Intruders In Dense Jungle, Work Resumes on Raided Rubber Plantation', ibid., Jan. 9, 1958.

41 '38 Killed, As Pirates Attack Rubber Plantation', *The Times of Viet Nam*, Aug. 12, 1958; Associated Press dispatch from Saigon in *The New York Times*, Aug. 12, 1958; and UPI dispatch from Dau Tieng in ibid., Aug. 18, 1958. See also *Cuoc Khang Chien Chong My Cuu Nuoc*, p. 25.

42 Commission for Foreign Relations of the South Vietnam National Front for Liberation, *Personalities of the South Vietnam Liberation Movement*, (1963) p. 29. Mon later became a member of the NFLSVN's Central Committee.

43   US Central Intelligence Agency, *Prospects for North and South Viet-nam*, National Intelligence Estimate 63–59 (May 26, 1959) in *United States–Vietnam Relations, 1945–1967*, Book 10, p. 1193.

44   Ta Xuan Linh, 'How Armed Struggle Began', *Vietnam Courier* (March 1974), p. 21.

45   'U.S. Perceptions of the Insurgency, 1954–1960', in *United States–Vietnam Relations, 1945–1967*, p. 26.

46   Republic of Vietnam, Ministry of National Defence, *Study of the Activation and Activities of R*, p. 47.

47   *Cuoc Khang Chien Chong My Cuu Nuoc*, p. 22.

48   *Tinh Hinh Nam Bo*, p. 37; *Tai Lieu Quan Nhu Tai Chanh Nam 1957*, in Race, *Vietnamese Materials*, Microfilm Reel 1, outlines the financial burdens of maintaining these forces.

49   'As far as the Viet-Minh arms and munitions are concerned, the national authorities, from September 1954 to June 1959, discovered 3561 dumps of arms and munitions of which 303 of the most important . . . have been brought to the attention of the International Commission for Supervision and Control'. Republic of Vietnam, *Violations of the Geneva Agreements by the Viet-Minh Communists* (July 1959), pp. 20–21.

50   Ta Xuan Linh, 'How Armed Struggle Began', *Vietnam Courier* (March 1974), p. 23.

51   ibid. See also *Cuoc Khang Chien Chong My Cuu Nuoc*, p. 24.

52   Race, *War Comes to Long An*, pp. 82–83.

53   Bernard B. Fall, 'South Vietnam's Internal Problems', *Pacific Affairs* (Sept. 1958), XXXI, 3, pp. 241–260.

54   Montgomery, *The Politics of Foreign Aid*, p. 40 and Robert F. Turner, *Vietnamese Communism: Its Origins and Development* (Stanford: Hoover Institution Press, 1975), pp. 174–176.

55   Race, 'Origins', op. cit., *Asian Survey* (May 1970) p. 369.

56   Fall, 'South Viet-Nam's Internal Problems', *Pacific Affairs* (Sept. 1958) p. 257.

57   Ta Xuyen Linh, 'How Armed Struggle Began', *Vietnam Courier* (March 1974) p. 22.

58   Sheehan, compiler, *The Pentagon Papers*, p. 75 cites a figure of 75 killed and kidnapped; Buttinger, *A Dragon Embattled*, Vol. 2, p. 982, cites RVN sources for the figure of 700.

59   Special Report on Current Internal Security Situation, cable from the American Embassy in Saigon to the Department of State (March 7, 1960), in *United States–Vietnam Relations*, Book 10, p. 1273.

60   Republic of Vietnam, *Violations of the Geneva Agreements by the Viet-Minh Communists*, p. 108. According to Sao Nam, a Party cadre, 'At first, the [RVN] agents took little notice, actually stepped up their terror. Our group would pay another visit, usually with two variants of hand-written leaflets. On one was written the biography and crimes of the local agents and the death sentence by the local organ of the People's Self-Defence Force; the other was similar except it contained a pardon with a warning not to commit any more crimes. If we found the chief agent at home, we executed him, leaving the execution slip with the body and posting up a few copies. For the others, and for the chief agent in case he happened to be away, we

posted up the pardon and warnings'. Burchett, *Vietnam: Inside Story of the Guerilla War*, p. 147.

61 Viet Nam Cong Hoa, *Bang Ke Khai Tong So Can Bo va Thuong Dan Viet Nam Cong Hoa Bi Cong San Bat Ciu Ke Tu 1954* [List of Civil Servants, Cadres and Civilians of the Republic of Viet Nam Abducted by the Communists Since 1954] (Saigon: Co So An Luat Trung Uong Phu Tong Uy Dan Van, March 23, 1973); these figures were tabulated from a list which included details on cases from 1954–1973. The yearly breakdown is as follows: 1954 (72); 1955 (15); 1956 (11); 1957 (9); 1958 (19); 1959 (25) and 1960 (69). The absence of data for certain provinces indicates that the figures may be incomplete.

62 United States Mission in Vietnam, *A Study—Viet Cong Use of Terror* (Saigon: May 1966), pp. 7–8.

63 Modelski, in Black, C. E. and Thornton, T. P., eds., *Communism and Revolution*, op. cit., p. 198, footnote 36.

64 Scigliano, *South Vietnam: Nation Under Stress*, p. 138.

65 Ta Xuan Linh, 'Armed Uprising by Ethnic Minorities Along the Truong Son', Part I, *Vietnam Courier* (Sept. 1974), New Series No. 28, p. 18. See also *Cuoc Khang Chien Chong My Cuu Nuoc*, pp. 25–26.

66 Republic of Vietnam, Ministry of National Defence, *Study of the Activation and Activities of R*, p. 22.

67 Ta Xuan Linh, 'Armed Uprising', Part I, *Vietnam Courier* (Sept. 1974), p. 19.

68 Ta Xuan Linh, 'Armed Uprisings by Ethnic Minorities Along the Truong Son', Part 2, *Vietnam Courier* (Oct. 1974), New Series No. 29, p. 18; Burchett, *Vietnam Will Win!*, pp. 144–145; and Montgomery, *The Politics of Foreign Aid*, p. 78.

69 Ta Xuan Linh, 'Armed Uprisings', Part II, *Vietnam Courier* (Oct. 1974), p. 18.

70 Burchett, *Vietnam Will Win!*, p. 116.

71 Ta Xuan Linh, 'Armed Uprisings' Part II, p. 19. The following paragraph is also drawn from this source.

72 ibid. The following quotation is also from this source. See also *Cuoc Khang Chien Chong My Cuu Nuoc*, pp. 25–26.

73 Wilfred G. Burchett, *The Furtive War: The United States in Vietnam and Laos* (New York: International Publishers, 1963), p. 125.

74 Race, 'Origins' *Asian Survey* (May 1970) p. 372 and 376.

75 Warner, *The Last Confucian*, p. 143. US Central Intelligence Agency, *Probable Developments in North and South Vietnam Through Mid-1957*, National Intelligence Estimate, (July 17, 1959), p. 1077; and MAAG–Vietnam, Country Statement on MDAP, Non-NATO Countries (Jan. 1957) in *United States–Vietnam Relations*, Book 2, IV.A.5 Tab 4, p. 16.

76 *Tinh Hinh Nam Bo*, p. 19.

77 Race, 'Origins', op. cit., *Asian Survey* (May 1970), p. 371.

78 *Tinh Hinh Nam Bo*, p. 37.

79 Ton Vy, op. cit., *Vietnamese Studies* (1966), p. 86.

80 Ta Xuan Linh, 'Armed Uprisings' Part II, *Vietnam Courier* (Oct. 1974), p. 19.

81   US Central Intelligence Agency, *Memorandum: The Organization, Activities, and Objectives of the Communist Front in South Vietnam* (Sept. 22, 1965), p. 2.
82   Ta Xuan Linh, 'How Armed Struggle Began' *Vietnam Courier* (March 1974), p. 23.
83   Republic of Vietnam, Ministry of Foreign Affairs, *Infiltration of Communist Armed Elements and Clandestine Introduction of Arms From North to South Vietnam* (Saigon: June 1967), pp. 8 and 34.
84   Vietnam News Agency, March 19, 1959 and *We Open the File* (Hanoi: Foreign Languages Publishing House, 1961), p. 71.
85   Interview with Phan The Ngoc, a member of the My Tho province committee specialising in 'arts and letters' (uy vien ban van nghe) who accompanied Le Duan as an escort officer during part of this trip in late 1958. Ministry of Open Arms, Saigon, June 8, 1972. Carver, op. cit., *Foreign Affairs* (April 1966) p. 359.

Chapter 8 Consolidating the north

1   Voice of Vietnam, March 4, 1957 Unattributed quotations in the following paragraphs are taken from this source.
2   Hanoi Radio, May 26, 1957.
3   Vietnam News Agency, April 23, 1957.
4   Voice of Vietnam, April 30, 1957.
5   *Nhan Dan*, January 27, 1957.
6   Vietnam News Agency, March 1, 1957.
7   Vietnam News Agency, May 12, 1957. Voroshilov's visit was a state, not party, visit.
8   Dispatch by Russell Baker from Washington in *The New York Times*, May 9, 1957.
9   Dispatch from Moscow in *The New York Times*, May 26, 1957, which cites a commentary by *Izvestia*.
10   Donald S. Zagoria, *Vietnam Triangle: Moscow/Peking/Hanoi* (New York: Pegasus, 1967), p. 102.
11   This is suggested by the inclusion of the Soviet Minister for Higher Education in the delegation and the visit to Hanoi Central University by Voroshilov and Ho.
12   TASS (Moscow), May 20, 1957; this passage was singled out by the VNA for special emphasis, Vietnam News Agency, May 21, 1957.
13   TASS (Moscow), May 21, 1957.
14   Herbert Feith, 'Indonesia', in George McT. Kahin, editor, *Governments and Politics of Southeast Asia* (Ithaca: Cornell University Press, 1964), pp. 205–209 and Leslie Palmer, *Communists in Indonesia: Power Pursued in Vain* (Garden City, New York: Anchor Press-Doubleday, 1973), pp. 180–181.
15   Hinton, *Communist China in World Politics*, op. cit., p. 32.
16   Vietnam News Agency, September 18, 1957; AP dispatch in *The Times of Viet Nam*, December 11, 1958 and 'Hanoi and the Insurgency in South Vietnam', in *United States–Vietnam Relations*, Book 2, IV.A.5. Tab. 3, p. 50.
17   This was alluded to by Ton Duc Thang who was quoted as observing that Voroshilov's visit would also contribute to the further strengthening of the socialist system; Vietnam News Agency, May 12, 1957.

18 Documentation for this section may be found in Carlyle A. Thayer, *The Origins of the National Front for the Liberation of South Vietnam*, unpublished Ph.D. thesis, The Australian National University, 1977, pp. 576–595.

19 ibid., Table 9–3, p. 578.

20 Yugoslavia was represented by its Under Secretary for Foreign Affairs, all other delegations sent their Foreign Affairs ministers. Vietnam News Agency, Sept. 1, 1957.

21 Vietnam News Agency, March 20, and Oct. 9, 1957; and Associated Press dispatch from Hong Kong in *The New York Times,* March 31, 1957.

22 Vietnam News Agency, Oct. 19, 1957.

23 'Ho's Travels', *The Economist,* July 27, 1957, p. 300; Associated Press dispatch from Berlin in *The New York Times*, July 29, 1957; and Vietnam News Agency, August 15, 1957. Other press accounts of Ho's visit raised the possibility that he might mediate between Albania and Yugoslavia; dispatch by Harrison E. Salisbury from Belgrade in *The New York Times*, August 6, 1957 and United Press dispatch from Belgrade in ibid., August 10, 1957.

24 Thayer, op. cit., unpublished Ph.D. thesis, The Australian National University, 1977, pp. 586–588, especially Table 9–4.

25 *President Ho Chi Minh's Visit to the Republic of India and the Union of Burma, February 4th–17th, 1958, Official Documents* (Hanoi: Foreign Languages Publishing House, 1958).

26 Dispatch from New Delhi in *The New York Times,* Feb. 6, 1958, reports that Ho received precisely the same welcome accorded Diem.

27 SarDesai, *Indian Foreign Policy,* pp. 111–112.

28 Thayer, Ph.D thesis, op.cit., Table 9–6, p. 592.

29 Dispatch from Hong Kong in *The New York Times*, Aug. 1, 1957 and Vietnam News Agency, April 1, 1958.

30 Vietnam News Agency, March 13 and Dec. 30, 1958.

31 Voice of Vietnam, June 30, 1957.

32 Voice of Vietnam, September 5, 1957.

33 Vietnam News Agency, Aug. 28, 1957.

34 ibid.

35 *An Outline History of the Viet Nam Workers' Party,* pp. 84–85.

36 The speech was carried in two instalments by Vietnam News Agency on September 13 and 14, 1957. Unattributed quotations in the following paragraphs are taken from this source.

37 Voice of Vietnam, Sept. 24, 1957

38 'The Origin and Development of the Differences Between the Leadership of the CPSU and Ourselves', in *The Polemic on the General Line of the International Communist Movement* (Peking: Foreign Languages Press, 1965), pp. 59–60.

39 ibid., pp. 64–65.

40 Donald S. Zagoria, *The Sino-Soviet Conflict, 1956–1961* (New York: Atheneum, 1964), p. 62.

41 David Floyd, *Mao Against Khrushchev* (New York: Frederick A. Praeger, 1964), p. 50.

42 The text of this document may be found in *The Polemic on the General Line of the International Communist Moverment*, pp. 105–108.

43 ibid., pp. 71–72.

44 Vietnam News Agency, October 28, 1957. A separate 25-member delegation led by Hoang Quoc Viet attended the celebrations marking the 40th anniversary of the October Revolution.

45 Latimer, op. cit., Ph.D. thesis, Georgetown University, 1972, pp. 53–54.

46 TASS (Moscow), Nov. 23, 1957

47 Voice of Vietnam, Dec. 5, 1957.

48 The communique was published three months later. 'Thong Cao cua Hoi Nghi Lan Thu 13 (mo rong) Cua Ban Chap Hanh Trung Uong Dang Lao Dong Viet Nam', [Communique of the Thirteenth (enlarged) Plenum of the Central Committee of the Viet Nam Workers' Party], *Nhan Dan*, March 23, 1958.

49 'Hanoi and the Insurgency in South Vietnam', in *United States–Vietnam Relations*, Book 2, IV.A.5. Tab 3, p. 52. The author was General Paul Gorman.

50 Vietnam News Agency, Jan. 1, 1958.

51 Vietnam News Agency, April 17, 1958. Unattributed quotations in the following paragraphs are from this source.

52 Vietnam News Agency, Oct. 24, 1958.

53 Vietnam News Agency, June 23, 1958 reports that the VWP delegation was led by Politburo member Nguyen Duy Trinh, a specialist on foreign aid and economic affairs.

54 Cameron, in Duncan, W.R. ed., *Soviet Policy in Developing Countries*, p. 199.

55 *An Outline History of the Viet Nam Workers' Party*, p. 90 and Vietnam News Agency, April 17, 1958.

56 Vietnam News Agency, May 8, 1958 and Associated Press dispatch from Washington in *The New York Times*, July 1, 1955.

57 Voice of Vietnam, March 26 and June 27, 1958.

58 Nhu Phong, in Honey ed. *North Vietnam Today*, pp. 84–89; Vietnam News Agency, April 15, 1958; Reuters dispatch from Saigon, April 22, 1958; and Voice of Vietnam, July 10, 1958.

59 An RLG delegation visited the DRVN in 1957 to discuss border problems and the withdrawal of military forces from the frontier, see: Vietnam News Agency, Oct. 4, 1957 and Reuters dispatch from Hong Kong in *The New York Times,* Sept. 23, 1957. A DRVN delegation attended celebrations in Phnom Penh marking the anniversary of Buddha's birth; Vietnam News Agency, May 23, 1957. Later in the year Cambodia and the DRVN held talks on the status of Vietnamese residents of Cambodia; Vietnam News Agency, Nov. 2, 1957.

60 Vietnam News Agency, June 12, 1957 and Associated Press dispatch from Saigon in *The New York Times*, June 13, 1956.

61 Vietnam News Agency, June 25, and Aug. 11, 1957, Jan. 30, 1958; and Voice of Vietnam, Sept. 24, 1957.

62 Vietnam News Agency, July 24, 1957 and Tillman Durdin dispatch from Hong Kong in *The New York Times*, July 21, 1958.

63 Vietnam News Agency, March 9, 1958.

64 New China News Agency (Peking), March 8 and March 9, 1958; and Radio Moscow, March 10, 1958.

65 Vietnam News Agency, May 8, 1958.

66 Vietnam News Agency, April 25 and 26, 1958, June 10, 1958
67 Vietnam News Agency, July 8, 23, and 31, 1958.
68 Vietnam News Agency, Dec. 26, 1958 and Hong Kong dispatch in *The New York Times*, Dec. 27, 1958.
69 Vietnam News Agency, March 19 and 20, 1958. March 19 was the anniversary of a 1950 public protest at the arrival in Saigon of American warships in support of the French.
70 Vietnam News Agency, June 9, 1958.
71 Voice of Vietnam, July 21, 1958 and Vietnam News Agency, July 23, 1958.
72 Voice of Vietnam, Sept. 10, 1958.
73 Vietnam News Agency, March 21, and Nov. 23, 1958; Hanoi Radio, May 28, 1958 and *The Times of Viet Nam*, Aug. 1, 1958.
74 Associate Press dispatch from Saigon in *The New York Times*, May 30, 1958.

Chapter 9 Founding the NFLSVN

1 Hinton, *Communist China in World Politics*, p. 266.
2 Associated Press dispatch in *The Times of Viet Nam*, April 2, 1958; 'Full Translation of the Government Communique,' in ibid., June 27, 1958; Reuters dispatch from Saigon in *The New York Times*, June 5, 1958; Associated Press dispatch in ibid., June 26, 1958; Reuters dispatch from Phnom Penh in ibid., July 1, 1958; and Tillman Durdin dispatch in ibid., July 2, 1958.
3 'Hoi Nghi Trung Uong Dang Lan Thu 14 Thao Luan Va Quyet Dinh Nhiem Vu Cai Tao Xa Hoi Chu Nghia Va Nhung Muc Tieu Phan Dau Cua Ke Hoach Ba Nam Phat Trien Xinh Te Va Van Hoa,' [The 14th Plenum of the Party's Central Committee Discussed and Resolved the Tasks of Socialist Construction and the Objectives of the Three-Year Plan of Economic and Cultural Development], *Nhan Dan*, Dec. 8, 1958.
4 *An Outline History of the Viet Nam Workers' Party*, p. 88.
5 Nguyen Duy Trinh, 'Economic and Cultural Development', in *The Problems Facing the Democratic Republic of Viet Nam in 1961* (Hanoi: Foreign Languages Publishing House, n.d.), pp. 9–10.
6 *An Outline History of the Viet Nam Workers' Party*, pp. 87–88.
7 'Hanoi and the Insurgency in South Vietnam', in *United States–Vietnam Relations*, Book 2, IV.A.5. Tab 3, p. 55, footnote 185.
8 Honey, 'The Problem of Democracy in Vietnam,' *The World Today* (Feb. 1960) op. cit., pp. 74–77; Lacouture, *Vietnam: Between Two Truces*, p. 29; and Republic of Viet Nam, *Violations of the Geneva Agreements by the Viet-Minh Communists*, pp. 106–108.
9 Vietnam News Agency, January 18, 1959; and *New Facts: Phu Loi Mass Murder in South Viet Nam* (Hanoi: Foreign Languages Publishing House, 1959) and *The Phu Loi Massacre in South Vietnam* (Hanoi: Foreign Languages Publishing House, 1959).
10 Race, 'Origins', *Asian Survey* (May 1970), p. 376.
11 *An Outline History of the Viet Nam Workers' Party*, pp. 108–109.

12   Carver, op. cit., *Foreign Affairs* (April 1966), pp. 359–360.

13   *Tinh Hinh Nam Bo*, p. 26.

14   ibid., pp 34 and 36. For a copy of the law see: Pham Van Bach, et al., *Fascist Terror in South Viet-Nam: Law 10/59* (Hanoi: Foreign Languages Publishing House, 1961), pp. 71–77. Warner, *The Last Confucian*, pp. 109–110, has written: '[d]uring the first year that the law operated, the tribunals investigated 431 incidents and tried 25 cases involving 131 accused, 27 were sentenced to death, 50 to life imprisonment, or 20 years, 47 to 10 years, and 7 others were acquitted.'

15   *Working Paper*, Appendices, Item 301, p. 10.

16   Ta Xuan Linh, 'Armed Uprising', Part II, *Vietnam Courier* (Oct. 1974), p. 20.

17   'Interrogation of a Senior Sergeant, a member of the Viet Cong [i.e., VWP] 5th Military Region,' *Working Paper*, Appendices, Item 73, p. 1; and 'Interrogation of a member of the 603rd Battalion, who was captured in Quang Ngai Province in 1960, and the interrogation of the commander of a company who was also captured in Quang Ngai Province in 1960', ibid., Item 72. According to Van Tien Dung, 'The 559th Troops, as their name indicates, came into being in May 1959 and are subordinate to the Rear Service General Department.' *Nhan Dan*, April 6, 1976. See also *Cuoc Khang Chien Chong My Cuu Nuoc*, pp. 30–31.

18   *Cuoc Khang Chien Chong My Cuu Nuoc*, p. 32. 'Interrogation reports of Viet Cong [i.e. VWP] agents dispatched by the maritime infiltration unit of Hanoi's Intelligence Directorate. The unnamed individuals were captured aboard a junk in July 1960', *Working Paper*, Item 75; and 'An intelligence summary on the interrogation of numerous Viet Cong [sic] agents captured along the coast of South Vietnam during June and July 1961', ibid., Item 76.

19   US Department of State, *Working Paper on the North Vietnamese Role in the War in South Vietnam*, reproduced in *Viet-Nam Documents and Research Notes* (June 1968), Nos. 36–37, Table I, p. 19.

20   US Department of State, *A Threat to Peace*, Part I, p. 13.

21   Ta Xuan Linh, 'Armed Uprisings', Part II, *Vietnam Courier* (Oct. 1974), p. 19. One group was named "339" after the date of its founding, March 3, 1959.

22   Ta Xuan Linh, Nguyen Ho and Nguyen Khanh Tuong, 'Cuoc Dong Khoi Tra Bong (28–8–1959)', [The Tra Bong Uprising of August 28, 1959], *Nghien Cuu Lich Su* (May–June 1971), No. 138, pp. 12–27. See also *Cuoc Khang Chien Chong My Cuu Nuoc*, p. 34.

23   Warner, *The Last Confucian*, pp. 159–160.

24   Charles W. Thayer, *Guerrilla* (London: Michael Joseph Ltd., 1963), pp. 25–29; and *Tinh Hinh Nam Bo*, p. 38. See also: *Cuoc Khang Chien Chong My Cuu Nuoc*, pp. 39–40.

25   An Bao Minh, 'Uprising in Ben Tre', *Vietnamese Studies*, (September 1968), Nos. 18/19, pp. 130–50; and An Bao Minh, 'Simultaneous Uprisings', *South Viet Nam in Struggle* (May 20, 1974), No. 249, p. 3. *No Other Road to Take: Memoir of Mrs. Nguyen Thi Dinh*, trans. Elliot, M. V., Southeast Asia Program Data Paper No. 102, Ithaca: Department of Asian Studies, Cornell University, June 1976.

26 'Tuyen Bo cua Nhung Nguoi Khang Chien Cu Ve Tinh Hinh Mien Nam Viet Nam' [Declaration of Former Members of the Resistance Concerning the Situation in South Viet-Nam] in Race, compiler, *Vietnamese Materials*, Microfilm Reel I, Document No. 1041. Burchett, *Vietnam: Inside Story of the Guerilla War*, p. 186; and Race, *War Comes to Long An*, pp. 120–121.

27 Le Duan, 'Political Report of the Central Committee of the Viet Nam Workers' Party (September 5, 1960)', in *Third National Congress of the Viet Nam Workers' Party, Documents*, (Hanoi: Foreign Languages Publishing House, 1961), Volume I, pp. 62–63.

28 Bernard B. Fall, 'The Roots of the Conflict', *International Affairs* [London] (January 1965), XL, 1 reprinted in Fall, ed., *Viet-Nam Witness*, p. 283. For details of this organisation-building period see the accounts by various Party cadres who were active in the 1959–60 period: Z-ZH Interviews, Nos. 41, 65, 117, 124, 127, 128, and 130 in Rand Vietnam Interview Series Z—Viet Cong Organization and Motivation and Experiences of Its Members, (Alexandria, Virginia: Defense Documentation Station for Scientific and Technical Information, March 1972), 2 Microfilm Reels; and Burchett, *Vietnam Will Win!*, p. 121.

29 Fall, *The Two Viet-Nams*, p. 362. See also: Z-ZH Interview No. 128, p. 7 in Rand Vietnam Interview Series Z.

30 Burchett, *Vietnam Will Win!*, p. 151. After reunification in 1975, the 'People's Revolutionary Party' was referred to as 'the party's southern branch' (dang bo mien nam); Carlyle A. Thayer, 'Political Developments in South Vietnam: Transition to Socialism', *South-East Asian Spectrum* [Bangkok: South-East Asia Treaty Organization], (July–September 1976), IV, 4, 30–39.

31 Ta Xuan Linh, 'How Armed Struggle Began', *Vietnam Courier* (March 1974), p. 19; and *10 Years of the PLAF* (South Vietnam: Giai Phong Editions, 1971), p. 50. The commander of these forces was Tran Nam Trung since identified as Tran Luong, then a member of the VWP Central Committee and a PAVN general.

32 Burchett, *The Furtive War*, pp. 95–106.

33 See the biographies in Commission for Foreign Relations of the South Vietnam National Front for Liberation, *Personalities of the South Vietnam Liberation Movement* (circa 1963).

34 Douglas Pike, *Viet Cong: The Organization and Techniques of the National Liberation Front of South Vietnam* (Cambridge: The M.I.T. Press, 1966), p. 115.

Conclusion

1 Jean Lacouture, *Vietnam: Between Two Truces*, pp. 53–57; Jean Lacouture, 'Le F.N.L. est-il bien le "Satellite" de Hanoi?', *Le Monde*, April 4, 1965; Kahin and Lewis, *The United States in Vietnam*, pp. 113–20; and Philippe Devillers, 'The Struggle for the Unification of Vietnam', *The China Quarterly* (Jan.–March 1962), 9, pp. 18–20.

2 *Tinh Hinh Nam Bo*, pp. 32–38.

3   In late 1958, for example, the Nam Bo Regional Committee was still asserting that the revolution could be advanced by peaceful means by exploiting the contradictions in South Viet-Nam. Xu Uy Nam Bo, *Tinh Hinh va Nhiem Vu 59* [The Situation and Tasks for 1959].
4   Lacouture, *Vietnam: Between Two Truces*, pp. 53–54.
5   *Tinh Hinh Nam Bo*, p. 32.
6   ibid., pp. 32–33, which states, 'moreover, until the beginning of 1959, the Party's Regional Committee still hesitated to explain its own problems and those of the Party organization (Dang bo) to the Central Committee.'

Bibliography

Manuscripts and unpublished sources

Documentary collections

Pike, D., compiler *Vietnam Reference Files* Files I–VIII Taipei: US Regional Information Office, 1972. These files have since been relocated to the Indochina Archive, The University of California at Berkeley.

Race, J., compiler *Vietnamese Materials* Microfilm Reels Nos. I–III Chicago: Center for Research Libraries, 1968.

Rand Vietnam Interview Series Z—Viet Cong Organization and Motivation and Experiences of Its Members AD 74132 2 microfilm reels Alexandria, Virginia: Defense Documentation Station for Scientific and Technical Information, March 1972.

United States Department of State *Working Paper on the North Vietnamese Role in the War in South Vietnam, Appendices* 1 microfilm reel Washington, D. C., 1968.

Unpublished theses

Donnell, J. C. 'Politics in South Viet-Nam: Doctrines of Authority in Conflict' Ph.D. thesis, The University of California, 1964.

Godfrey, E. J. 'The Emergence of a Communist State in Vietnam' M.A. thesis, Cornell University, 1962.

Latimer, T. X. 'Hanoi's Leaders and Their South Vietnam Policies 1954–1968' Ph.D. thesis, Georgetown University, 1972.

MacAllister, R. 'The Great Gamble: United States Policy Toward South Viet-Nam From July 1954 to July 1956' M.A. thesis, The University of Chicago, 1958.

Ngo Ton Dat 'The Geneva Partition of Vietnam and the Question of Reunification During the First Two Years (August 1954 to July 1956)' Ph.D. thesis, Cornell University, 1963.

Pearce, R. M. 'Land Tenure and Political Authority: Changes in Land Attitudes and Land Relations in Vietnamese Villages of the Mekong Delta Since 1954' Ph.D. thesis, The University of Washington, 1968.

Thayer, C. A. 'The Origins of the National Front for the Liberation of South Vietnam' Ph.D. thesis, The Australian National University, 1977.

Turley, W. S. 'Army, Party and Society in the Democratic Republic of Vietnam: Civil-Military Relations in a Mass-Mobilization System' Ph.D. thesis, The University of Washington, 1972.

White, C. P. 'Agrarian Reform and National Liberation in the Vietnamese Revolution: 1920–1957' Ph.D. thesis, Cornell University, 1981.

US Joint Publications Research Service translations

Bui Cong Trung 'The Food Problem' *Nghien Cuu Kinh Te* (Economic Research) February 1961. JPRS No. 10, 1974.

Bui Cong Trung 'Aid by Countries in the Socialist Camp in Restoring and Developing the National Economy of the Democratic Republic of Vietnam' in *Demokratichevskaya Respublika V'yetam* Moscow: Institute of the Peoples of Asia of the Academy of Sciences USSR, 1960. JPRS No. 4,925, 1961.

Nam Moc 'A Few Observations on Our Literary Theory and Criticism During the Past Fifteen Years' *Nghien Cuu Van Hoc* (Literary Research) October 1960. JPRS No. 8304, Selected Translations on North Vietnam No. 3, May 1961.

War Experiences Recapitulation Committee of the High-Level Military Institute, *Cuoc Khang Chien Chong My Cuu Nuoc, 1954–1975: Nhung Su Kien Quan Su* (The Anti-U.S. Resistance War for National Salvation, 1954–1975: Military Events) Hanoi: Nha Xuat Ban Quan Doi Nhan Dan, 1980. JPRS Translation No. 80968, June 3, 1982.

Vietnamese language primary sources

Duong Loi Cach Mang Mien Nam ('The Line of Revolution in the South'), 1956.

Xu Uy Nam Bo (Nam Bo Regional Committee), *Ban So Ket Hoc Tap Ve 'Duong Loi Cach Mang Mien Nam'* (Preliminary Report on the Study of 'The Line of Revolution in the South'), 1956.

—— *Chanh Sach Dien Dia* (Policy on Land), October 1957.

—— *Tinh Hinh Nam Bo Tu Sau Hoa Binh Lap Lai Den Hien Nay* (The Situation in Nam Bo from the Restoration of Peace to the Present), circa 1960.

—— *Tinh Hinh Phong Trao Dau Tranh Chinh Tri O Nam Bo Tu Hoa Binh Lap Lai Den Hien Nay* (The Situation of the Political Struggle Movement in Nam Bo from the Restoration of Peace to the Present), circa 1960.

—— *Tinh Hinh va Nhiem Vu 59* (The Situation and Tasks for 1959), circa 1959.

Newspapers

The Bangkok Post
The Daily Worker
France-Soir
Journal d' Extreme-Orient
La Depeche du Cambodge
Le Monde
The New York Herald Tribune
The New York Times
Nhan Dan
The Observer
South Viet Nam in Struggle
The Times
The Times of Vietnam
The Times of Vietnam Weekly
Vietnam Courier

Official publications

China

Eighth National Congress of the Communist Party of China Documents Peking: Foreign Languages Press, 1956.

The Polemic on the General Line of the International Communist Movement Peking: Foreign Languages Press, 1965.

Communist Vietnamese sources

An Bao Minh 'Uprising In Ben Tre' *Vietnamese Studies*, Nos. 18/19, September 1968, pp. 130–150.

An Outline History of the Viet Nam Workers' Party Hanoi: Foreign Languages Publishing House, 1970.

Ban Nghien Cuu Lich Su Dang Thanh Pho Ho Chi Minh (Ho Chi Minh City Party Department of Historical Research) *50 Nam Dau Tranh Kien Cuong cua Dang Bo va Nhan Dan Thanh Pho* (Fifty Years of Steadfast Struggle of the City Party Organisation and People) Thanh Pho Ho Chi Minh: Nha Xuat Ban Thanh Pho Ho Chi Minh, 1981.

Ban Nghien Cuu Lich Su Dang Trung Uong (Party Central Committee Department of Historial Research) *Bon Muoi Lam Nam Hoat Dong Cua Dang Lao Dong Viet Nam* (Forty-five Years of Activities of the Viet-Nam Workers' Party) Hanoi: Nha Xuat Ban Su That, 1976.

Commission for Foreign Relations of the South Vietnam National Front for Liberation *Personalities of the South Vietnam Liberation Movement*, circa 1963.

Documents Related to the Implementation of the Geneva Agreements Concerning Viet-Nam Hanoi: Press and Information Department, Ministry of Foreign Affairs, 1956.

Ho Chi Minh *Nhung Chang Duong Lich Su Ve Van* (Episodes from a Glorious History) Hanoi: Nha Xuat Ban Quan Doi Nhan Dan, 1973.

—— *Selected Works* 4 vols. Hanoi: Foreign Languages Publishing House, 1961–1962.

—— *Selected Writings (1920–1969)* Hanoi: Foreign Languages Publishing House, 1973.

New Facts: Phu Loi Mass Murder in South Viet Nam Hanoi: Foreign Languages Publishing House, 1959.

Pham Thanh Bien et al. 'Ve Cuoc Khoi Nghia Tra-Bong Va Mien Tay Quang-Ngai Mua Thu 1959' (The Tra Bong and Western Quang Ngai Uprisings) *Nghien Cuu Lich Su*, No. 146, September–October 1972, pp. 11–22.

Pham Van Bach, et al. *Fascist Terror in South Viet-Nam: Law 10/59* Hanoi: Foreign Languages Publishing House, 1961.

The Phu Loi Massacre in South Viet Nam Hanoi: Foreign Languages Publishing House, 1959.

President Ho Chi Minh's Visit to the Republic of India and the Union of Burma, February 4th–17th, 1958, Official Documents Hanoi: Foreign Languages Publishing House, 1958.

The Problems Facing the Democratic Republic of Viet Nam in 1961 Hanoi: Foreign Languages Publishing House, 1961.

Quang Loi *Growing Oppression, Growing Struggle* Hanoi: Foreign Languages Publishing House, 1961.

—— *South of the 17th Parallel* Hanoi: Foreign Languages Publishing House, 1959.

Ta Xuan Linh 'Armed Uprisings by Ethnic Minorities Along the Truong Son' Part I *Vietnam Courier*, New Series No. 28, September 1975, pp. 15–20.

—— 'Armed Uprising by Ethnic Minorities Along the Truong Son' Part II *Vietnam Courier*, New Series No. 29, October 1975, pp. 18–21.

—— 'How Armed Struggle Began in Viet Nam' *Vietnam Courier* New Series No. 22, March 1974, pp. 19–24.

—— 'South Viet Nam at the Time of Dien Bien Phu' *Vietnamese Studies* No. 42, 1976, pp. 53–78.

Ta Xuan Linh et al. 'Cuoc Dong Khoi Tra Bong (28–8–1959)' (The Tra Bong Uprising of August 28, 1959) *Nghien Cuu Lich Su,* No. 138, May-June 1971, pp. 2–27.

10 Years of the P.L.A.F South Vietnam: Giai Phong Editions, 1971.

Third National Congress of the Viet Nam Workers' Party, Documents 3 vols. Hanoi: Foreign Languages Publishing House, 1961.

To Minh Trung 'The Students' and Pupils' Struggle' *Vietnamese Studies*, No. 8, 1966, pp. 112–180.

Ton Vy 'The Workers' Struggle' *Vietnamese Studies*, No. 8, 1966, pp. 78–111.

Truong Ngoc Khang et al. 'Dan Toc Cor Tra Bong Truoc Cuoc Khoi Nghia Ngay 28–8–1959' (The Cor Peoples of Tra Bong Before the Uprising of August 28, 1959) *Nghien Cuu Lich Su*, No. 148, January-February 1973, pp. 11–25.

The Truth About Viet Nam – China Relations Over the Last 30 Years Hanoi: Ministry of Foreign Affairs, 1979.

Tran Van Giau and Le Van Chat *The South Viet Nam Liberation National Front* Hanoi: Foreign Languages Publishing House, 1962.

Viet Hong 'Vai Net Va Dau Tranh Vo Trang Va Luc Luong Vo Trang O Nam Bo Truoc Cuoc Dong Khoi 1959–1960' (The Armed Struggle and the Armed Forces in Nam Bo Before the 1959–1960 General Uprising) *Nghien Cuu Lich Su*, No. 155, March–April 1974, pp. 39–55.

Vu Can 'The People's Struggles Against the US–Diem Regime from 1954 to 1960' *Vietnamese Studies*, Nos. 18/19, 1968, pp. 55–129.

Vietnam Peace Committee *Five Years of the Implementation of the Geneva Agreements in Viet Nam* Hanoi: Foreign Languages Publishing House, 1959.

—— *The Peace Movement in Viet Nam* Hanoi: Foreign Languages Publishing House, 1958.

We Open the File Hanoi: Foreign Language Publishing House, 1961.

Who's Who of the Republic of South Viet Nam Giai Phong Editions, 1969.

Great Britain

Documents Relating to British Involvement in the Indo-China Conflict 1945–1965 Misc. No. 25 (1965, Command Paper Cmnd. 2834) London: HMSO, 1966.

Further Documents Relating to the Discussion of Indochina at the Geneva Conference Misc. No. 20 (1954, Command Paper Cmd. 9239) London: HMSO, 1954.

Vietnam and the Geneva Agreements: Documents Concerning the Discussions Between the Representatives of Her Majesty's Government and the Government of the Union of Soviet Socialist Republics held in London in April and May 1956 Vietnam No. 2 (1956, Command Paper Cmd. 9763) London: HMSO, 1956.

India

Foreign Policy of India: Texts of Documents, 1947–1959 New Delhi: Lok Sabha Secretariat, 1959.

International Commission for Supervision and Control

First and Second Reports of the International Commission for Supervision and Control in Vietnam, August 11, 1954 to December 10, 1954 and December 11, 1954 to February 10, 1955 Vietnam No. 1 (1955, Command Paper Cmd. 9461) London: HMSO, 1955.

Third Interim Report of the International Commission for Supervision and Control in Vietnam, February 11, 1955 to April 10, 1955 Vietnam No. 2 (1955, Command Paper Cmd. 9499) London: HMSO, 1955.

Fourth Interim Report of the International Commission for Supervision and Control in Cambodia for the Period 1 April to 30 September, 1955 Cambodia No. 1 (1956, Command Paper Cmd. 9671) London: HMSO, 1956.

Fourth Interim Report of the International Commission for Supervision and Control in Vietnam, 11 April to 10 August 1955 Vietnam No. 3 (1955, Command Paper Cmd. 9654) London: HMSO, 1955.

Fifth Interim Report of the International Commission for Supervision and Control in Vietnam, August 11, 1955 to December 10, 1955 Vietnam No. 1 (1956, Command Paper Cmd. 9706) London: HMSO, 1956.

Sixth Interim Report of the International Commission for Supervision and Control in Vietnam, December 11, 1955 to July 31, 1956 Vietnam No. 1 (1957, Command Paper Cmd. 31) London: HMSO, 1957.

Seventh Interim Report of the International Commission for Supervision and Control in Vietnam, August 1, 1956 to April 30, 1957 Vietnam No. 2 (1957, Command Paper Cmd. 335) London: HMSO, 1957.

Eighth Interim Report of the International Commission for Supervision and Control in Vietnam, May 1, 1957 to April 30, 1958 Vietnam No. 1 (1958, Command Paper Cmd. 509) London: HMSO, 1958.

Ninth Interim Report of the International Commission for Supervision and Control in Vietnam, May 1, 1958 to January 31, 1959 Vietnam No. 1 (1959, Command Paper Cmd. 726) London: HMSO, 1959.

Tenth Interim Report of the International Commission for Supervision and Control in Vietnam, February 1, 1959 to January 31, 1960 Vietnam No. 1 (1960, Command Paper Cmd. 1040) London: HMSO, 1960.

Eleventh Interim Report of the International Commission for Supervision and Control in Vietnam, February 1, 1960 to February 28, 1961 Vietnam No. 1 (1961, Command Paper Cmd. 1551) London: HMSO, 1961.

Special Report to the Co-Chairmen of the Geneva Conference On Indo-China Vietnam No. 1 (1962, Command Paper Cmd. 1755) London: HMSO, 1962.

Republic of Viet-Nam

Bang Ke Khai Tong So Can Bo va Thuong Dan Viet Nam Cong Hoa Bi Cong San Bat Giu Ke Tu 1954 (List of Civil Servants, Cadres and Civilians of the Republic of Viet Nam Abducted by the Communists Since 1954) Saigon: Co So An Luat Trung Uong Phu Tong Uy Dan Van, 1973.

Bilan des realisations gouvernementales Saigon: State Secretariat for Information, 1961.

Committee for the Denunciation of Communist Subversive Activities *Achievements of the Campaign of Denunciation of Communist Subversive Activities, First Phase* Saigon: The People's Directive Committee for the National Congress of Denunciation of Communist Subversive Activities, May 1956.

Ministry of Foreign Affairs *Infiltration of Communist Armed Elements and Clandestine Introduction of Arms From North to South Vietnam* Saigon: June 1967.

Ministry of National Defence Joint General Staff, J2 *Study of the Activation and Activities of R* Saigon: Combined Document Exploitation Center, 1969.

Viet Nam Nien Giam Tong Ke (Statistical Yearbook of Viet Nam) vols 4–6, Saigon: Bo Kinh Te Quoc Gia, 1952–1956.

Violations of the Geneva Agreements By the Viet-Minh Communists Saigon: n.p., July 1959.

United States

Central Intelligence Agency *Memorandum: The Organization, Activities, and Objectives of the Communist Front in South Vietnam* September, 1965.

Department of Defense *United States–Vietnam Relations, 1945–1967* 12 vols, Washington, DC: US Government Printing Office, 1971.

Department of State *A Threat to Peace: North Viet-Nam's Effort to Conquer South Viet-Nam* 2 parts, Washington, DC: Bureau of Public Affairs, Office of Public Services, December 1961.

—— *The Communist Subversive Threat in Vietnam, Cambodia and Laos* Washington, DC: Office of Intelligence Research, December 1955.

—— Office of the Historian, Bureau of Public Affairs *Foreign Relations of the United States, 1955–1957*, vol. 1, Washington, DC: US Government Printing Office, 1985.

—— *Intelligence Report: The Outlook for North and South Vietnam* No. 8008, Washington, DC: Bureau of Intelligence and Research, May 1959.

United States Mission in Vietnam, *A Study—Viet Cong Use of Terror* Saigon: May 1966.

Books and articles

Andrews, W. R. *The Village War: Vietnamese Communist Revolutionary Activities in Dinh Tuong Province* Columbia: University of Missouri Press, 1973.

Black, C. E. and Thornton, T. P. (eds) *Communism and Revolution: The Strategic Uses of Political Violence* Princeton: Princeton University Press, 1964.

Burchett, W. G. *The Furtive War: The United States in Vietnam and Laos* New York: International Publishers, 1963.

—— *North of the Seventeenth Parallel* Delhi: People's Publishing House, 1956.

—— *Vietnam: Inside Story of the Guerilla War* New York: International Publishers, 1968.

—— *Vietnam Will Win!* New York: Monthly Review Press, 1970.

Buttinger, J. *Vietnam: A Dragon Embattled* 2 vols, New York: Frederick A. Praeger, 1967.

Cameron, A. W. 'The Soviet Union and Vietnam: The Origins of Involvement' in W. R. Duncan (ed.) *Soviet Policy in Developing Countries* Waltham, Massachusetts: Ginn-Blaisdell, 1970. pp. 106–205.

Carver, G. A. 'The Faceless Viet Cong' *Foreign Affairs,* Vol. 44, No. 3, April 1966, pp. 347–372.

Chaffard, G. *Indochine: Dix ans d'independance* Paris: Calmann–Levy, 1964.

Chen, K. C. *Vietnam and China, 1938–1954* Princeton: Princeton University Press, 1969.

Child, F. C. *Essays on Economic Growth, Capital Formation, and Public Policy in Vietnam* Saigon: Michigan State University Vietnam Advisory Group, May 1961.

Cole, A. B. (ed.) *Conflict in Indo-China and International Repercussions: A Documentary History, 1945–1955* Ithaca: Cornell University Press, 1956.

Corley, F. J. 'Viet Nam Since Geneva' *Thought* (Fordham University Quarterly), Vol. 33, No. 131, Winter 1958/59, pp. 546–547.

Brian, C. 'The International Situation in Indochina' *Pacific Affairs,* Vol. 19, No. 4, December 1956, pp. 309–323.

Devillers, P. 'The Struggle for the Unification of Vietnam' *The China Quarterly,* No. 9, January–March 1962, pp. 2–23.

Devillers, P. and Lacouture, J. *End of a War: Indochina, 1954* London: Pall Mall Press, 1969.

du Berrier, H. *Background to Betrayal: The Tragedy of Vietnam* Boston: Western Islands Press, 1965.

—— 'Report from Saigon' *American Mercury,* Vol. 87, No. 416, September 1958, pp. 43–51.

Duiker, W. J. *The Communist Road to Power in Vietnam* Boulder, Colorado: Westview Press, 1981.

—— *The Rise of Nationalism in Vietnam, 1900–1941* Ithaca: Cornell University Press, 1976.

Duncan, W. R. (ed.) *Soviet Policy in Developing Countries* Waltham, Massachusetts: Ginn Blaisdell, 1970.

Duchacek, I. D. *Nations and Men: An Introduction to International Politics* 3rd edition, Hinsdale, Illinois: The Dryden Press, 1965.

Duncanson, D. J. *Government and Revolution in Vietnam* London: Oxford University Press, 1968.

Easton, E. *A Framework for Political Analysis* Englewood Cliffs, New Jersey: Prentice-Hall Inc., 1965.

Ely, P. *L'Indochine dans la Tourmente* Paris: Librairie Plon, 1964.

Fairbank, J. K. et al. *A History of East Asian Civilization* 2 vols, Boston: Houghton Mifflin Co., 1965.

Fall, B. B. 'Crisis in North Viet-Nam' *Far Eastern Survey*, Vol. XXVI, No. 1, January 1957, pp. 12–15.

—— 'The Political–Religious Sects of Vietnam' *Pacific Affairs*, Vol. 28, No. 3, September 1955, pp. 235–253.

—— 'South Viet-Nam at the Crossroads' *International Journal*, Vol. XIX, No. 2, Spring 1964, pp. 139–154.

—— 'South Viet-Nam's Internal Problems' *Pacific Affairs*, Vol. 31, No. 3, September 1958, pp. 241–260.

—— *The Two Viet-Nams: A Political and Military Analysis* rev. ed. New York: Frederick A. Praeger, 1967.

—— *The Viet Minh Regime: Government and Administration in the Democratic Republic of Viet Nam* New York: Institute of Pacific Relations, 1956.

—— 'Viet Nam in the Balance' *Foreign Affairs*, Vol. 45, No. 1, October 1966, pp. 1–18.

—— (ed.) *Ho Chi Minh On Revolution: Selected Writings, 1920–66* New York: Frederick A. Praeger, 1967.

—— (ed.) *Viet-Nam Witness 1953–1966* New York: Frederick A. Praeger, 1966.

The Fight Against The Subversive Communist Activities in Vietnam Saigon: Review Horizons Special Edition, 1956.

Fifield, R. H. *The Diplomacy of Southeast Asia: 1945–1958* New York: Harper & Brothers, 1958.

Floyd, D. *Mao Against Khrushchev* New York: Frederick A. Praeger, 1964.

Gittinger, J. P. 'Communist Land Policy in North Vietnam' *Far Eastern Survey*, Vol. XXVIII, No. 8, August 1959, pp. 113–126.

—— 'Rent Reduction and Tenure Security in Free Vietnam' *Journal of Farm Economics*, Vol. XXXIX, No. 2, May 1957, pp. 429–440.

Hall, M. 'The Dragons Lash Their Tails in Indo-China' *Journal of the Royal Central Asian Society*, Vol. XLIII, No. II, April 1956, pp. 113–120.

Henderson, W. 'South Viet Nam Finds Itself' *Foreign Affairs*, Vol. 35, No. 2, January 1957, pp. 283–294.

Hendry, J. B. *The Small World of Khanh Hau* Chicago: Aldine Publishing Company, 1964.

Hickey, G. C. *Fire in the Forest: Ethnohistory of the Vietnamese Central Highlands, 1954–1976* New Haven: Yale University Press, 1982.

—— *Sons of the Mountains: Ethnohistory of the Vietnamese Central Highlands to 1954* New Haven: Yale University Press, 1982.

Hinton, H. C. *Communist China in World Politics* Boston: Houghton Mifflin Co., 1966.

Hoa Mai (ed.) *The 'Nhan Van' Affair* Saigon: Asian People's Anti-Communist League, Vietnam Chapter, 1958.

Hoang Van Chi *From Colonialism to Communism: A Case Study of North*

Vietnam New York: Popular Library, 1964.

Hoang Van Hoan 'Distortion of Facts About Militant Friendship Between Viet Nam and China is Impermissible' *Beijing Review* No. 49, December 7, 1979, pp. 11–23.

Honey, P. J. *Communism in North Vietnam: Its Role in the Sino-Soviet Dispute* Cambridge: The M.I.T. Press, 1966.

—— 'North Vietnam's Party Congress' *The China Quarterly*, No. 4, October–December 1960, pp. 66–75.

—— 'The Problem of Democracy in Vietnam' *The World Today* Vol. 16, No. 2, February 1960, pp. 71–79.

—— 'The Revolt of the Intellectuals in North Vietnam' *The World Today*, Vol. 13, No. 6, June 1957, pp. 250–260.

—— (ed.) *North Vietnam Today* New York: Frederick A. Praeger, 1962.

Hudson, G. F. et al., *The Sino-Soviet Dispute* New York: Frederick A. Praeger, 1961.

Huntington, S. P. *Political Order in Changing Societies* New Haven: Yale University Press, 1968.

Huynh Kim Khanh *Vietnamese Communism, 1925–1945* Ithaca: Cornell University Press, 1982.

Jumper, R. 'The Communist Challenge to South Vietnam' *Far Eastern Survey*, Vol. 25, No. 11, November 1956, pp. 161–168.

—— 'Sects and Communism in South Vietnam' *Orbis*, Vol. III, No. 1, Spring 1959, 85–96.

—— 'Mandarin Bureaucracy and Politics in South Vietnam' *Pacific Affairs*, Vol. 31, No. 1, March 1957, pp. 47–58.

Jumper, R. and Normand, M. W. 'Vietnam' in G. McT. Kahin (ed.) *Governments and Politics of Southeast Asia*, 2nd ed. Ithaca: Cornell University Press, 1964.

Kahin, G. McT. *Intervention: How America Became Involved in Vietnam* New York: Alfred A. Knopf, 1986.

Kahin, G. McT. (ed.) *Governments and Politics of Southeast Asia* Ithaca: Cornell University Press, 1964.

Kahin, G. McT. and Lewis, J. W. *The United States in Vietnam: An Analysis in Depth of the History of America's Involvement in Vietnam* rev. ed. New York: Dell Publishing Co., 1969.

Kattenburg, P. M. 'Viet Nam and U.S. Diplomacy, 1940–1970' *Orbis*, Vol. XV, No. 3, Fall 1971, pp. 818–841.

Kaye, W. 'A Bowl of Rice Divided: The Economy of North Vietnam' in P. J. Honey *North Vietnam Today* New York: Frederick A. Praeger, 1962, pp. 105–116.

Kolko, G. *Vietnam: Anatomy of a War, 1940–1975* Sydney: Allen and Unwin, 1986.

Lacouture, J. *Vietnam: Between Two Truces* New York: Vintage Books, 1966.

Lancaster, D. *The Emancipation of French Indochina* New York: Octagon Books, 1974.

Lansdale, E. G. *In the Midst of Wars: An American's Mission to Southeast Asia* New York: Harper and Row, 1972.

Lindholm, R. W. (ed.) *Viet-Nam: The First Five Years: An International*

Symposium East Lansing: Michigan State University Press, 1959.

McAlister, J. T. *Viet Nam: The Origins of Revolution* New York: Alfred A. Knopf, 1969.

McAlister, J. T. and Mus, P. *The Vietnamese and Their Revolution* New York: Harper and Row, 1970.

McLane, C. B. 'The Russians and Vietnam: Strategies of Indirection' *International Journal*, Vol. XXIV, No. 1, Winter 1968–69, pp. 47–64.

Marr, D. G. *Vietnamese Anticolonialism 1885–1925* Berkeley: The University of California Press, 1971.

—— *Vietnamese Tradition on Trial, 1920–1945* Berkeley: The University of California Press, 1981.

Mecklin, J. *Mission in Torment* New York: Doubleday & Co., 1965.

Mehnert, K. *Peking and Moscow* New York: Mentor, 1964.

Modelski, G. 'The Viet Minh Complex' in C. E. Black and T. P. Thornton (eds.) *Communism and Revolution: The Strategic Uses of Political Violence* Princeton: Princeton University Press, 1964, pp. 185–214.

Moise, E. E. 'Land Reform and Land Reform Errors in North Vietnam' *Pacific Affairs*, Vol. 49, No. 1, Spring 1976, pp. 70–92.

—— *Land Reform in China and North Vietnam* Chapel Hill: The University of North Carolina Press, 1983.

Montgomery, J. D. *The Politics of Foreign Aid: American Experience in Southeast Asia* New York: Frederick A. Praeger, 1962.

Murti, B. N. S. *Vietnam Divided: The Unfinished Struggle* New Delhi: Asia Publishing House, 1964.

Nguyet Dam and Than Phong *Chin Nam Mau Lua Duoi Che Do Gia Dinh Tri Ngo Dinh Diem* (Nine Years of Blood and Fire Under the Nepotism of Ngo Dinh Diem) Saigon: n.p., 1964.

No Other Road to Take: Memoir of Mrs. Nguyen Thi Dinh trans. Elliot, M. V. Southeast Asia Program Data Paper No. 102, Ithaca: Department of Asian Studies, Cornell University, June 1976.

Nutt, A. L. *Troika on Trial: Control or Compromise?* 3 vols, Washington, DC: US Department of Commerce, 1967.

O'Neill, R. J. *General Giap: Politician and Strategist* Melbourne: Cassell Australia, 1969.

—— *Vietnam Task: The 5th Battalion, The Royal Australian Regiment, 1966/67* Melbourne: Cassell Australia, 1968.

Palmer, L. *Communists in Indonesia: Power Pursued in Vain* Garden City, New York: Anchor Press–Doubleday, 1973.

Pike, D. *Viet Cong: The Organization and Techniques of the National Liberation Front of South Vietnam* Cambridge: The M.I.T. Press, 1966.

Popkin, S. 'South Vietnam: Villages Under Diem' in S. Spiegel and K. Waltz (eds.) *Conflict in World Politics* Cambridge, Massachusetts: Winthrop Pub. Inc., 1971, pp. 267–268.

Porter, D. G. *The Myth of the Bloodbath: North Vietnam's Land Reform Reconsidered* International Relations of East Asia Project Interim Report No. 2, Ithaca: Cornell University, September 1972.

—— 'The Myth of the Bloodbath: North Vietnam's Land Reform Reconsidered' *Bulletin of Concerned Asian Scholars*, Vol. 5, No. 2, September 1973, pp. 2–15.

The Quynh Luu Uprisings Saigon: The Asian People's Anti-Communist League, Vietnam Chapter, 1957.

Race, J. 'How They Won' *Asian Survey*, Vol. X, No. 8, August 1970, pp. 628–650.
—— 'The Origins of the Second Indochina War' *Asian Survey*, Vol. X, No. 5, May 1969, p. 359–382.
—— *War Comes to Long An: Revolutionary Conflict in a Vietnamese Province* Berkeley: The University of California Press, 1972.
Radanyi, J. *Delusion and Reality: Gambits, Hoaxes, and Diplomatic One-Upmanship in Vietnam* South Bend, Indiana: Gateway Editions Limited, 1978.
Randle, R. F. *Geneva 1954: The Settlement of the Indochinese War* Princeton: Princeton University Press, 1969.
Rocolle, P. *Pourquoi Dien Bien Phu?* Paris: Flammarion, 1968.
Sainteny, J. *Ho Chi Minh and His Vietnam: A Personal Memoir* Chicago: Cowles Book Co. Inc., 1972.
Sansom, R. L. *The Economics of Insurgency in the Mekong Delta of Vietnam* Cambridge: The M.I.T. Press, 1970.
SarDesai, D. R. *Indian Foreign Policy in Cambodia, Laos and Vietnam, 1947–1964* Berkeley: The University of California Press, 1968.
Schlesinger, A. M. Jr, *A Thousand Days* Boston: Houghton Mifflin Co., 1965.
Schram, S. (ed.) *Mao Tse-tung Unrehearsed: Talks and Letters, 1956–1971* Harmondsworth: Penguin Books, 1974.
Scigliano, R. C. *South Vietnam: Nation Under Stress* Boston: Houghton Mifflin Company, 1964.
Scigliano, R. C. and Fox. G. H. *Technical Assistance in Vietnam: The Michigan State University Experience* New York: Frederick A. Praeger, 1965.
Shaplen, R. *The Lost Revolution: The U.S. in Vietnam, 1946–1966* New York: Harper and Row, 1966.
Shaw, B. 'China and North Vietnam: Two Revolutionary Paths' Part I, *Current Scene*, Vol. IX, No. 11, November 7, 1971, pp. 1–12.
Sheehan, N. S., (compiler) *The Pentagon Papers as Published by 'The New York Times'* New York: Bantam Books, 1971.
Smith, R. B. *An International History of the Vietnam War Vol. 1: Revolution Versus Containment, 1955–61* London: Macmillan, 1983.
Smyser, W. R. *The Independent Vietnamese: Vietnamese Communism Between Russia and China, 1956–1969* Papers in International Studies Southeast Asia Series No. 55, Athens, Ohio: Ohio University Center for International Studies, Southeast Asia Program, 1980.
Spiegel, S. and Waltz, K. (eds.) *Conflict in World Politics* Cambridge, Massachusetts: Winthrop Pub. Inc., 1971.
Spector, R. H. *Advice and Support: The Early Years of the U.S. Army in Vietnam 1941–1960* New York: The Free Press, 1985.
Talbot, S. (ed. and trans.) *Khrushchev Remembers* London: Sphere Books Ltd., 1971.
Taylor, M. C. 'South Viet-Nam: Lavish Aid, Limited Progress' *Pacific Affairs*, Vol. 34, No. 3, 1961, pp. 242–256.
Thayer, C. A. 'Political Developments in South Vietnam: Transition to Socialism' *South-East Asian Spectrum* (Bangkok: South-East Asia Treaty Organization), Vol. IV, No. 4, July–September 1976, pp. 30–39.
—— 'Southern Vietnamese Revolutionary Organizations and the Vietnam

Workers' Party: Continuity and Change, 1954–1974' in J. J. Zasloff and
M. Brown (eds) *Communism in Indochina: New Perspectives* Lexington,
Massachusetts: D. C. Heath and Company, 1975, pp. 27–56.
Thayer, C. W. *Guerrilla* London: Michael Joseph Ltd., 1963.
Tram Hoa Dua No Tren Dat Bac (The Blooming of the Hundred Flowers
in the North) Saigon: Mat Tran Bao Ve Tu Do Van Hoa, 1959.
Turner, R. F. *Vietnamese Communism: Its Origins and Development* Stanford: Hoover Institution Press, 1975.
Topping, S. *Journey Between Two Chinas* New York: Harper and Row, 1972.
Truong Nhu Tang *Vietcong Memoir: An Inside Account of the Vietnam War and Its Aftermath* New York: Harcourt, Brace, Jovanovich Publishers, 1985.
Vu Quoc Thuc 'National Planning in Vietnam' *Asian Survey*, Vol. I, No. 7, September 1961, pp. 3–9.
Warner, D. *The Last Confucian: Vietnam, Southeast Asia, and the West* Baltimore: Penguin Books, 1964.
Weinstein, F. B. *Vietnam's Unheld Elections: The Failure to Carry Out the 1956 Reunification Elections and the Effect on Hanoi's Present Outlook* Southeast Asia Program Data Paper No. 60, Ithaca: Cornell University, Department of Asian Studies, July 1966.
Woodside, A. B. *Community and Revolution in Modern Vietnam* Boston: Houghton Mifflin Company, 1976.
Wright, E. R. *Barriers to Progress in South Vietnam: The United States Experience* Seoul: Pomso Publishers, 1973.
Wurfel, D. 'Agrarian Reform in The Republic of Vietnam' *Far Eastern Survey*, Vol. XXVI, No. 6, June 1957, pp. 81–92.
Zagoria, D. S. *The Sino-Soviet Dispute, 1956–1961* New York: Atheneum, 1964.
—— *Vietnam Triangle: Moscow/Peking/Hanoi* New York: Pegasus, 1967.
Zasloff, J. J. *Origins of the Insurgency in South Vietnam, 1954–1960: The Role of the Southern Vietminh Cadres* Memorandum RM-5163/2-ISA/ARPA, Santa Monica: The Rand Corporation, May 1968.
Zasloff, J. J. and Brown, M. (eds) *Communism in Indochina: New Perspectives* Lexington, Massachusetts: D.C. Heath and Company, 1975.

Radio monitoring services

British Broadcasting Corporation *Summary of World Broadcasts, The Far East,* Part III (1954–1959) and Part V (1959–1960).
United States Central Intelligence Agency Foreign Broadcast Information Service *Daily Report,* 1954–1961.

Index

delegations to DRVN, 164–5, 177; economic and cultural agreements, 177; party delegations to 1957 Moscow Conference, 170; relations with DRVN, 29, 45, 98, 100, 109–10, 191; support for national liberation, 174; visit by Ho Chi Minh, 163
socialist construction, xxv, 175, 181, 194
socialist transition, *see also* socialist construction, xxiv
South Korea, 2, 25, 123, 159–60, 163
South Vietnamese (defined), xxvi–xxx
Southeast Asia Treaty Organisation (SEATO), 13, 25, 28, 30–1, 65–6
Soviet Union (USSR), xx, xxv; aid to Viet-Nam, xxv, 62, 64, 161, 166, 174, 191; delegations to DRVN, 164–5; diplomatic support for DRVN, 6, 79, 161–3, 174, 178, 192; foreign policy, 5; Geneva Conference Co-Chairman; 73–4; reconvening Geneva Conference; 58, 73, relations with DRVN, 1, 6, 29, 33, 44, 60–3, 66, 99, 110, 174, 191–2; trade with DRVN, 60; visits by Ho Chi Minh, 33, 35–7, 41, 44, 165, 184
Special Forces, xvii
Stalin, *see also* de-Stalinisation, xxv, 62, 95–6, 169–70, 192; denunciation by Khrushchev, xxv, 62, 95, 169, 192
State of Viet-Nam (SVN), *see also* National Army (State of Viet-Nam); xxvii, 2, 14, 16–17, 21, 25, 33, 44, 48; Bandung Conference 34; consultative conference with DRVN, 34,
strike(s) 40, 42–3, 70–1, 118, 134

struggle movement *see* political struggle
Suez, 102, 110
Sukarno, 162

Ta Quang Buu, 2
Ta Xuan Linh, 88, 141–3, 150, 185
Taiwan, *see* Republic of China
Tam Ngan, 149
Tan Viet Minh (New Viet Minh), 56
Tay Ninh province, xvii, 48–9, 86, 117, 135, 141–2, 153, 187; Duong Minh Chau area, 135; Trang Sup, 187; Vam Co river, xvii; Xom Giua hamlet, xvii
Temporary Equipment Recovery Mission (TERM), 126–7
terrorist incidents *see* killing tyrants
Thanh My resettlement camp, 149
That Son, *see* Seven Mountains
Thu Dau Mot, 117, 135, 139, 141–2, 153, 183
Thua Thien province, 39, 82, 115
Tinh Hinh Nam Bo (The Situation in Nam Bo), 131, 138, 143, 153–4
Ton Duc Thang, 76–7
Ton Vy, 134–5
Tonkin, *see also* Bac Bo xxvi
Topping, Seymour, 7
Tra Bong district, *see* Quang Ngai province
Tra Vinh province, 131
Training Relations and Instruction Mission (TRIM), 127
Tran Chanh Thanh, 81–2
Tran Cong Truong, 91
Tran Nam Trung, 150
Tran Quang, 54
Tran Trung Dung, 58
Tran Van Huu, 77
Tran Van Soai, xvi, 22–3, 39, 52–5, 57